East Harlem
Remembered

ALSO BY CHRISTOPHER BELL
*Scapegoats: Baseballers Whose Careers
Are Marked by One Fateful Play* (McFarland, 2002)

EAST HARLEM REMEMBERED
Oral Histories of Community and Diversity

Christopher Bell

McFarland & Company, Inc., Publishers
Jefferson, North Carolina, and London

LIBRARY OF CONGRESS CATALOGUING-IN-PUBLICATION DATA

Bell, Christopher, 1968 –
　　East Harlem remembered : oral histories of community and diversity / Christopher Bell.
　　　　p.　　cm.
　　Includes bibliographical references and index.

　　ISBN 978-0-7864-6808-9
　　softcover : acid free paper ∞

　　1. East Harlem (New York, N.Y.) — History.　2. New York (N.Y.) — History.　3. East Harlem (New York, N.Y.) — Biography.　4. New York (N.Y.) — Biography.　5. Oral history — New York (State) — New York.　6. Community life — New York (State) — New York — History.　7. Cultural pluralism — New York (State) — New York — History.　8. East Harlem (New York, N.Y.) — Social life and customs.　9. New York (N.Y.) — Social life and customs.　I. Title.
　　F128.68.H3B452　2013
　　974.7'1 — dc23　　　　　　　　　　　　　　　　　　2012044046

BRITISH LIBRARY CATALOGUING DATA ARE AVAILABLE

© 2013 Christopher Bell. All rights reserved

No part of this book may be reproduced or transmitted in any form or by any means, electronic or mechanical, including photocopying or recording, or by any information storage and retrieval system, without permission in writing from the publisher.

Front cover photograph: 116th Street open air market between Lexington and Third Avenues, Harlem, ca. 1965 (photograph by Hiram Maristany)

Manufactured in the United States of America

McFarland & Company, Inc., Publishers
　Box 611, Jefferson, North Carolina 28640
　www.mcfarlandpub.com

To Robert DeLeon, Michael Rivera, Vincent Murphy,
Rose Pascale, Manny Diaz, Jr., Raquel Villegas, Wally Lambert,
Yolanda Sanchez, Peter Rufano, Helen Rubenstein
and anyone else who may have passed away
before the book is published.

And to all East Harlemites.

Table of Contents

Preface 1
Introduction 3

1. Planting Roots (1900–1920) 9
2. The Great Depression and World War II (1930s–1940s) 45
3. Marc (Vito Marcantonio) 58
4. Planting Roots II (1945–1950) 75
5. Community and Diversity 91
6. 1950s—Three Strikes: Public Warehousing, Drugs, Tribalism of Gangs 103
7. 1960s—Decade of Change 146
8. 1970s—Fruits of Labor 186
9. 1980s—Dr. King's Dream Lives On 199
10. 1990s—Rebirth of East Harlem 207

Epilogue 219
Chapter Notes 223
Bibliography 229
Index 231

Preface

This is an oral history of East Harlem, where I had the pleasure of being raised by my godmother and my mother. Each one helped me love and appreciate my neighborhood. And despite some trying times in East Harlem, it's still my home. My mother, like many before, came here to East Harlem to seek a better life for her and her family. During my formative years my godmother and mother both regaled me with stories of their East Harlem experiences. My godmother, born at the turn of the twentieth century, and my mother, a baby boomer, had plenty of stories to share. My godmother, who by this time was well into her seventies, often mentioned the Great Depression, World War II and iconic figures like Adam Clayton Powell, Jr., Martin Luther King, Jr., and Presidents Franklin D. Roosevelt and Harry S Truman. In fact, she recalled seeing Truman enter the Waldorf Astoria Hotel when she worked there. In East Harlem, my godmother appreciated the diversity of the neighborhood. She learned a few Spanish words by conversing with her Puerto Rican co-workers and at home she spoke broken Spanish to her neighbors.

In adulthood I have worked in several government positions that provided city services to the East Harlem community. One day an elderly Italian gentleman accompanied by his daughter arrived seeking assistance at the city councilman's office where I worked as a community associate. He sat down and took off his fedora. The old man asked where I was raised, and I told him I grew up in East Harlem. He responded that he, too, grew up in East Harlem and remarked that many years ago the neighborhood was heavily Italian and was called "Little Italy."

Before my position in city government I worked at a private law firm. The old Italian's story instantly reminded me of when a Jewish lawyer once told me that Jews also lived in East Harlem. I found it curious that East Harlem, then a predominantly Puerto Rican and black neighborhood, once was heavily populated with East European immigrants. There were still were more lessons to learn, and I eagerly soaked up the knowledge.

Their stories have never left me and spurred me to conduct and record an oral history of East Harlem.

Introduction

Organized chronologically, this book is about several ethnic groups who immigrated and migrated to East Harlem. They include blacks, Irish, Jews, Italians and Puerto Ricans. Each group established a presence in the neighborhood for a considerable time starting in the early 20th century. Next, the oral histories will focus on the depression and World War II, a period when New York City developed plans to transform East Harlem through public housing and when the controversial Congressman Vito Marcantonio came to the forefront. The post–World War II era saw two significant changes in East Harlem: the departure of the East European population and the growth of the Puerto Rican and black populations in the neighborhood. Most notably, Langston Hughes, the "Poet Laureate of Harlem," came to East Harlem around this time.

The 1950s saw Marcantonio's political reign, marked by extensive community activism, ended. Afterwards, the neighborhood turned to social services agencies and churches to receive the services once supplied by Marcantonio's office. But gangs emerged, too. When urban renewal caused scores of tenements and small stores to be demolished, many East Harlemites scattered throughout the city. The burgeoning housing projects replaced the tenements and transformed the neighborhood forever. The Italian population of East Harlem was dramatically reduced, and the neighborhood left East Harlem a quasi segregated community.

In the 1960s, the revolutionary spirit arrived in East Harlem, and blacks and Puerto Ricans challenged the white Democratic leadership. East Harlemites embrace the leadership of Antonia Pantoja, and Puerto Rican American Piri Thomas' book *Down These Mean Streets*, became popular. Puerto Rican Americans in the 1970s showed cultural pride in Taller Boricua, El Museo Del Barrio. But in the 1980s, East Harlem bottoms out with urban blight; however, during this period a former East Harlemite shared his dream and developed a program which helped many high school students enroll in college. By the late twentieth and into the twenty-first century, East Harlem's resurgence has begun, but gentrification leaves the neighborhood's future in question. I hope that the reader will realize this book is not an urban story in America but an American story in an urban neighborhood.

The original inhabitants of what we know as East Harlem were the Weckquaesgeeks, Native Americans. They derived from the Delaware tribe and lived on the land of Manhatta ("hilly island") known today as Manhattan.[1] Henry Hudson's arrival in North America in 1609 ushered a new era in Dutch exploration.[2] Seventeen years later, Peter Minuit purchased Manhattan from the Native Americans for twenty-four dollars.[3] In 1658, the village of Nieuw Haerlem (New Harlem) was founded, years before Manhattan Island became New Amsterdam.[4] One of the last major events of this period was the construction of the first Dutch Reformed Church of Harlem, located at what is now 121st Street and Third Avenue.[5]

By this time, the Weckquaesqeks had moved on to what later became the Western part of the United States.[6] In 1664 England conquered and supplanted the Dutch and New Amsterdam became New York.[7] But England, too, would lose New York after the American Colonists defeated the British in the Revolutionary War in 1783. New York became the first location of the nation's capital.

As for East Harlem during the next century, the village of Nieuw (East) Harlem changed little. Several farmers who resided in Nieuw Harlem during in the late seventeenth and the eighteenth century became wealthy. A large government in the area was not needed as committees and civil officers resolved all relevant conflicts. This system remained in effect through the late 1660s to the early nineteenth century.[8]

In 1811, New York City was laid out in a grid plan.[9] Fifth Avenue separated the East and West Side of Manhattan.[10] The Harlem area now had a distinction and the east side of Harlem would be known as East Harlem. By the early nineteenth century, East Harlem was no longer an attractive place for the wealthy as it had deteriorated for decades. The decline in value led several East Harlemites, among them James Roosevelt, the great-grandfather of Franklin Delano Roosevelt, to sell their properties to a prosperous gentleman who sold them to the city.[11]

After several formerly formed parcels were auctioned off, East Harlem's rural landscape dissipated. Also during this period, the neighborhood's transportation system changed, first from ferry boats to horse-drawn carriages and finally to steam locomotives that traveled along the Fourth Avenue tracks. To this day, commuters can enjoy this route on the Metro North Railroad which stops at the Park Avenue station on 125th Street in East Harlem.[12] Later, hotels were constructed along several stations at 109th, 115th, 125th and 133rd Streets respectively.

African American farmers settled in East Harlem near 130th Street followed by German and Irish immigrants who lived in shanties throughout the neighborhood.[13] By mid-century East Harlem was part of the Twelfth Ward, which began at 96th Street and ended in upper Manhattan.[14] East Harlem's population stood at 1,500.

The neighborhood had three municipal officeholders: Health, Warden Commissioners of Tax and Assessments and Commissioners of Jurors. The Twelfth Precinct stood at 126th Street between Third and Fourth (Park) Avenues. Three of eighteen fire engines within the Twelfth Ward were located in East Harlem, along with the assistant fire commissioner's office, which was located on 128th Street and Fourth Avenue (Park). These engine companies were aided by several hose and hook-and-ladder companies. Six public and four primary schools served the entire Twelfth Ward. Public School 39 existed on 125th Street between First and Second Avenues. Primary School 4 was located on 120th Street between Second and Third Avenues. Finally, a separate school for African-Americans was located one block west, between Third and Lexington Avenues.[15]

Though East Harlem possessed a school, police, health and fire departments, it was still a remote neighborhood. This would change during the early 1880s when the construction of the Second and Third Avenue elevated subways connected lower and upper Manhattan. Also, the elevated subways reduced commuter time between East Harlem and City Hall to forty-five minutes. Before the elevated subways were built, the commute time between both places was twice as long.[16] Finally, the street-level trolley cars complemented the elevated subways. For the next seventy-five years, East Harlemites rode the elevated subways. Though the Second and Third Avenue Els ceased operation in 1942 and 1955, respectively, East Harlemites remember them fondly.[17]

Willie Lopez: *Third Avenue El was very slow and it used to make a lot of stops and it had interwoven straw seats. Then there were cigarette advertisements: Lucky Strike and Kool. You looked out your window and you saw the tenements and sometimes you saw people during their private moments when they undressed themselves.*

Father Peter Rufano: *I remember the Third Avenue El and I also remember the Second Avenue El. I took the Second Avenue El to school for years from 111th Street to 33rd Street. The Third Avenue El was out of my section. I only used the Third Avenue El when it was necessary, but I loved the Second Avenue El, it was convenient. Then, you would connect to 125th street and 138th Street and to the Bronx.*

Dr. Alvin Poussaint: *I took the Third Avenue El everyday to go down to Stuyvesant High School. I thought it was fun to ride the El and I liked it better than the subway, it was open air transportation. You chugged along past the buildings and it was very convenient.*

Arnie Segarra: *I broke my arm at the El Station on 116th Street. When I was about ten years old, I was fooling around on the tracks after the El stopped running at night. The El had old cars and I rode it to the Bronx as often as I could and it was the above like subway. And you could travel to certain parts of the city and could look out and see many neighborhoods.*

Johnny Colon: *The El's cars were old army dark green, and they had rickety-rackety seats made out of woven-straw. Then you had the small fans, along with the poles which were porcelain and they were always polished. The El made the same squealing sound you hear on the subway. Also on the Third Avenue El you passed the Rupert Brewery and you smelled the yeast.*

The elevated subways moved real estate developers to build in East Harlem. Soon 100th to 125th Streets were lined with "dumbbell" tenements (so called because of their layout) built near the Second and Third Avenue elevated subways. Brownstones, flats and private houses were also constructed in the neighborhood, and the spate of housing construction reflected an immediate change in East Harlem. In 1885 the neighborhood was home to twenty churches, nine primary and grammar schools, St. Joseph's Hospital, three consolidated car companies, rubber and sewing machine factories, and numerous coal, stone, lumber and timber factories from Second Avenue to the East River. Entrepreneurialship was evident as many small stores existed throughout East Harlem. You could choose from soda manufacturers, bakeries, stationery stores, toy stores, furniture stores, greenhouses, pharmacies, jewelers, ice cream parlors, plumbers, breweries, hotels and a market.[18]

Housing construction continued in the next decade and new tenements sprouted all over the neighborhood. Real estate developers raced to finish construction before new building codes were implemented in 1901.[19] East Europeans moved into East Harlem and were joined by African Americans who now resided throughout the neighborhood. With the growth of the community came a need for social agencies. Several churches and settlement houses opened and provided the community with spiritual and social services. Union Settlement and Home Garden House (which became Harlem House in 1890) were two of the settlement houses that served in the neighborhood during this period. In 1956 Harlem House became LaGuardia Memorial House.

The population increase led to a housing deficit. Years before, there had been a surplus of apartments. Now a dry period prompted some developers to stop building in East Harlem. Passage of the Tenement House Act of 1901 resulted in "new law" tenements, an improvement from the "old law" dumbbell tenements constructed in the nineteenth century. Airshafts were widened, a water closet for each apartment was installed, and windows appeared in the hallways on each floor. Lastly, better fire escapes, fireproof halls, stairs and lightened interior rooms were added to improve health and minimize the chance of fire. However, the act was unenforceable. By 1903, loopholes were discovered and builders circumvented the 1901 Tenement House Act, and construction resumed. Thousands of small three-story private houses that had been constructed in East Harlem during the last decades of the nineteenth century were razed and replaced by six-story tenements.[20] Despite — or because of — the density, tenement life allowed East Harlemites to establish a close relationship with each other.

Nicholasa Mohr (Writer whose books include *Nilda* and *El Bronx Remembered*): *There were tenements all over Madison Avenue from 96th to 106th Streets. There you had beauty shops and mom-and-pop stores. I lived across from Mount Sinai Hospital on 100th Street and Madison Avenue. But we didn't stay there for long and my family moved to 105th Street. Today the building is next to El Museo del Barrio. Several memories stand out. The building had an alleyway and stoops which were connected to each building. The stoops allowed each tenant to sit down with their family and friends. My family also lived in a tenement building on Madison Avenue between 107th and 108th Streets, but there were no stoops there. I look at the stoops today and I realize there's a real discrepancy in how I communicated with my neighbors and played in the streets.*

Yolanda Sanchez (Executive Director of the Puerto Rican Association of Community Affairs): *Common vacancy rate was high in East Harlem because the landlord gave you a month's free rent. There were so many apartments you would move in and take an apartment for free or pay what you could. Then if you fell back on your rent you left and moved on to the next apartment.*

Humberto Cintron: *In reality the tenant got two or even three months free rent. What the tenants did was, after their free rental expired they found another apartment. Then when that rental expired the tenant moved again. So for the year they only paid six months rent for twelve months.*

Judge Eugene Nardelli: *Tenements, you had stores on both sides of the entrance. In some tenements you had a basement and inside there was a bakery. Here was where the baker did the baking. They would sell their merchandise on the ground floor and the store was clean and properly used. Every block from 99th to 106th Streets had a bakery. It was common to see people eating fresh bread three times a day. The baker would bring the bread to your local grocery store. And there was a butcher on every block, and you tell them how you want you meat cut, through the machine.*

Angela Bella Puco: *Within each tenement you had the airshaft, the space that stood between each tenement. From this location you could see your neighbor's window. I remember looking out of my window and I was able talk to my next door neighbor.*

Marilyn Goodman: *The tenements also allowed you to have the clothesline. We didn't have a dryer, so we needed a clothesline. You went to the hardware store and bought the rope and you would anchor it across the backyard by someone else's tenement apartment. But you had to get in touch with the other person across the yard. Let's say if you lived on 112th Street then you went around to 113th Street to locate the building in front of you. Sometimes you would be able to see the person across the yard and you would motion the person to put up the line. Most often the owner said yes, because that's what we did. The owner gave you the address and you went to the same floor at the opposite building. Hopefully, there wasn't a dog or vagrant around. Next, you would go up to the fire escape and somebody from your family, or your block would swing the line with this knot on the end until you caught the line and placed it on the pulley. If not a pulley then there was a hook to put the line on and that's how it worked.*

1
Planting Roots (1900–1920)

This chapter will focus on several groups that remained in East Harlem for a considerable period: Jews, Italians, blacks and Puerto Ricans. Each group settled in East Harlem in the late nineteenth century, but their oral histories will begin in the early twentieth century. This story concludes with the onset of the Great Depression.

Jewish East Harlem

In the late fifteenth century, Sephardic Jews living in Spain and Portugal were exiled to Holland. Jews found brief refuge there and in several other Dutch territories, but this respite was short-lived and these Jews fled again, this time to New Amsterdam in 1654. The first Hebrew school and synagogue were established here in 1728 and 1730 respectively.[1] After the Civil War, a cadre of German-Jewish merchants from the Lower East Side settled in East Harlem. Upon their arrival these merchants built homes and opened stores along the Third Avenue commercial strip.[2]

Morton Ross, the son of Simon and Mildred Ross, is a Jewish entrepreneur who was raised in East Harlem. He still travels to work in the neighborhood. Though not a German Jew, Ross's family arrived in East Harlem at the time when many German Jews first settled in the neighborhood. Like the German Jews of that era, Ross' family were also entrepreneurs.

My grandfather, Henry Ross, was from Hungary and he met my grandmother in Europe and he brought her over here. He came to East Harlem during Abraham Lincoln's presidency. After his arrival he kept in contact with his brothers by writing back to them in Hungary. My grandfather like every immigrant had to make a living and when he lived in Europe he got into the wine business. Henry Ross went into the vineyards, got the grapes, cleaned it and he'd bottled it and that was his business. My father Simon Ross was the youngest of five children and he was born in the neighborhood. My grandfather spoke a little Hungarian, and a little Polish, Italian and Yiddish. I can tell you this, Yiddish is a language spoken all over the world. It is a combination of several languages like German, Polish and Czechoslovakian [sic] *and my grandfather spoke it all over the world.*

After their arrival to the neighborhood, German Jews resided next to one another and later established several Jewish organizations in East Harlem and found work. The German Jewish laborers during this period worked in such trades as construction, painting, paper hanging, carpentry and decorating. Though German Jews established themselves in East Harlem, they were separated from their brethren in downtown Manhattan were they could worship and partake in the daily activities of Jewish life. This separation motivated them to build a synagogue in 1873, a Hebrew school in 1876 and other social organizations that were conducive to Jewish life in East Harlem. Other Jewish organizations that followed were the Harlem YMHA (Young Men's Hebrew Association) and B'nai B'rith, the former founded in 1879 and the latter in 1882.[3]

Some wealthy Jewish New Yorkers then living in lower Manhattan abandoned the area and settled in East Harlem, and before long German Jews became a part of the neighborhood that included Germans, Irish and later Italians. German Jews became affiliated with many German immigrant associations. To affirm their solidarity with Irish East Harlemites, German Jews sponsored a charity event to assist the Irish Relief Fund.[4]

Unfortunately some attempts at acclimation were not unsuccessful. Jacob Cantor, a New York state senator, applied and was rejected for membership to an exclusive gentleman's club because he was Jewish. Only after his rejection was made public was Cantor accepted. Many of East Harlem's German Jewish organizations succeeded as a result of the community's population surge. For example, at first Synagogue Hand in Hand, like many Jewish organizations, struggled to find participants. Fortunately Hand in Hand added congregants which allowed the synagogue to move from its modest location on 110th and Third Avenue to a more spacious edifice on 125th Street and Fifth Avenue. The move coincided with a new name: Temple Israel.[5]

Women played an important role in German-Jewish East Harlem. Temple Israel's female congregants established a sewing circle for poor Jewish East Harlemites and a free kindergarten class for disadvantaged children. Another successful venture was the (Uptown) Talmud Torah, the congregation's first school, founded in the 1890s. The final wave of German Jews transplanted themselves from downtown to East and West Harlem by the end of the century. Jewish immigration into East Harlem continued into the next century, but this group hailed from Eastern Europe. They followed in the footsteps of earlier immigrant German Jews to East Harlem. However, a small number of East European Jews had resided in East Harlem since 1890. Five years later this population expanded.[6]

When the twentieth century began, 17,000 Russian Jews of every economic class resided in the Harlem area.[7] By 1929 tens of thousands of East European Jews resided in both East and West Harlem. Many East European Jews were attracted to the neighborhood by the possibility of financial prosperity and better housing. The tenements and brownstones in East Harlem were structurally sound and less expensive in contrast to the tenements on the Lower East Side. Also, Jews on the Lower East Side lost their residences when their apartments were destroyed and replaced by factories, parks and the Manhattan and Williamsburg bridges.

Finally, nearly one million Jews fled to America to escape the Kishinev and Gomel massacres in 1903 and the Russo-Japanese War (1904–05).[8] Here two Jewish former East Harlemites whose families hailed from Eastern Europe recall their East Harlem connection. Businessman Meyer Kukle, born in 1920, grew up in East Harlem. He remembers when his father immigrated to the neighborhood.

My father immigrated to the United States from Latvia on May 8, 1909, when he was twenty years old and moved to East Harlem and lived on 109th Street. Before he came to America he was a solder for Czar Nicholas of Russia which owned Latvia in those years. And my father ran away from the Russian army. [His cousins] became his patron and signed the papers so the public wouldn't be responsible for his welfare. He rented a room and received a couch for two dollars a week and obtained his first job through his cousins which was a furniture business on the Lower East Side. My father made four dollars a week and he later worked at Peck Slip at the Fulton Fish market. He pulled a bucket of fish with a hook over the cobblestones. His next job was with a local man from East Harlem who had a wholesale food business, and lots of food and vegetables were sold there. And many Germans and Jews also worked there and the food was sold on a horse and wagon and my father sold his produce along 125th Street. My mother, Sara Laurie, arrived from New Jersey and it was my father who went to New Jersey and met my mother through a Latvian friend.

Eugene Sklar, former director of Union Settlement in East Harlem, also recalls when his parents came to East Harlem. Like Kukle, his parents arrived from Eastern Europe after the Russian conflict in 1905.

Eugene Sklar: *My father boarded a ship in Rotterdam, in the Netherlands and arrived in East Harlem in 1912. He was originally from Odessa, Russia, and my father was exposed to many Russian Jews with radical viewpoints. This happened after the Russians were defeated by the Japanese in the 1905 Russo-Japanese War and this was a period of radical thinking. Upon his arrival he moved with his cousins, a working-class family, on 110th Street and Lexington Avenue. His uncle owned an old-fashioned fish store and there was a huge tank with live fish swimming around.*

You went and picked out a fish and they would kill it and skinned the fish. Afterwards, my father worked for a taciturn and tyrannical German Jewish grocery store owner. He never gave my father anything to eat. And my father would have to buy his food which was a can of sardines and that would be his lunch. After working there for a number of years he moved to Chicago and later enlisted in the service. After he was discharged, he returned to New York and bought a laundry store on 135th Street. There he met more Jewish craftsmen who bought and rehabilitated buildings.

My mother arrived in about 1921 before the second Anti-Immigration Act [of 1924] which further curtailed East European immigration. She lived with sister at the YWHA on 110th and Fifth Avenue. My parents' first home was on 100th Street and Lexington Avenue, owned by Sephardic Jews. My grandparents on the mother's side were Orthodox and they never learned English, and they spoke only Yiddish. However, my father being the more radical person learned English.

East European Jews replaced the Irish and German immigrants in the neighborhood and became the main group west of Third Avenue and below 125th Street. Prosperous Jews lived in the tenements and brownstone flats located west of Lexington Avenue and south of 110th Street and many were employed in high or low white-collar positions. Within this group one-fourth worked as manufacturers, businessmen, or other white-collar professionals. In contrast the other three-fourths worked as clerks, sales people or semi-professionals. And the lower-class segment of East European Jews resided in the congested tenement district east of Lexington Avenue. Many in this section were employed as skilled and unskilled laborers. These Jews worked in menial positions, and only one-fourth of Jews who resided in this part of the neighborhood worked in white collar jobs.[9]

East of Third Avenue to the East River was dominated by the Italians in the Little Italy section of East Harlem. Only a small percentage of East European Jews lived in Little Italy.[10] Meyer Kukle's parents were blue-collar laborers who sold produce to make ends meet.

Mom and Pop had a pushcart business under the New York Railroad (Metro North) on Park Avenue at 111th to 112th Streets and they placed their supplies in the nearby cellar. For instance they sold onion and potatoes per pound now they put it in cans. At night you would wrap up the pushcart with a blanket and ropes.... and my parents did this routine six days a week. My father obtained his produce at the Harlem wholesale market on 100th Street and First Avenue. The market was composed of four square blocks and the men who provided our produce came from Staten Island and Bergen County, New Jersey. These men stayed at the farmer's hotel on 101st Street and First Avenue. At 4:00 A.M. they'd go to the market and take the covers off their trucks and the store keepers would buy their fresh vegetables. My father would arrive at 6:00 A.M. and buy the vegetables and put them on my mother's pushcart. On Saturdays he'd go before 9:00 A.M. and see what the farmers were stuck with, because at 9:00 A.M. the farmers had to leave. At 6:00 A.M. the farmer sold his spinach at fifty cents a box and three hours later the price was lowered to twenty-five cents. The food was healthier back then, for it wasn't sprayed with too many chemicals like many of today's canned foods.

With the relocation of many Jews from Lower Manhattan to East Harlem, two disparate East European Jewish groups emerged. The first group aimed to divorce itself from the old world culture in lower Manhattan. To accomplish this, these East European Jews established several social and cultural associations. In short, they created what author Jeffrey Gurock termed "American Judaism," a form of Judaism that in his view remained committed to the Jewish tradition combined with the American way of life.[11]

The latter group of East European Jews chose to retain their identification with the old world culture. These Jews used institutions based on the old world culture that were instrumental in solving the social and financial situations of many Jews. Before long, many Jewish houses of worship and organizations moved from the Lower East Side to East Harlem. Synagogues and yeshivas helped Jews maintain the old world customs. Non-religious organizations also helped to perpetuate old world customs. The Workmen's Circle Branch No. Two, established in the late nineteenth century, became a cultural center for progressive-minded Jews and provided death benefits or catered to those who were ill. Later, the Workmen's Circle expanded and included educational and fraternal associations.[12] In addition to the Workmen's Circle, other socialist organizations addressed the day-to-day concerns of many Jewish East Harlemites. Meyer Kukle recalls the Workmen's Circle and the socialists' presence in East Harlem.

> The socialists had different chapters and they gathered on the corner of 110th Street and the Lexington Avenue subway and would congregate and make speeches. Other political parties were also there as the Democrats would convene on another corner. And across the street on another corner was composed of the communists. The Republicans didn't come around much for the Republicans in East Harlem was what La Guardia was, the fusion party. My father read the Forward, a socialist paper. The Forward informed you of all the socialist parties and politicians like Jasper McGreevy and the socialist mayors throughout the country.
> On 106th Street between Lexington and Park Avenues on the north side of the street was a settlement house called the Federation, a four-story building which was like a community center. Right next to the Federation was a big seven-story office building. There the socialist branches held their meetings. My friends' parents belonged to the Arbeter Ring, of the Workmen's Circle, which was a Jewish organization. All the members were socialists and they were fine organizations and they were Jewish-oriented but not religious.

Meyer Kukle pictured here in 2004 at the CUNY Graduate Center. Mr. Kukle grew up in the Jewish section of East Harlem. Later, he became an executive of an outerwear company. Mr. Kukle received his bar mitzvah at the Uptown Talmud Torah on East Harlem on 111th Street and Lexington Avenue. The person next to him is unknown.

The socialists' presence coincided with the progressive movement in East Harlem. Through their affiliation with the labor unions, Jewish East Harlemites participated in rents strikes and demonstrated against exorbitant food prices. These protests culminated in the quest for political power.[13] Like other organizations, the socialists sought to become a political force in the neighborhood. However, it took a decade and a half before they made their mark in East Harlem. The socialists had established a base in East Harlem and advocated on the behalf of the Jewish community. The socialists participation in the neighborhood's rent strikes, consumer and worker protests paid off. The socialists made modest steps in the 1912 congressional race, but unfortunately their party's candidate finished in fourth place.[14]

On the Lower East Side the socialist congressional candidate, Meyer London, successfully won his seat with a door-to-door campaign. This inspired East Harlem socialists, and in late 1916 they recruited Morris Hillquit, a champion of labor issues from the Lower East Side, to run in the 20th Congressional District. Hillquit challenged incumbent Republican congressman Siegel and Democrat Bernard Rosenblatt for the congressional seat. Despite support from five of the city's biggest unions and a very impressive door-to-door campaign, Hillquit lost to Siegel by only four hundred votes out of twelve thousand ballots cast. Hillquit was not successful in the next two Congressional races either.

Nevertheless, Hillquit mobilized the socialist Jewish vote in the neighborhood and demonstrated how Jews could affect the outcome of a political race. Later, Hillquit became an advisor to East Harlem socialists Bernardo Vega and Norman Thomas. William Karlin succeeded Hillquit as the socialist congressional candidate in 1922 but he lacked Hillquit's charisma. After Hillquit left East Harlem, the Socialist Party's appeal waned in the neighborhood and many Jews moved back to the Democratic Party.[15]

Religious institutions helped Jews retain an attachment to the old traditions, yet they also helped Jews acclimate themselves to the American culture. The Harlem Federation and the Uptown Talmud Torah were two organizations that were instrumental in this endeavor. The Harlem Federation, founded in 1905, resulted from a September 1903 newspaper article that asserted young Jewish children could convert to Christianity. Soon Jewish leaders founded synagogues and religious schools for Jewish children.

The Harlem Federation provided its members with a variety of social services. For example, the educational committee provided instruction in Yiddish and in English, and the employment committee secured jobs for many of its members. The social work committee established recreational activities, and the civics committee encouraged its members to seek U.S. citizenship and be active in their community. Within five years the Harlem Federation building located on 105th Street between Second and Third Avenues served over 1,000 children.[16]

Another organization which helped East Harlem Jews to maintain their Jewishness was the Uptown Talmud Torah Association (UTTA). Established in 1892, the UTTA met the religious and educational needs of Russian Jewish children. A new Uptown Talmud Torah was created in 1905 when it merged with the Harlem Educational Institute. It also acquired property on 111th Street and Lexington Avenue. This new organization garnered community support by helping Jewish youth retain their culture and focused on teaching Judaism and Hebrew. The UTTA also began a breakfast program for impoverished children in the neighborhood. Around 1912 it was estimated that 8,000 people from the immediate area were associated with the Uptown Talmud Torah. Meyer Kukle recalls his time at the UTTA.

I went to P.S. 101 on 111th Street and Lexington Avenue right next to the Uptown Talmud Torah Hebrew School. [Later the UTTA would become Commander John J. Shea School under the auspices of St. Cecilia Church. This building would change hands again when the school closed in 1971. Since then, the Highway Church of Christ has occupied this building.] The Uptown Talmud Torah taught you how to read Hebrew and translate the words and also prepared you for your bar mitzvah by studying the Torah. You didn't go to your regular teacher, you went to a special rabbi.

Meyer Kukle also recalled how the UTTA served as a community center for Jewish youth in East Harlem.

Downstairs is where we had our prayers and the older people met upstairs. The UTTA taught Hebrew school from 3:30 P.M. until 6:30 P.M., and after 6:30 it became a recreational center called the Harlem Hebrew Institute. The Harlem Hebrew Institute put on plays. And we also had a basketball team composed of blacks, Puerto Ricans, Panamanians and Italians. We also had different clubs and some of them were religious, while other clubs were nonreligious. For example we had a Boy Scout troop.... Georgie Sandler, who was a member of the Boy Scouts, also happened to be black, and he was my best friend who spoke excellent Yiddish.

Despite the establishment of the UTTA and the Harlem Federation some East Harlem Jews still feared Jewish youth might acclimate to American culture and reject their Jewish heritage. In fact, many adolescents had become more Americanized. Along with the assimilation of American culture, some Jewish leaders concluded that intermarriage was another reason the old world customs had lost their appeal. Jewish leaders answered with the establishment of the "American" synagogue.[17]

At that point in time, the Talmud Torah helped bridge both Judaism and American ideals. But some believed it was insufficient for it only reached Jews in the East Harlem area. So Jewish leaders conceived the idea of an American synagogue. They felt this was needed because the traditional synagogues failed to reach the broad East Harlem Jewish community. One reason was the synagogues hired American-born rabbis who spoke English, while many adherents desired Yiddish instruction. They discovered the American synagogue could bring Jews together and serve as both a house of worship and social organization, also hosting dances and athletic events.[18]

But the Harlem Young Men's Hebrew Orthodox League and the Harlem Hebrew League were social organizations. The next organization founded to help Jewish youth retain their heritage was the Central Jewish Institute (CJI).

The CJI combined Jewish social, cultural and recreational services with religious instruction, supposedly under the authority of a sanctioned orthodox synagogue. But the Central Jewish Institute was not a synagogue and though the CJI's tried to help Jewish youth embrace old world customs, it was not enough and Jewish leaders still looked for answers. Nevertheless, the CJI continued to operate in nearby Yorkville well into the 1940s.[19]

Undaunted, the Jewish leaders pressed on. Rabbi Herbert S. Goldstein, once associated with CJI, gained valuable experience from that venture and transformed his ideas into the Institutional Synagogue. The Institutional Synagogue in Central Harlem concentrated on connecting second-generation Americanized Jews with Jewish culture. However, the Institutional Synagogue had its detractors. Some adherents felt the institution was composed only of the upper crust of Jewish East Harlem. And the synagogue also charged dues, which some members viewed as an effrontery. Lastly, Rabbi Goldstein was accused of employing the theatrics of a Christian minister. However, Goldstein said that his contributions were religious oriented and helped bring many Jewish youth to the synagogue.[20]

Little Italy in East Harlem

Italian immigrants succeeded East European Jews and settled in East Harlem. In the late 1870s, J.D. Crimmons, a wealthy Irishman and contractor, hired Irish laborers to work on the horse car lines situated on 125th Street and First Avenue, but the laborers went on strike. Undeterred, Crimmons replaced the Irish laborers with Italian laborers from Lower Manhattan. However, more men were needed so Crimmons requested and hired more Italian laborers from Italy.[21] Italian immigrants lived near Mount Morris Park (today called Marcus Garvey Park and located at 121st–124th Streets, Madison to Fifth Avenues). Later, they moved to 106th Street and First Avenue and lived in shanties near the East River Creek, then called the Jones Woods an area once known as a location for target practice.[22] In 1878, the first assemblage of Italian immigrants from Italy to East Harlem hailed from the town of Polla in the province of Salerno. As it had been for Jews, East Harlem was a respite compared to the overpopulated Lower East Side. Many Italians moved to East Harlem and upon their arrival, they roomed with relatives or friends who already lived in the neighborhood.[23]

Italian immigrants moved into many of the four- and five-story tenements that were constructed east of Third Avenue to the East River. Italian East Harlem slowly began to emerge and by 1884, four thousand Italian immigrants lived in East Harlem. Southern Italians immigrated to East Harlem to avoid unemployment, overpopulation, disease, excessive taxes and infighting that transpired in Italy.[24]

Angela Bella Puco: *My great-grandfather, Stefano Puco, hailed from Sant' Antimo, Italy, near Naples. He was born there in 1871 and landed at Ellis Island in 1901. According to the Ellis Island files, my great-grandfather's relatives were living in East Harlem when he arrived in the neighborhood. His choices limited, Stefano left his family behind in Sant' Antimo. During his two-week transatlantic voyage to America, Stefano traveled with other men from his hometown. In America, he worked hard as a laborer, saved his money, and later returned to Naples. Stefano brought his wife, my great-grandmother Teresina Milo, and his daughter Rosina to America in 1905. My grandfather Antimo remained in Italy. And he followed in the Italian tradition of the first male child being named after their paternal grandfather. Hence, Antimo is my great-great grandfather's name. My grandfather Antimo was born in Sant 'Antimo, Italy, in 1896, and arrived in America at age nine. He should have arrived eight months earlier with his mother and sister, but his name had been crossed out of the ship's manifest on July 3, 1905.*

When a passenger's name was crossed out on the ship's manifest page this indicated that a person never boarded the ship. Back in Naples, all immigrants were carefully inspected by the Italian authorities to see if you were "fit to travel." If one's name was crossed out, it was most likely due to an illness. Antimo Puco arrived on Ellis Island in March, 1906, chaperoned by his uncle, Antonio Ligouri. My grandfather and his uncle traveled on the Steamship Cretic, *which was the sister ship to the SS Romanic. Both ships were part of the White Star Line. According to the ship's manifest document, Antimo and his uncle told the inspectors at Ellis island that they were going to stay with Stafano Puco at 2123 First Avenue between 109th and 110th Streets. The tenement building was demolished many years ago. Today only an empty lot remains.*

The burgeoning Italian enclave led to the development of several mutual aid societies in East Harlem which helped Italian immigrants. Many of these societies were named after towns or provinces in Italy. These societies allowed Italian immigrants to socialize with one another or help procure money to bury recently deceased Italian immigrants. Furthermore, they sustained the values and customs brought to the new world. One of these societies was founded by Italian immigrants from Polla. They named it in honor of the Madonna di Constantinopoli, known as the Protectress of Polla. A *festa* was held to pay homage to the Madonna on 110th Street near the East River. A year later the festivities took place in a house on 111th Street near the East River.[25] The homage to the Madonna occurred almost simultaneously with the construction of the church of Mount Carmel. East Harlem still pays homage to the Madonna in mid–July when the church of Mt. Carmel holds its annual festa. Al Loungo, executive coordinator of the Mount Carmel Festival, explains.

Al Loungo: *The tradition goes back, 1500 years and many Italians who worshipped the Madonna retained this tradition when they came to America. In the early twentieth century it might have been supported by an Italian club or society, and these clubs were located near small stores where many Italians met. Years ago, during the festa people set up stands and sold food, et cetera, and by the early 1960s, the Giglio was located on 106th Street and Second Avenue. But it moved to 108th Street because of the construction of the Benjamin Franklin Plaza. Then, it stopped entirely because of the housing construction in the area and by the mid-1960s, Italians moved to the Bronx or Long Island. The Italians wanted to transfer the tradition to those areas. And it was not the same because the area included homes and houses and it was a more rural area. Father Rufano, the pastor of our Lady of Mount Carmel and other old-time Italians who once lived in the neighborhood wanted to bring the festa back to East Harlem. Myself, my cousin Andy Rocco and my wife all decided to bring it back. When the festa returned, there was only one stand, then it grew and there were many stands and people sold food, games, et cetera. We added rides and other events to make it a more festive atmosphere. Then, the Giglio Society saw the festa and they realized it was once again alive in the neighborhood. Many people joined the Giglio society of East Harlem.*

Emiliano Kirner, a Pallotine priest, settled in the neighborhood in 1880s and worked with the Italian community to build the church. The neighborhood's commitment to the church's construction was boundless and both Italian men and women in East Harlem helped in the church's construction.

The Church of Mt. Carmel was completed in 1885 and held its first baptism on November 29. Since many Italians built the church it was unofficially called the "Church of the Italians." But for many years Italian East Harlemites were confined to the church's basement to worship, while Irish and German parishioners attended the church's services upstairs. Father Kirner insisted that the church was not complete unless a school was constructed. Inspired by Father Kirner, Our Lady of Mount Carmel School was completed the same year, but in 1887 tragedy struck. Father Kirner was inspecting the school's roof when a wall fell in and he died the next day.[26] A key voice was gone, but soon more Italian immigrants arrived from southern Italy to East Harlem. These immigrants came to East Harlem from Sicily, Calabria, Basilicata and Naples; however, Italian immigration was fraught with problems. Scores of Italian immigrants settled in the neighborhood through the "padrone method." The *padrone*, usually an Italian, offered friendship to recently arrived and confused Italian immigrants and guaranteed the men employment working on the railroads.[27]

The padrone's task was to recruit a group of Italian laborers and lead them to the worksite. If the padrone's efforts at recruitment were unsuccessful, the banks would take over. The bank's messenger would gather a group of Italian located at the docks or place an advertisement in a window. Work was available, but there was no guarantee that the laborer would find employment. Furthermore, the padrone or banker both might exploit these laborers. For example, both men could conveniently fail to mention the exact payment, worksite or conditions. More problems persisted for the Italian laborers since they purchased their food and work gear from the padrone at exorbitant prices. And the padrone billed the laborers to find employment. If too many laborers were recruited for employment, this quota could exceed the amount of available work and the laborers remained idle. Conversely, if the work quickly dissipated the laborers were dismissed without pay.[28] The padrone method continued until the 1935 Foran Act outlawed this type of employment practice.

Angela Bella Puco: *My great-cousin Anna Rose recounted the story how my great grandfather was a victim of the padrone system. And the padrone was very manipulative because these men took your hard earned money. They forced their employees into certain types of unsavory labor systems. Also some even worked in the mines which mirrored a labor camp and the men were housed if they were prisoners. And many Neapolitans and southern Italians traveled to West Virginia to obtain work. In 1906* Outlook *magazine did an expose on the padrone system. Fortunately, my grandfather escaped the padrone in West Virginia and returned to New York.*

Factory work or taking in boarders was another way to increase a family's income. Italian immigrants who roomed with their family or relatives paid women to do their laundry. Boarders cooked their own meals and ate alone, except on Sundays when they could eat with the family. Even if a boarder found a home in East Harlem, he still faced life without his family. The Italian immigrants longed to reunite with their family, and one immigrant labored for years until he acquired enough money to bring his siblings over from Italy.[29]

George Di Martino: *My grandfather came here to East Harlem from Naples at age 12 in 1908 and he lived with my great-grandparents on 110th between First and Second Avenues. Later, he went back to Italy in 1914 during the Italian-Turkish War and served in the cavalry and kept his Italian citizenship. After the war my grandfather came back to America and brought my grandmother with him.*

Even after their arrival in East Harlem these immigrants lived very frugally.

Rose Savatelli: *Both of my parents hailed from Naples and they came to this country to seek a better life. But growing up in East Harlem we didn't have* *many things like a washing machine and we didn't eat meat except on Sunday. We had pasta three or four times a week and I'll tell you one thing, the food we ate was healthier compared to today's food.*

In Italian East Harlem the family became a buffer as Italian immigrants acclimated themselves to the United States. But first-generation Italian immigrants maintained some attachment to Italy. Some Italian families returned to Italy to attend a family member's wedding or during the Christmas season. Unfortunately, the same problems that compelled Italians to immigrate to America existed in East Harlem: overpopulation, disease, and unemployment. By the early twentieth century Italian East Harlem was a dense and overpopulated area. Ten, twelve or fourteen people might live in an apartment meant for four or five. Air and light were scarce in the neighborhoods' old law tenements. And Italian East Harlemites developed many health problems living in these tenements, including diarrhea, respiratory diseases, diphtheria and tuberculosis. These causes led to many deaths in the neighborhood.[30]

Few, if any, new-law tenements that included expanded airshafts, better fire escapes, and windows on every floor were built in Italian East Harlem.[31] Despite the harsh realities Italians remained undaunted and Italian East Harlem, fondly known as Little Italy, continued to expand throughout the neighborhood. Its unofficial boundary lines were 102nd to 120th Streets from Third Avenue to the East River. Numerous family-owned businesses were part of Italian East Harlem.[32] Michael Lentini, who grew up in Italian East Harlem, is the head of the Fathers and Sons stickball league. Lentini's family were entrepreneurs. His father owned a funeral home on 118th Street and Second Avenue where his uncles also worked. Another important business was the Italian Bank that served Italian East Harlem. More than just dispensing money, it provided needed services like a small discount store.

Rose Pascale: *Today there is a pet shop on 116th Street between First and Second Avenues, but before when many Italians lived here, it was an immigrant Italian bank. And one of the first Italian banks in East Harlem. The Italians obtained their mail from Italy and they also brought Italian stamps and envelopes to write back to their families or send money back to Italy.*

Hundreds of grocery and candy stores, restaurants and bars were part of Italian East Harlem. Italians bought their favorite foods there.[33] Rao's restaurant and Patsy's Pizzeria were just two of the restaurants in the neighborhood. Rao's opened in 1896.

Jim Arless: *Pasquallie Lancieri, my father-in-law, opened Patsy's in 1933. Patsy's started out as a single store located at 2287 First Avenue between East 117th and 118th Streets. Patsy's had a clam bar in the window, a few tables and a bar, a pizza oven, and behind the pizza oven was a stove, sink, and refrigerator. Patsy's* *gradually expanded to what it is now. We used to buy our pizza by the slice. I remember working and it was open until four or five in the morning.*

Patsy's became a successful establishment. George Arless recalls some of the celebrities who have eaten at Patsy's.

Jim Arless: *Frank Sinatra was a regular customer or the New York Yankees would eat here. I remember as a teenager, my friends and I waited until the Yankee players ate here and we got their autographs. One autograph I got was Joe Page, the Yankees relief pitcher. [Other] celebrities who came to Patsy's were Anthony Quinn, Bill Murray, Rodney Dangerfield with his son, Faye Dunaway, and Linda Ronstadt.*

Italian immigration occurred in the areas once dominated by the Irish and Germans. At first both groups took umbrage to the Italian incursion into East Harlem and the Italians fought with the Irish. Eventually, the Italians supplanted the Irish and German immigrants in East Harlem and became the majority. Here is how one building became totally occupied by Italian immigrants. If there was an Italian custodian, he used his position to rent to other Italian immigrants. Before long the tenement became predominantly Italian.[34] Residents from particular provinces in Italy were located on certain blocks throughout Italian East Harlem. Father Peter Rufano remembers.

Father Peter Rufano: *Italians who lived on 104th–106th Streets hailed from northern Italy; and residents on 107th Street hailed from Sicily and the Italians who resided on 108th Street were from Calabria; while other families who lived on 109th Street hailed from Naples. My family came from Salerno and we lived on 110th Street and my mother was a housewife with ten children and my father was a laborer. He came over and worked with the so-called green lines, what was then known as the Lexington Avenue trolleys. And finally there were Italians who lived on 111th–112th Streets and they were Abruzzians and Neapolitans.*

Work for many Italians improved in the early twentieth century as Italian East Harlemites held various forms of employment. In his thesis, Robert Freeman studied census data from 1900 in two districts of Italian East Harlem. This employment data from enumerated 126 workers. Fifty percent of them were employed as day laborers. The rest of the workforce was composed of carpenters, tailors, masons, barbers, shoemakers and saloon owners. A decade later, the workforce doubled but also became more diverse. The percentage of day laborers was reduced to 28 percent while masons, barbers and tailors remained the same. New categories of truck drivers, street sweepers, piano factory workers, store owner, hat and fruit stands and cafés were added. Several decades later, Italians were still employed in these same businesses.[35]

Rose Savatelli: *Men worked as bricklayers or in construction and the women worked in the house and did piece work or made fake flowers. My father was a barber* who worked on 125th Street and Second Avenue and he earned fifteen dollars a week with tips. If he received a quarter or fifty cent tip that was a big deal then. We also had small buildings and there were adjacent stores near those buildings. On 115th Street we had grocery stores, pizza parlors and pastry shops like Cincotti's, where my daughter worked.

George DiMartino: *There were pushcarts along First Avenue and my grandmother and I shopped there with a paper bag. We would go up and down First Avenue to 110th Street where you could buy potatoes, calzones, meat, cheese, pastas, greens and other foods.*

Many Italian laborers lived in Little Italy, but upper-class Italians lived in Italian East Harlem on First Avenue near 116th Street to the East River, an area called Doctor's Row.[36] For many years Italian East Harlemites were treated by these doctors who made house calls with their familiar black bag. Or Italian East Harlemites traveled to the doctor's office. However, some of these doctors had their own idiosyncrasies.

Father Peter Rufano: *On 116th Street and Pleasant Avenue there were private houses and brownstones and doctors, lawyers or all professional people lived there.*

Rose Savatelli: *Ten doctors were on one street like Dr. Cafeeli, Dr. Longo, Dr. Septi, or Dr. Qualio. We never went to the emergency room and you said, "Take the kid to the doctor over here." And it was clean.*

Ann Poliseo: *Then there was Dr. Constantine. I remember him because he was a very big, heavy man and there are some things you don't forget. Dr. Constantine had the messiest office that I have ever seen and paper was strewn everywhere in his office. I remember going there with my grandmother and she would say, "How can he find anything in here?" But he did, and he found his notes and gave us the right prescriptions.*

We will now look at the people of Italian East Harlem. In the nineteenth century, many Italian women worked in the garment industry. Italian women worked under arduous conditions in dimly lit locations without proper ventilation. These insufferable conditions did not end until the 1930s. Though Italian women were seldom seen in the neighborhood, they were not confined to their apartments. As Orsi writes, "Italian women were sheltered, but not imprisoned." They spent their time indoors with the exception of work, conversing with friends, or tending to their children. Women placed their pillows on the windowsills and leaned out and saw what transpired below.[37]

Rose Pascale: *Yes, I remember the lady in the window. I was talking with a group of older people about that lady, my friend said, "Yeah, she used to rat on us to our mother."*

Lois Pascale Evans, daughter of Rose Pascale: *I recall how the people sat outside in front of their buildings on the lawn chairs. The women leaned out* *of their windows with their arm on their pillows. In the buildings all of the doorways were open and every body knew everybody and you were close with your neighbor. Your brought your neighbor a dish to eat and your neighbor reciprocated and brought you a dish to eat. It was back and forth and it was a lot of sharing then.*

Father Peter Rufano: *You never went out of your block because if you went two or three blocks away you were a bad boy and you were accused of mixing up with others. For some reason you had to be seen by your family and we were restricted except when I grew up and went to vaudeville or to the movies.*

Though Italian East Harlemites lived and worked in some of the most unenviable conditions imaginable, they refused to be downtrodden. Instead many Italian East Harlemites came together.[38] Audrey Berghaus recalls how her community became a unit.

Audrey Berghaus: *Our borderline extended from 112th to 115th Streets and you never really ventured out of that world. All the grocery stores were there on your block and everything was in walking distance. Ten families lived in my building and every building in my neighborhood was a tenement. We didn't have hot water or steam heat in our building but we made out okay. In fact, we had our own forms of communication which was a signal in our building. If a neighbor needed a favor she would knock once on the pipe. Now if a family member was sick then you heard two knocks on the pipe.*

In the summer we barely had a fan, and we'd go up to the roof—"Tar Beach." The only problem was that the tar got stuck on you. You'd put out a blanket or a sheet and you'd sit up there or you sit on the fire escapes to cool off.

The Italian family formed a tight bond which trusted no one outside of the immediate family. Many southern Italians adhered to *Campanilismo* (Territorial) and what followed was the concept of La Famiglia. This translated to "blood relatives" or those married into the family. Those not related to the immediate family were viewed as *forestiere* (foreigners). Many times the *forestiere* were shunned by the tight-knit Italian family. If needed, some Italian East Harlemites made contact with *paesani*, or someone from the same town in Italy.[39] Throughout many Italian neighborhoods in the city, Italian immigrants met their friends or future spouses through the *paesani*.[40]

Ann Poliseo: *My grandparents emigrated from Italy, outside of Bari, called Toritto. They didn't know each other before they met. My grandmother was twenty-one and my grandfather was twenty-nine and they only knew each other for two weeks when they were married. The paesani or family friends matched them together and they were married at Our Lady of Pompeii Church on the Lower East Side. Later they moved to the West Side and finally to East Harlem and lived on East 112th Street between Park and Madison Avenues. Later they moved to the same street between Second and Third Avenues.*

However, the Italian immigrants from the same provinces did not live in total isolation. Daily exchange among the *paesani* from the other towns and other ethnic groups in East Harlem made such isolation impossible.[41]

Italian East Harlem was very patriarchal community. Men were the dominant force in the family. Italian men also spent many hours in the numerous social clubs in the neighborhood. Social clubs provided a venue where Italian men felt free to let their guard down. They talked politics, listened to sporting events or played card games. They played bocce or dominoes on folding tables and, like the women, congregated on the sidewalk or the streets. Social clubs also organized social and athletic functions and outings. They held events intended to promote Italian heritage and instructed Italian immigrants on obtaining their U.S. citizenship.[42]

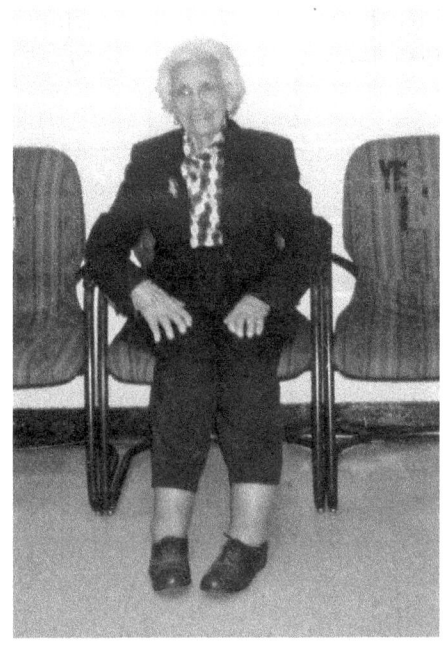

Rose Pascale lived her entire life in East Harlem. Years after her retirement, she continued to serve the neighborhood, volunteering at the Fiorello LaGuardia House on East 116th Street between First and Second Avenue, where this photograph was taken.

Mike Lentini: *Right here on 118th Street and Pleasant Avenue it is a parking lot now. Back then my friend's grandfather owned it and the men played bocce all of the time. And there were numerous clubs in the area. This club here [between 117th and 118th Streets on Pleasant Avenue] has been around here since 1945. It's called the Friends of Victory Club and when I was growing up we called it the old man's club. The old men ran the club and they had the mustaches dressed in suits and ties.*

But social clubs, and even the coffee and barber shops, had one thing in common: women were denied admittance. In addition to social clubs, the mutual aid societies continued in the twentieth century and became more than bereavement associations. Like social clubs, mutual aid societies sponsored social events such as parades, picnics and dances. By the mid–1930s, over one hundred mutual aid societies existed in the neighborhood. Political clubs were also part of Italian East Harlem and these clubs helped elect a rising or established politician. For example, Fiorello La Guardia won an East Harlem congressional seat in 1922 with the assistance of local political club.[43]

At its zenith the population of Italian East Harlem was estimated at 80,000 residents and East Harlem became one of the largest Little Italys in America.[44] Italian East Harlemites were on the streets as they were in their apartments. In fact, the streets became a continuation of the Italian neighborhood. Besides the street life many Italian East Harlemites traveled to the East River. Though the East River was dirty, young men were not deterred and dove off the banks for a swim.[45]

Father Peter Rufano: *From 105 to 108th Street there were the piers along the East River. People jumped in the East River to cool off and they became great swimmers. I never, did for I was not that courageous.*

Central Park posed a problem for Italian children to play for it was too far away, but Jefferson Park, located on 112th to 114th Street and First Avenue, was convenient. In 1934, Jefferson Pool was constructed and many Italians went to the pool. Jefferson Park was also place where many Italian East Harlemites listened to many musicians.

Rose Pascale: *No bridges were up here and there was no East River Drive, but we had Jefferson Park. When I was growing up you had no pool and you went to the park. There was a house in the middle of the Park which we called it the White House. The reason why it was the called the White House, it was white like concrete and with a big staircase. In the summer they had concerts there in Jefferson Park.*

Besides Jefferson Park, Italian adolescents looked to settlement organizations for enjoyment. Harlem House, Union Settlement, and La Casa del Popolo (The People's House) were some of the places that provided recreational space for Italian American youth. Young Italian East Harlemites also frequented dance halls and cabarets in the neighborhood. They also played in the streets throughout the neighborhood, but the streets could also be very dangerous.[46]

Rose Pascale: *You played in the street, even though there were trolley cars. There was not much traffic, also you played stickball, or played on the sidewalk. We made our skateboards with the box crates. And the cop knew your mother and he came after you when you did something wrong.*

First-generation Italian immigrants wanted their children to retain some of their Italian heritage, and this was accomplished through customs or language. Leonard Covello, principal of Benjamin Franklin High School, established the Italian American Students League, which helped Italian youth learn the Italian language.[47] Pre-adolescent Italian girls bided their time in movie theatres, read books, congregated on the building stoops or played on the sidewalk. But when they became adolescents and old enough to work, Italian boys and girls were both viewed as financial providers to the family. Many Italian parents distrusted the educational system, which they looked upon as a form of elitism as the teacher represented the upper class. The law mandated that children attend school, but southern Italians viewed formal education unfavorably. Since southern Italians failed to expand their horizons, they felt their children would follow in their footsteps. Student absenteeism and low marks became frequent and tolerated by some parents in Italian East Harlem.[48] Audrey Berghaus' relatives immigrated to East Harlem in 1910 from a town called San Fratello, a province in Messina. Audrey recalls that her grandmother worked in a factory to support her family and sacrificed any form of education.

Audrey Berghaus: *The minute my grandmother arrived in East Harlem she went to live on 103rd Street. The next day she was working in a factory doing piecework making men's shirts, collars and sleeves. And she had no real formal education in the United States, maybe she had some in Italy. My grandmother was in her twenties and was unmarried, because she had to work to support her family. There were seven of them and every child worked except the two youngest family members. Every time a suitor came over, my great-grandfather said, "I have no daughters to get married." My grandmother finally married my grandfather at twenty-five. They met through a family friend.*

Little Italy in East Harlem was alive, but Italian East Harlem soon disappeared under the guise of redevelopment and changing demographics.

This short story focuses on the Irish in East Harlem. The potato famine of the mid–1840s led to a mass exodus from Ireland. A decade later, over 130,000 Irish immigrants lived in New York City. As the nineteenth century ended, 409,924 Irish New Yorkers resided in the city[49] and some settled in East Harlem. When the twentieth century began, many Germans, Italians, Jews and Irish lived in the neighborhood. One Irish East Harlemite, actor James Cagney, who achieved fame as George M. Cohan in the film *Yankee Doodle Dandy*, lived on 96th Street and attended St. Francis de Sales Church on the same block.

By the 1920s many Irish East Harlemites left the neighborhood. But some Irish families remained in East Harlem, like Vincent Murphy who along with his family lived in the Harlem Courthouse from 1920 to 1931. The courthouse was located on 121st Street between Lexington and Third Avenues. Murphy's father and mother had six children.

Vincent Murphy: *My mother, Lucy Ellen Phippes, nicknamed Nellie, came here from Leicester, England, with my grandmother, Amos Phippes, to escape my* *grandfather, whom I guess was very tyrannical. After mom arrived in America she worked in a small dry goods store. My father, Daniel K. Murphy, was born in County Cork in Ireland. He left Ireland when he was accused of tickling the fish, which is taking the fish and probably other items without paying for them, and this was a major offense. My father's uncle, Tim Crimmins, worked as a butler in a fancy apartment on Seventy-Fourth Street and Madison Avenue. My father was visiting my great-uncle when he met my mother who happened to be at the apartment that day. They returned to Ireland on the Lusitania and married. My mother eventually converted to Catholicism.*

After Murphy's parents returned to America, they first lived in Hell's Kitchen (today Clinton) on Fifty-Fourth Street and Eleventh Avenue, where young Vincent was born. Later, the family lived in Astoria, Queens, then Palisades Park in New Jersey. Murphy recalls how his family arrived in East Harlem. Like most immigrants Murphy's father had high aspirations for himself and his family. Interestingly, Murphy attended a segregated school in the black part of East Harlem. Here he recounts the school and his neighborhood.

Vincent Murphy: *My father was a smart man who studied a lot and he took many city tests to obtain work. Before you found work through the Tammany machine, but he passed the test and obtained work at the Harlem Courthouse. There*

Vincent Murphy lived with his parents and siblings from 1921 to 1930 at the Harlem Courthouse on 121st Street between Lexington and Third Avenue. Murphy's father once worked at the courthouse as a foreman. Murphy is seen here in the living room of his home in New Jersey. During the early twentieth century, East Harlem was home to many European immigrants.

my father supervised seven people who worked under him and the men worked as porters and mopped the floors while the women cooked the meals. Because he worked at the courthouse his apartment was rent free. I first went to St. Paul's Church (117th Street between Madison and Park Avenues), but my father was dissatisfied with the education at that school and he transferred me to All Saints School on 129th Street and Madison Avenue. At the school we put on plays that were boring and there was no speaker system. The school was in a black neighborhood, but there weren't any blacks in the school.

There wasn't much to do so we'd walk a lot, played football, roller skate to school or to the Macomb's Dam Bridge near the Polo Grounds. You also walked along 125th Street which was wonderful. There you had restaurants, theatres, movie houses and vaudeville which took place mostly in the afternoon though it was on the way out. A guy from Atlantic City, New Jersey, would perform and sing. As for the movies they cost a nickel or fifteen cents. You saw a slide show like Billy Watson, Douglas Fairbanks, William S. Hart, and lots of Westerns. Once in a while they showed a mystery and every block had a museum. There was a guy named Walter Huston and he played the soprano organ and sang in a high voice. Before the Apollo Theater opened it was a burlesque house.

Every year the merchants on 125th Street got together and promoted a parade and my whole family was in it. You won a prize for the most original costume and my father had the idea to dress our family like carrots. All of his children, including me, there were four of us in the family then, had red hair and we were dressed up like carrots with the orange and green paper draped around us. The winner had two choices and one of the two prizes was a Kodak box camera or a five-dollar gold coin which was real money then. My family won, and we chose the Kodak box camera and my family was filmed winning the prize.

Vincent Murphy describes this community near the Harlem courthouse.

The names they had for Irish, they called you a Mick. There was an Irish section on the next block on 120th Street but they were roughnecks. On 121st Street between Second and Third Avenues was where we shopped. You bought your food from the Jewish merchants who owned the pushcarts. Two families lived at there at Five and Seven Sylvan Place. One girl came from Armenia, and a couple of boys who were Irish lived around there also. At Mount Morris Park we would have sleigh rides, but we mostly played at Sylvan Place.

In the early twentieth century, many East Harlemites still lived in a nineteenth-century world.

There was wet wash and a guy would come around in a horse and buggy. The small stuff you washed, but the big stuff you sent it to the wet wash and then it was sent back to you and you put your clothes on the clothesline. There were no big stores, *just small chain stores like Butler Brothers, A&P or Gristedes, but there was a supermarket on 125th Street which was run by German merchants. They had delivery boys, but I was employed as a baggage preparer. The store had the wicker basket and you put your food in it. Then, I would prepare the grocery bags and placed it in the chute. Later, the store would package it and someone would deliver it.*

Drugs later became a major problem in East Harlem, but they existed in another form during Murphy's youth. Here he recalls the effects of drugs in the neighborhood. Living in the Harlem Courthouse, Murphy saw these drug addicts sentenced to prison. Unfortunately, it was in East Harlem where young Vincent and his family were dealt a serious blow.

In the Harlem Courthouse they had a prison section to hold the guys who used opium. And many people who went to jail were high on opium. We'd say as a joke what's wrong with him, oh, he's on opium. After a while in jail, the effects of opium was noticeable, so they would give him some type of shot to quiet him.

As for my family, Pop had just taken a test for a promotion which would have paid him more money, but he got sick. The night he died, Pop didn't feel well and he didn't go to sleep, but instead he sat in a large chair. I went to bed, and when my mother woke me and my siblings up she told us Pop had died. After Pop died, mom received the notice that he'd passed the test. His co-workers collected $1,000 which was a lot of money back then. A keener (a tradition brought over from Ireland) came by and sang at his wake. Someone must have told that person that Pop had died.

After his father's death Vincent Murphy quit school during his adolescent years to support his family. Here Murphy recalls his entry into the workforce where many odd jobs were available before the Depression.

A year after my father died I started working at fifteen to support my family who still lived in the courthouse. Another gentleman replaced my father, and he told my family, I don't need the apartment so you can stay there, and we did. I started working and I remember my first job delivering false teeth. I was playing with kids on Sylvan Place, then someone comes up and says, "Hey, you want a job, kid?" I delivered false teeth for Zuckerman and Lefkowitz, two dentists who worked on 120th Street and Third Avenue. I'd take the train to up to New Rochelle, but the trains went on strike and I couldn't work and we had no telephone. Later, I read in the newspaper that the strike was over, and I went back to work, but the dentist said, We don't need you now," and I lost my job. I found another job at Bonwit Teller on Thirty-Eighth Street as an errand boy and I delivered packages. After that I worked at Con Edison and finally I worked at UPS.

Murphy's family left the courthouse and lived in the neighborhood for a while before they left East Harlem for good.

After six years living in the courthouse the original person who turned down the apartment now wanted it back, and we moved to 124th Street and Madison Avenue right opposite Mount Morris Park [Marcus Garvey Park]. They were nice apartments. It was a mostly white neighborhood then. Later my family moved to Queens.

El Barrio in East Harlem

Thousands of Puerto Ricans migrated to America and especially New York City after World War II, but America's connection with Puerto Rico can be traced to the mid-1700s. These immigrants came to America in three stages during the nineteenth century. The first stage occurred when Puerto Rico and the American colonies engaged in a secret trading policy where the island bartered its sugar and molasses for food and other supplies. The northeast coast benefited the most from this partnership and by 1830s this successful venture led to the creation of the Cuban and Puerto Rican Benevolent Society in New York (Sociedad Beneficio Cubano y Puertorriqueña). Entrepreneurs from Cuba, Puerto Rico and the United States were part of this consortium.[50] In addition, North America and European countries aided Puerto Rico with equipment to harvest and plant the island's crops. This development influenced many Puerto Ricans to immigrate to America.

In modern times, one of the first Puerto Ricans to immigrate to America were the merchants, students, and factory laborers. In *Memoirs of Bernard Vega,* Vega recounts how his Uncle Antonio emigrated from Puerto Rico to New York City during the late 1850s. Vega's uncle boarded with an Irish family and found work in a cigar factory in Lower Manhattan. There, he met and befriended other Latinos including some fellow Puerto Ricans.[51]

The second stage of Puerto Rican immigration to America during this period occurred with the independence leaders and their fight against Spain's Colonialism. During the Civil War, Puerto Ricans and Cubans lived in New York City and also New Orleans, Louisiana. But after the Union Army captured New Orleans, racial animosity from the Union soldiers compelled the independence leaders to return to New York City. Nineteenth-century Puerto Rican immigration continued with the island's political activists. In the late 1890s Puerto Rican political activists established an offshoot of the Cuban Revolutionary Party which supported both Cuban and Puerto Rican independence against Spain.[52] This action also led skilled and unskilled laborers to settle in New York City.

Despite the charismatic fire of Jose Martí, the independence movement struggled. But the movement was kept alive through an organization called La Liga de Artesanos and Los Dos Antillas located in the city. One of the members of La Liga Antillana was Arturo Alfonso Schomburg. Schomburg along with Rosendo Rodriguez and Raphael Serra established Los Dos Antillas (the two Antilles), located in East Harlem on Ninety-Seventh Street at 1758 Third Avenue, with twenty-three members. Rodriguez served as its president and Schomburg served as its secretary. Los Dos Antillas supported Martí's ideas and vowed to cooperate with their Cuban counterparts to achieve independence for both islands.[53]

But financial constraints, Jose Martí's death in 1895 and other events weakened the movement. The final blow to the independence movement came after the United States defeated Spain in the Spanish-American War of 1898. Several members still wanted to maintain the independence movement. Many felt Cuba and Puerto Rico were still colonized, by either Spain or the United States. This sentiment did not prevail, and the members voted to dissolve the independence organizations. Later Arturo Alfonso Schomburg moved to nearby West Harlem and became one of the foremost historians of African culture in the United States.[54]

The third stage of nineteenth-century Puerto Rican immigration occurred immediately after the Spanish-American War. After the war the nature of Puerto Rican immigration to America changed. The immigration of political exiles to America declined, but Puerto Rican immigration still continued. In *From Colonia to Community*, Virginia E. Sánchez Korrol cites two theories about increased Puerto Rican immigration to America. The first theory was predicated by Lawrence R. Chenault and Oscar Handlin, who believed the United States' possession of Puerto Rico upgraded the island's health care and medical services. and increased population on the

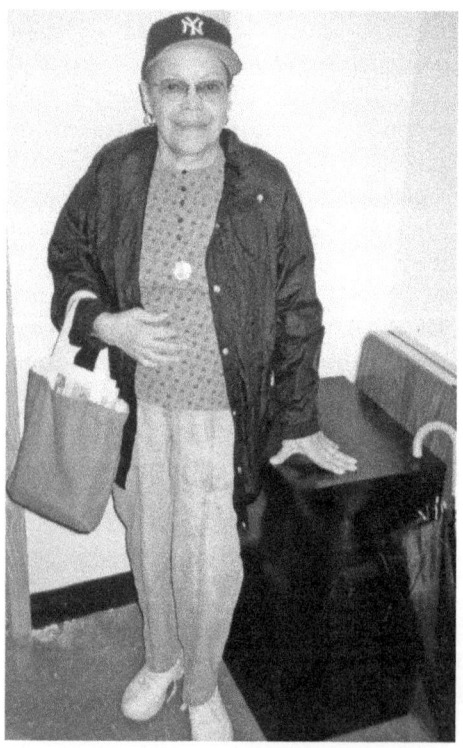

Juanita Rickoff arrived in East Harlem from Puerto Rico on the steamship *Cuoamo* in the early 1920s. She spent many years on East 112th Street between Park and Madison Avenue. She is seen here at the James Weldon Johnson senior citizen center.

1. Planting Roots (1900–1920)

island. The second theory was put forth by the Center for Puerto Rican Studies (CPRS, or Centro de Estudiad de Puerto Rico). The CPRS stated that new forms of production and land ownership led to an abundance of displaced laborers in Puerto Rico. Both the population surge and the displaced labor force compelled Puerto Ricans to immigrate to America. Another factor that influenced Puerto Rican immigration was the island's poor economy and the potential employment opportunity in New York. However, prior to the twentieth century, a small group of Puerto Ricans immigrant tobacco workers (*tabaqueros*) settled in lower Manhattan.[55] Finally, the 1917 Jones Act granted American citizenship to Puerto Ricans. This legislation benefited Puerto Ricans especially after the 1921 and 1924 anti-immigration statutes curtailed European migration to the United States to three and two percent respectively. With these statutes in effect America experienced a drought of semi-skilled and unskilled workers before and after World War I. The shortage of European immigrants and loss of potential laborers created a labor vacuum. Unskilled employment was available and Puerto Ricans and African Americans met this demand.[56] Many Puerto Ricans traveled to the United States by steamship to find work.[57] Texas and the other Gulf Western states offered a warm climate and less travel time from the island, but the ports in these regions were unequipped to receive passenger ships from Puerto Rico. By contrast, passenger ships from Puerto Rico to New York could dock in the city without any difficulty.[58]

Despite New York's cold climate, Puerto Ricans took the opportunity and moved to New York City. The average time to travel from Puerto Rico to New York City was estimated at three to five days. The *Cuoamo* was one of the ships that traveled from Puerto Rico to the United States. We shall hear from several Puerto Ricans who came as children or whose family immigrated to the United States during the 1920s. Each person's story presents a wide spectrum of the Puerto Rican migration during this period. **Joe Monseratt**, born in Bayamon, Puerto Rico, arrived in East Harlem as a child.

It is difficult to talk about Puerto Ricans as if they were a single group because they are not. People who were poor in Puerto Rico came to New York City looking for work while other people came to New York to expand their horizons. My father was a cigar maker and he considered himself middle class and most Puerto Ricans who came to the United States in the early twentieth century were of the middle class. Middle class being somewhat different than what people think in New York.

It was this chance to expand one's horizons which led Albert Medina's family to travel to East Harlem.

Albert Medina: *My parents lived in Aquadilla, Puerto Rico, and my father came here as a farm worker after World War I. He came here to investigate New*

York City because my father found life in Puerto Rico too demanding and lacked of opportunities to develop economically. He made plans to come to New York City which is why he came here and my father never spoke to me about life in Puerto Rico. He said he didn't want to look back at the economic deprivation of those times.

Juanita Rickoff was raised on 112th Street between Madison and Park Avenues and also came to East Harlem as a child.

Juanita Rickoff: *I came to Spanish Harlem on a boat called the Cuoamo when I was four yeas old. I think my mother said it took three days and we landed someplace downtown and my father and my grandparents picked us up. My grandparents and two uncles were the first to arrive. After their arrival they got a nice big apartment and they found work while my grandmother stayed home. Afterwards, my relatives raised enough money and they sent for us. My family came to New York to better themselves, because it was very hard in Puerto Rico since the only work there was rolling tobacco. My father was a farmer, but he never liked farming so he learned to cook. He landed a restaurant job and he made eighteen dollars a week which was good money then. As for my, mother she sewed clothes.*

Manny Diaz, Jr., born in Humacao, Puerto Rico, in 1922, came to the city and lived on 114th Street between Madison and Fifth Avenues.

I came here on the steamship SS Cuoamo and back then there were three boats to and from Puerto Rico. It would take five days to travel and I arrived with my Uncle Victor on April 18, 1927, my mother having arrived in New York ahead of the family. My parents boarded with another family, from Spain, on 112th and Lenox Avenue for six months. This arrangement saved us, but the food we received was boiled gumbo and eggplant. My family ate this five days a week and I hated it and even today I won't eat it.

COMMUNITY

Virginia E. Sánchez Korrol again sites Lawrence R. Chenault and Jose Hernandez Alvarez with reference to the Puerto Rican community. Sánchez Korrol used the term *Colonias* to describe several Puerto Rican communities in New York City. *Colonias* were dense enclaves that helped Puerto Ricans adjust to life in New York City and keep their social identity. Most Puerto Rican migrants who arrived here between 1915 and 1920 were tobacco workers. During the mid–1920s, a survey reported that many migrants were male, urban, Caucasian, skilled or semi-skilled laborers and between 15 and 35 years of age. These migrants worked in the hotels, restaurants, or as cigar makers.[59]

The Puerto Rican population in New York City was estimated at 100,000. However, some organizations estimated that 200,000 Puerto Ricans lived in the city. Three-fourths of the Puerto Rican population resided in Manhattan in East and Central Harlem and the last fourth lived in Brooklyn. East Harlem was known as El Barrio or La Cuna (the cradle) and it became the most prominent Puerto Rican community during this period. Over two hundred grocery stores (bodegas) and nearly one hundred restaurants served the Puerto Rican communities in the city. And East Harlem's inexpensive apartments and access to the many transportation outlets appealed to many Puerto Rican immigrants.[60] In his memoirs, Bernardo Vega remembered when El Barrio was a small community ensconced between Jewish and Italian East Harlem, from 110th to 117th Street between Madison and Park Avenue.[61] Later, El Barrio's unofficial boundary lines was from 100th Street to 116th Street and Fifth to Lexington Avenue. The neighborhood described in Vega's book stood intact for many decades until it was destroyed to make way for public housing. Efrain Marzan later arrived in East Harlem and lived on 109th Street and Madison Avenue. He recalls the many businesses on the same blocks mentioned in Vega's book.

Efrain Marzan: *On the south side of 109th Street was the flower shop, next to it was a dry cleaner called El Maraquero. The owner once sponsored a baseball team in Central Park. Next was a Cuban restaurant called El National on 110th Street and Madison Avenue. Also on the block were two bars called Blanco's and Calle de Oros. Then our barbershop, which was closed on Sundays or Mondays. And the next block we had Bobbyan Department Store on 111th Street and a drugstore on 112th Street and this is all on one side of the street. Followed by the drugstore was Dr. Reinhardt, our local dentist. Upstairs you had a Jay Club on 112th to 113th Streets; 113th to 114th Streets was my aunt Petra's restaurant. Finally, on 115th Street there were two businesses, Monje's funeral parlor and Duarte's photo shop. Then, coming back from the west side of the block on 114th Street was the Municipal movie theater. Brownstones existed there followed by tenements on 113th to 112th streets and El Cenepo restaurant. Next to the movie theater were candy stores and el lechonera or the meat market. On top of those establishments was Casa Estrella, a social club where I used to play with my band as the sax player. From 110th to 109th Streets another pharmacy, a bodega and on the corner was Gonzalez's Funeral home. Now going south from 108th to 107th Street you had Regina's Bar and a pool hall. Today it is Public School 108. Before the school was constructed it was an empty lot where people played baseball or held carnivals.*

The original *La Marqueta* (The Market) was also part of El Barrio. La Marqueta was where East Harlemites shopped for certain foods not found in the neighborhood's stores. La Marqueta first operated outdoors until it was enclosed after Fiorello La Guardia became mayor.

Albert Medina: *La Marqueta was an open air market from Madison to Park Avenues. We had a pickle vendor on the corner and residential buildings on* both sides of the market. In essence La Marqueta was the outpost of the existing population.

George Espada: *I sold shopping bags at La Marqueta and it was good for the neighborhood. La Marqueta was a Caribbean center and people from East Harlem, Brooklyn, or other parts of the New York City bought their foods there. Those foods that were sold back home in Puerto Rico and other parts of the Caribbean, say like fish, fruits and collard greens et cetera. Back then the bodegas or supermarkets didn't carry those items and everybody went to La Marqueta. It was always crowded until other stores began to carry those items that La Marqueta once sold.*

Robert Espier: *In its popularity, the variety of products, produce and volume, La Marqueta could really be compared to the great traditional markets of Mali and Marrakech. My grandmother never paid list price for anything because watching her negotiate discount prices was a workshop in haggling. The price reduction didn't have to be great, but there had to be one. This was understood by the vendor and in La Marqueta's stretch from 111th to 116th Streets, the merchants knew the women, and the women knew all of the merchants. In the 1950s, much of the Puerto Rican immigrant experience was still fresh. Many of the vendors had very strong accents from their respective languages—immigrants themselves. Among them were Jews, Italians, Greeks in that regard, buyer and seller were bonded.*

Olga Quinones: *If you made $24 a week, you could buy a week's food on $10, like the meats and other foods, and season it up. I used to go every Saturday and I went to different vendors where I bought my eggs, rice and bananas. One side was strictly for food and the other side was for clothes.*

Louis Rosaly details the business that surrounded La Marqueta. Like Efrain Marzan's, this description details how El Barrio was a community within a community.

If you went alongside the Marqueta, from 116th Street all the way down to 111th Street was the fish market. On the outside of La Marqueta was Siegel's Liquor Store and then you went down towards 114th Street and you had hat and clothing stores like you see on Delancey Street. From 114th to 113th Streets was the Day Shop Well store on Park Avenue and that was their first store. They sold cheeses and the store looked like a super delicatessen and they had every kind of cold cuts. The next block on 112th Street was a chicken place and you bought the chickens in the wooden cases or you could buy it on the other side where there was a poultry place. There you walked into a building and you saw the chickens running around. Basically, what you had was a living neighborhood.

Puerto Ricans in New York City maintained communication links between themselves and Puerto Ricans on the island. Newspapers and magazines such as *El Grafico* and *La Prensa* (later *El Diario/La Prensa*), kept the community in touch with other Puerto Ricans in East Harlem and throughout the city. These

1. Planting Roots (1900–1920) 37

periodicals also offered advertisements, job vacancies and community events. In addition to the newspapers, Puerto Rican and other Latino workers enjoyed Mexican and Argentine films shown in El Barrio's movie theaters.[62]

WOMEN

To earn income Puerto Rican women did domestic work or worked in the garment industry. In the garment industry, piecework emerged as the great source of employment for those women who wished to work at home. A contractor or subcontractor compensated the women upon the completion for a specified number of items. Some of these items were imitation flowers, hair, or jewelry, and there were advantages and disadvantages to this arrangement. The plus side to piecework allowed Puerto Rican women to work at their own speed, employ their sewing prowess, communicate in Spanish and, finally, removed the prospect of commuting to an unfamiliar section of New York City.[63] Two Puerto Ricans recall their piecework experience. Ray Rodriguez grew up with his family in East Harlem and though Rodriguez's mother did piecework, young Raymond made the deliveries. The second person, Olga Quinones, actually did piecework and she gives her insight into the practice.

Ray Rodriguez: *We lived on 100th Street between First and Second Avenues and my mother took in piecework from the factory. The owner would give you hair that you had to separate. It was animal hair or fur and the colors were light, medium and dark. The owner gave you the hair in bunches which was tied up and you had to sort them out. After I did my homework, I helped out my mother by taking her work downtown to the foremen. I took the Second Avenue El on Ninety-Ninth Street and went downtown to Chatham Square. There the foreman would look at my mother's work and he'd give me the money. I don't remember the amount, but I got paid for that work. Then they would give me more work to bring home. Coming back, I would take the Third Avenue El to 42nd Street and got a free transfer to the Second Avenue El. Then you had to walk the Second Avenue El, where I took it to Ninety-Ninth Street. Or sometimes I took the Third Avenue El to Ninety-Ninth Street.*

Olga Quinones: *I did piecework in a factory downtown and I made the dresses on the sewing machine. You get a certain section of the dress and you do a certain amount of that section to fix the dress. And they paid you twenty-five cents a garment or sixty cents a garment. That's what they call piecework and you made as many of them as you can and they added it up and that's what they pay you.*

Conversely, piecework had its drawbacks. Working in factories, these laborers faced exploitation, long hours and low pay. Like the men, the original

Puerto Rican women garment laborers entered New York City's during the early 1920s. A full account of these workers is unknown, but a 1925 census reported that 600 of nearly 3,500 (17 percent) who worked as dressmakers and seamstresses, resided in East Harlem.[64]

A small group of Puerto Rican women found white-collar positions as clerical workers, while other women became community activists or did volunteer work. Finally, Puerto Rican women earned income by housing boarders or child care.[65]

ORGANIZATIONS

Puerto Ricans in El Barrio in the 1920s and 1930s coalesced around similar interests and established organizations that covered the social, cultural and political aspects of their community. In El Barrio, like their brethren from the Lower East Side, established mutual aid societies often named after a town in Puerto Rico.[66]

But the 1920s witnessed a shift of priorities within Puerto Rican communities throughout the city. Improvements in technology canceled the need for cigar makers, who now competed with other unskilled ethnic workers for jobs. This also led to the reduction of many mutual aid societies in East Harlem and other Puerto Rican communities.[67] Yet with over 100,000 Puerto Ricans in New York City, an organization was still needed to represent them individually and as a whole group. Two organizations adequately filled this void. One organization was the Porto Rican Brotherhood of America (PRBA, or *Hermandad Puertorriqueña*). Established in the early 1920s, this organization furnished a meeting place and it brought its members together. Ateneo Obrero Hispano, headquartered in East Harlem on 106th Street, was a subsidiary of the Porto Rican Brotherhood. Its working-class members focused on Latino literature, the arts and the educational progression of New York–born Puerto Ricans. The Porto Rican Brotherhood dealt with numerous themes. Some of them were unity, friendship and mutual aid. Furthermore, the PRBA concentrated on representation rather than politics.[68] The PRBA's mettle was tested during the 1926 El Barrio race riots. But the roots of this disturbance were predicated on financial matters as well. For several weeks New York City was mired in a heat wave. This prompted many in El Barrio to seek refuge in the streets or on the tenement rooftops to avoid the unbearable hot weather. The Puerto Rican population growth in East Harlem also coincided with the growth of many Latino business establishments in El Barrio. Though Jewish East Harlemites were leaving East Harlem during the 1920s (see next chapter) Jewish entrepreneurship still remained in the neighborhood. Some Jews objected to the presence of the burgeoning Puerto Rican entrepreneurs in their community. The intense heat only heightened tensions in the neighborhood which led to several skirmishes between the two groups. Some Puerto Ricans were harassed and several Puerto Rican businesses were broken into. Soon Puerto Rican and Jewish customers and owners boycotted each other's businesses.

The PRBA responded to this crisis by sending a representative to the local police precinct to demand security for those not involved in the melee. The PRBA also requested restitution from all parties convicted of the crime. The group also advocated a truce in the Latino press. Finally, the PRBA contacted several local elected officials to restore peace to the neighborhood.[69] Though the PRBA achieved some degree of respectability during this period, the episode highlighted the need to bring all of the Latino groups into one centralized organization. This led to the formation of La Liga Puertorriqueña e Hispana (LLPRH). Like the Puerto Rican Brotherhood, La Liga abstained from politics, but the LLPRH promoted civic defense and general welfare for the Puerto Ricans and Latino community. Its objectives were as follows: (1) To strengthen the social, political and economic situation of both mainland and island Puerto Ricans. (2) Unify all Latinos regardless of their economic backgrounds; furnish referral and educational services; advocate on the behalf of Latinos before the authorities and become a benevolent institution and to increase the Puerto Rican vote.[70]

POLITICS

From the 1920 to the 1930s, the Puerto Rican vote was small. However, several factors contributed to this statistic. Eligible Puerto Rican voters were required to take and pass an English examination. Local political clubs customarily controlled by the Irish or Italians were unreceptive to the small number of registered Puerto Rican voters. But the city's attitude changed after the anti-immigration laws restricted European immigration. The loss of East European registrants opened the door for the Puerto Rican vote and some politicians quickly responded to this opportunity.[71] In the late 1920s, Congressman Fiorello La Guardia sought the out the Puerto Rican vote. And he asked a Puerto Rican activist in El Barrio about the number of Puerto Rican organizations in his district and their interests. La Guardia also inquired if there was any form of legislation that the Puerto Rican community sought so he could advocate on their behalf in Congress.[72] Unfortunately, La Guardia failed to maintain his alliance with the Puerto Rican community as he lost his congressional seat to Democrat James Lanzetta in 1932.[73]

Puerto Ricans showed their diversity throughout the decade as they voted for the Democrat Franklin D. Roosevelt for president, while supporting then

Republican Congressman Vito Marcantonio, La Guardia's successor. Later, Marcantonio enrolled in the American Labor Party and overwhelmingly won the Puerto Rican vote. Though Marcantonio was admired by many Puerto Ricans in El Barrio, the community made history in 1937 when Republican Oscar Garcia Rivera, a lawyer born in Mayagüez, Puerto Rico, was elected to the New York State Assembly. Once in office Garcia Rivera clashed with his fellow Republicans and adopted a socialistic approach to government.[74] Garcia Rivera won reelection in 1938, but he was defeated two years later by Democrat Hulan Jack, a black West Indian. This leads to black East Harlem.

Blacks in East Harlem

The history of blacks in East Harlem has been marginally explored. Many historians have focused on blacks in nearby West and Central Harlem. Their numbers were small during the late nineteenth and early twentieth centuries, but blacks have lived on the island since the days of the Dutch colonists. After Peter Minuit purchased Manhattan from the Native Americans, eleven African men became the first people of African descent to reside in Manhattan.

Shortly thereafter, several enslaved African women arrived and joined their male counterparts.[75] Originally, these enslaved Africans were bondservants who worked on farms.[76] Slowly, the African population increased, but the Dutch couldn't decide how to use these enslaved Africans and released them. When the English supplanted the Dutch in 1664, Africans were subjected to a more repressive form of slavery. By the end of the seventeenth century over 2,000 enslaved Africans resided in New York.[77] After their death, their remains were laid to rest in the city's two Negro burying grounds. The most famous one is located in lower Manhattan; however, another Negro burial ground was in East Harlem. Its present location is on 126th Street near the FDR Drive.[78]

The New York State Legislature abolished slavery on July 4, 1827. Three years later, African American farmers arrived in East Harlem on 130th Street and founded the African Methodist Episcopal Zion Church (Little Zion). Over sixty African Americans founded another church in a small brick building on East 117th Street.[79] In the 1850s African Americans continued establishing religious and educational institutions. The Bethel African Methodist Church and a Negro public school were built.

In nearby Harlem throughout the nineteenth century, African Americans resided in various parts of the city and many were employed as unskilled laborers: servants, porters, waiters, waitresses, laundresses and janitors. An African

American middle class existed that was estimated at four hundred and fifty. They worked as clerks, actors, musicians or music teachers, doctors and lawyers.

Several factors contributed to the African American migration. After the Civil War the Jim Crow laws, brutal mistreatment and limited prospects for southern blacks led to migration up north, while other African Americans came out of curiosity. Finally, the industrial revolution enticed many African Americans to seek employment. African Americans established mutual aid societies to maintain friendships, provide health care and death coverage. Several mutual aid organizations were named after southern states. These organizations were important, for mortality rates for African Americans were enormous during slavery and remained unchanged after slavery was abolished. Tuberculosis and pneumonia were some of the diseases which felled many African Americans.[80]

Dr. Alvin Poussaint. This Harvard psychologist served as an advisor on the Bill Cosby television series. His grandfather emigrated from Guadalupe as a child. Dr. Poussaint spent his early years on East 98th and 102nd Streets (Harvard College, Liza Green).

In East Harlem by 1898, African Americans resided on East 122nd, 124th and 126th Streets. In the early twentieth century, African American families were scattered throughout East Harlem. Some black families lived on 96th and 97th Streets between Second and Third Avenue; 97th and 98th Street between Second and Fourth Avenue (Park Avenue); 99th and 100th Street between Second and Lexington Avenues; 102nd and 104th Street between Second and Third Avenue; 114th and 115th Street between Madison and Fifth Avenue; 121st and 123rd Street between First and Second Avenue; 123rd and 125th Street between Pleasant and First Avenue and 126th and 128th Street between Second and Third Avenue.[81]

COMMUNITY

Jesse Hamilton's forbears were an African American family who lived in East Harlem during this time. Hamilton was six years old when he moved from Florida to East Harlem with his mother in 1944 and became the fourth generation of Hamiltons to reside at 59 East 100th Street between Madison and Park Avenues. Like many blacks in the south, Hamilton's family ventured up north to find employment. Hamilton describes how his family helped his mother settle in the neighborhood.

Our family had a tradition and we had some family members that already lived here in New York City. They developed a flagship for those who came up from the south to give you a start. My great grandmother and grandmother lived here in that apartment and they passed it down to my family.

James Bryant, a black East Harlemite born to Caribbean parents, lived with his family on Ninety-Ninth Street. Later, his family moved several blocks north between Park and Madison Avenues.

James Bryant: *The block was seventy-five percent African American and Caribbean blacks and there also were some Jews and Puerto Ricans. The tenements were old railroad flats and most of the hallways had two entrances. Basically, most of the apartments were five rooms, all walk-ups, and there were little stores downstairs—candy stores, cleaners and other different businesses. The most stable business was the meat market on the corner and for years there was the storefront church on one side of the streets.*

WORK

Bryant and Hamilton's parents were semi-skilled laborers who obtained similar types of employment comparable to many other ethnic groups profiled earlier in the book.

James Bryant: *Work for blacks in East Harlem was a scuffle, for blacks had the lowest-paying jobs and lots of layoffs. And not many people in my neighborhood went to college and when you did it was a celebrated act. I remember my mother saying, "Get yourself a high school diploma and you got it made." This is what you did back then. My mother was a domestic who worked for Jewish people and my father drove a truck. Later, he worked at Bellevue Hospital and performed housekeeping chores.*

Jesse Hamilton: *It took a while to find work, for you had to search for it. However, some family members helped you get your act together until you obtained a job or found a place to live and then you moved out. This is why we lived with my grandmother. Despite this difficulty there was always something to eat. Blacks did factory work or found piecework in the garment industry.*

Some blacks in East Harlem were from the West Indies. Like their Puerto Rican and East European counterparts, West Indians maintained their cultural roots and values upon their arrival in East Harlem. Two people interviewed here have families from the Caribbean islands. Helen Licorish Rudder, aged ninety-nine, arrived in East Harlem with her parents at the turn of the twentieth century.

1. Planting Roots (1900–1920)

My mother and I both arrived from Barbados and settled in East Harlem. My father worked in the city as an elevator man and he sent for us. We lived on 133rd Street near Fifth Avenue and our apartment was a straight-through railroad flat. They weren't too many blacks from Barbados, but there were some black families from North and South Carolina. My sister and I went to P.S. 19 near Eighth Avenue and after school my sister and I always went home. My mother who worked as a seamstress was a very gentle person and she told us to stay in the house which is why we didn't go out, because the streets were tough. Young men were rowdy and if you went out of your neighborhood the white boys called you "nigger." Blacks worked as a porter or did housework, for there was nothing but hard work for blacks. They (whites) didn't have any use for blacks for only fair (skinned) people caught a break. The black women minded the children, but the relationship gradually changed. Black people worked for whites, but when the white children became fifteen or sixteen they [white parents] hired they own care for their children. Black and white schools were separated, for they had white public schools, however, many white people sent their children to Catholic schools. There was not too much traffic and it was only a horse and buggy or mules that were found on the streets. The streets were clean, for you didn't see paper around unless the wind blew it. Each nationality dressed differently and you could tell a person's nationality by the clothes they wore.

The 1920 anti-immigration statues scarcely applied to the West Indians. And this situation paved the way for the massive influx of West Indian immigrants to East and West Harlem. They came from Jamaica, Barbados, Antigua, Bermuda, Martinique, St. Vincent, Trinidad, St. Lucia, the Virgin Islands, and St. Kitts.[82]

Dr. Alvin Poussaint also grew up in East Harlem. The famed Harvard psychologist was instrumental in the development and presentation of *The Cosby Show* in the mid 1980s to early 1990s. Dr. Poussaint relates a detail from his family history.

Both of my parents were born in the United States, but my grandfather was a man named Poussaint and he was brought over to the United States from Guadalupe by a white family as a young boy. No one seems to know about him and apparently they abandoned him when he was sixteen to be left on his own. Interestingly, my family believes the people who bought him over at age ten were named Toussaint. And when he was discarded by the white family the T was changed to a P. I have encountered many Poussaints and these people who are named Poussaints are in some way related to my family. Maybe the immigration officials changed it.

Most West Indian immigrants retained their roots upon their arrival to America. This allowed many West Indians to remain nationalistic and pro– American. West Indians primarily were English speaking, but some of these immigrants spoke in French and Spanish. West Indians were Catholic or Episcopalian. Many West Indians felt themselves to be middle class. Also, they rejected all forms of second class citizenship and demonstrated against this treatment whenever possible. West Indians abhorred menial work, and some rationalized menial labor as a temporary way to improve oneself.[83] Collectively they were imbued with the entrepreneurial spirit. In the West Indian family, the father was in charge and his word was law. Finally, he felt obligated to provide for his loved ones and felt insulted to do household chores.[84]

After their arrival to East Harlem in the late nineteenth and twentieth centuries, our next stories focused on how these East Harlemites lived during the depression. This story ends with World War II.

2

The Great Depression and World War II (1930s–1940s)

> When you are poor, you don't feel poor or have a sense that you are poor.—Manuel Diaz, Jr.

This chapter will cover East Harlem in the 1930s beginning with the Great Depression and end with the redevelopment of East Harlem through public works projects. The depression of the 1930s was perhaps the most difficult economic period in the country's history. October 29, 1929, was the unofficial start of the depression, but for many East Harlemites who always struggled to make ends meet, the depression wasn't anything new. Franklin Roosevelt's New Deal financially helped some Americans, but the country did not fully recover from the depression until World War II. East Harlemites vividly recall that era.

Father Peter Rufano: *Most of our people, except the middle class professionals who lived on 116th Street, worked as manual laborers or bricklayers. These people didn't feel the depression too much because they never made much money to begin with. My father worked all the time and the rent was $18 and there was no money in the bank."*

Other East Harlemites used their own ingenuity to survive the depression.

Manny Diaz, Jr.: *Nobody had a job during the depression and we managed to get through the depression on marginal work because we produced liquor. It was still Prohibition back then and you went to the Woolworth store and you bought everything you needed to make wine, beer or gin except for the basic ingredients. My mother worked as a seamstress, but my father struggled to find work. During the winter months, when it snowed, my father would line up at the city's sanitation garage with two hundred men when snow shovelers were needed. If you were handed a shovel, you could get a dollar a day for shoveling snow down the sewer. When you are poor you don't feel poor, or have a sense that you're poor, and people shared their* *possessions with your neighbors. Our neighbor was an Italian merchant marine seaman and he'd ship out for three months. He'd come back with a wad of money. He would buy a pig and shared that pig with everyone and the whole building had food. And if we had wine we shared the wine because everybody shared their food during the depression. When FDR was elected, we danced in the streets. Not because he was a great guy, but because we knew Prohibition would end and you could buy liquor. [Prohibition was repealed in 1933, FDR's first year in office.]*

Olga Quinones (whose mother was an associate of Dutch Schultz): *My mom made liquor to survive by making bathtub gin, and it was good. People came all the way from Brooklyn to buy it. She got busted a couple of times when the cops came and broke the still, but the next day she had a new one. My mother hid the barrel for fermenting and you couldn't tell it was there, and then she would take it out and start boiling this big kettle. My mom also ran the numbers and had a couple of candy stores. One of the candy stores where she worked was located on 59 East 99th Street.*

Albert Medina: *My mother was a homebody and my father was a WPA worker. He filled the swamps throughout parts of New York State. I never felt we were poor because my parents provided [for] me. I was conscious that we received home relief, but it never affected me as it did other people. At that time home relief gave you knickers for young boys and milk for the family.*

Piri Thomas: *People waited on long lines to obtain canned corned beef, powdered sugar or eggs. There were lots of little stores, but we didn't have a lot of money, so the store proprietor had a little blue credit book and we signed it. We owed the proprietor for the food, but when my family got paid, he got paid.*

Meyer Kukle: *We managed to survive by selling our produce on the pushcarts. All the businesses on 125th Street closed down and I remember you went down the street you'd say, Hi, how are you doing?" The next question was, "Are you working?" I remember in the early 1930's children left school because you had to support your family. Many unemployed people walked the street and even if you graduated from high school or college there were no jobs to apply for. If you were lucky, like my friend who got into the bagel business, you found work. The Jews got into civil service sector and maybe they found jobs teaching or in the police department. During the depression, the private sector didn't hire Jews or hire blacks and it was a hard struggle. People had their apartments [seized] and the city Marshal put your furniture on the street. You had to raise enough money to get your apartment back.*

In 1937 the mayor's Committee on City Planning (MCCP) issued a report on East Harlem. This report would be used by city officials and alter the neighborhood's physical structure for decades. The MCCP reported that most of New York City never looked to East Harlem for business or industry and seemed less likely to do so in the future.[1] Out of the 271 blocks that existed in East Harlem, all but 42 of them were residential and hardly any blocks were suitable for businesses. Only the first-floor stores adjacent to the tenement buildings provided any room for entrepreneurship. And one-tenth of those business industries were located in non-buildable sections in East Harlem.[2] The buildings along the East River, once a suitable location for entrepreneurship, were closed for the development of the East River Drive. A produce market was once headquartered in East Harlem on First Avenue and provided consistent business for the neighborhood, had moved to the Bronx.[3]

When the twentieth century began, the neighborhood's population stood at a crowded 300,000. For instance, a single block could hold from 1,350 to 4,000 residents. In fact 90 percent of East Harlemites resided in only 60 percent of the neighborhood. East Harlem's population accounted for 10 percent of the city's population, yet the neighborhood's space comprised only 6.6 percent of Manhattan. The old law tenements built in the nineteenth century were never remodeled, and they violated city and state building codes. As stated earlier the abhorrent tenement conditions led to many health problems in the neighborhood.[4]

East Harlemites who left the neighborhood, coupled with the anti-immigration laws, reduced East Harlem's population to 206,000. The MCCP speculated that the Italian East Harlemites, the largest neighborhood group, would continue to live in East Harlem. The rest of the racial breakdown included African Americans, Russians, Irish, Germans, Polish, Austrians and other foreign-born immigrants. Puerto Ricans, American citizens since 1917, were counted as native born Americans.[5]

The MCCP selected several locations throughout East Harlem for possible housing construction. The study drew two conclusions: (1) East Harlemites needed to take action to better their neighborhood; (2) if they did not, the neighborhood would inevitably decline and East Harlemites would move to other neighborhoods throughout the city and elsewhere.[6] The MCCP also knew that redevelopment would not happen overnight, but if the status quo persisted, decent tenements would deteriorate until habitation was impossible. Apartments were available, but despite low rents the landlords could not find any new tenants. And it was difficult for the landlord to acquire capital to upgrade and maintain property. This resulted in unpaid taxes, and foreclosure became imminent.

With an unstable real estate market, the committee concluded, when the financial situation improved, the tenants who resided in the old-law tenements would not be able to pay the rising rents so renovation was in order. The committee made recommendations to improve the neighborhood. It said it would be futile to rehabilitate individual tenement buildings. The committee felt that many cross streets should be eliminated, allowing several blocks to be combined into a super-block, where public housing would be built. Housing projects should be executed on a large scale with the assistance of local, state and federal governments. Also, the neighborhood lacked recreational space, such as parks and playgrounds. These, too, would be created through the combination of super-blocks.[7]

The MCCP reported that new zoning in East Harlem should be studied and revisions should be implemented. But the committee issued one warning which was ignored and left devastating consequences on the neighborhood.

> The importance of having corrected zoning in an area such as East Harlem cannot be overstated. Much of the area must inevitably be rebuilt. Unless the zoning is such as to guide the type of new building into economically sound channels, irreparable harm can be done. Illogical, lax zoning regulations encourage a short-sighted owner to upset the well-conceived development plans of the majority of his fellows. By erecting tall massive buildings that would effectively destroy the new amenity and attraction of the neighborhood, wise zoning, by contrast, will set the pattern for uniform economic rebuilding of the area in the best way suited to its prospective future place in the city.[8]

The report was hopeful that these recommendations in housing, businesses, space and recreation would provide a more comfortable and attractive place for East Harlemites to live. As we shall see, this did not happen.

The Jewish Exodus from East Harlem

At its zenith, the population of East European Jews in both East and West Harlem totaled over 178,000.[9] The end of World War I brought immediate changes in New York City. During the war, many construction materials went to support the war and real estate developers could not invest in East Harlem. The neighborhood's housing stock declined after the war and landlords took advantage of this housing shortage and increased the rents. The housing deficit and landlords' failure to maintain their properties convinced many in Jewish East Harlem to leave the neighborhood.[10]

New homes and apartments were erected in the Bronx, Brooklyn and Queens. New housing was also built in Manhattan, but it was south of 96th Street, on Park Avenue, in Washington Heights, and on Riverside Drive. These apartments were more expensive, but Jews jumped at the chance to improve their living conditions. And, as mentioned before, the anti-immigration laws (insured the rapid downturn of Jewish East Harlem. By the mid–1920s, one-fourth of Jews had left East Harlem and the number shrunk to 123,000. Two years later, the number of Jews had dropped to 88,000.[11]

As the 1930s began, the Jewish population in East Harlem was estimated at 25,000. African American migrants from the South replaced many Jews in West Harlem and upper East Harlem. In the lower part of East Harlem, Jews were replaced by Puerto Ricans. Two East Harlem Jews remember when they left the neighborhood for available apartments in the Bronx.[12]

Eugene Sklar: *My parents went to the Bronx in the 1920s.*

Meyer Kukle: *I left East Harlem in 1944 and my family found out about a better apartment in the Bronx.*

When Jews vacated East Harlem during the 1920s, their synagogues and organizations followed them. Workmen's Circle Branch No. 2 relocated to the Bronx by decade's end. But unlike Jews in West Harlem who transferred their organizations to the West Side and upper Manhattan, many of these Jewish organizations in East Harlem transferred their services to the Bronx at a much later date.[13] The Harlem Hebrew Institute remained in East Harlem at 111th Street between Lexington and Park Avenue throughout the 1930s. As late as the 1940s, pockets of Jews still lived in East Harlem. The Rev. Norman C. Eddy, who arrived in East Harlem in 1949, remembers.

Rev. Norman C. Eddy: *There was a Jewish synagogue in a tenement building on 317 East 101st Street. The Orthodox Jews had taken the whole ground floor and that became their synagogue. But they were not allowed to turn on the lights on their Sabbath because that was work and they would pay little Puerto Rican boys to turn on their lights.*

Ray Rodriguez was one of the Puerto Rican boys entrusted to turn off the lights for the Orthodox Jews who worshipped in the 101st Street synagogue.

Ray Rodriguez: *Jewish people had a synagogue on 317 East 101st Street. On the Sabbath they would not light a candle, nor do any type of work. They liked me for I was quiet and the rabbi asked me to go upstairs to put out the candle on Friday or Saturday. I got paid a penny or two for this gesture, but when I came back from the service in 1953 the synagogue was gone.*

East Harlem's First Housing Project

The Mayor's Committee on City Planning culminated in East Harlem's first housing project. When Franklin Delano Roosevelt became president in 1933 he introduced several New Deal programs, one of which was the National Recovery Act (NRA). From this program came the Public Works Administration (PWA). A housing division was also part of the PWA. Next, city, state and federal governments passed several measures to end slum clearance.

Shortly thereafter the New York City Housing Authority was created. In 1937 Senator Robert F. Wagner, Sr., of New York helped pass the Wagner Act, which appropriated half a billion dollars towards public housing. East Harlem took notice and Leonard Covello, principal of Benjamin Franklin High School in East Harlem, spearheaded the fight for public housing. In 1939 Covello, with the aid of several neighborhood and civic organizations, won approval for public housing in East Harlem.[14]

The location for the new project, called the East River Houses, was chosen along the erstwhile East River business mart once located on First Avenue between 102nd and 105th Street. Nearly 17,000 East Harlemites applied for 1,166 available units of the East River Houses. The applicants selected for the East River Houses were those residents who lived in the most atrocious housing conditions in East Harlem. On March 2, 1940, East Harlemites gathered on 104th Street and First Avenue as Mayor La Guardia broke ground on the East River Houses, the ninth housing project in New York City.[15] Fourteen months later, on May 28, 1941, East River Houses were completely tenanted. There were 1,166 families, plus one field officer and three residential employees for a total of 1,170 residents comprised in 5,000 rooms.[16]

Apartments ranged from two to six and a half rooms. A two-room apartment cost $16.65, while 6 rooms were priced at $31.66. Each apartment was equipped with these amenities: refrigerator, gas stove, running hot water, state-of-the-art bathrooms and kitchen. An elevator, incinerator, laundry, and indoor and outdoor recreation and playgrounds were also part of the East River Houses. Ten housing projects were constructed. Seven were six stories high. Two were ten stories and one was eleven stories. The projects were built on a diagonal plan near the East River which allowed more sunlight into each room. Finally, Green lawns complemented each new public housing project. The cost for the East River Houses was nearly $5.5 million.[17] Ray Grist and his family, originally from Jamaica, Queens, were one of the first families to live in the East River Houses. Ray, an artist, is the brother of world renowned soprano Reri Grist. His father worked as a clerk and his mother was a housewife. Ray Grist recalls the racial make-up in East River Houses.

> *East River was the first multiracial housing project in the city. Before the East River Houses were built, housing was segregated across the city. East River was built primarily for the Italian community because at that time many Italian families lived in East Harlem. Congressman Vito Marcantonio convinced the housing authority to allow all races to apply for the East River Houses. Every race lived there except the Germans and Japanese because of World War II. Italians, Jews, Puerto Ricans, Filipino, Dutch, southern blacks and West Indian blacks all lived in the East River Houses.*

2. The Great Depression and World War II (1930s–1940s) 51

Eugene Nardelli, who emigrated from Italy with his parents in the 1930s, lived in a nearby tenement when the East River Houses were constructed. He saw the immediate differences between the tenements and public housing.

Eugene Nardelli: *I watched the construction of the East River Houses from my third-floor tenement. The projects also have elevators and an incinerator. They also had grass, clean floors which were installed as tiles or marble, all of which were all shiny. It was just another world and except for the lack of stores, it was a nice place.*

Public housing rules were strictly enforced when the East River Houses first opened. Later these rules were relaxed but recently, public housing has reverted back to this strict enforcement. Public housing residents saw an opportunity for progress and advancement in society.

Ray Grist: *One of the stipulations of public housing back then was that each apartment was rented to two-parent families and at least one of them worked. There was stability. You had the potential to build a stable family and build stable lives. I lived at 425 East 102nd Street. The area where I lived was industrial, for there was a hotel on the corner of 102nd Street and First Avenue and a big sign read "60 beds for farmers only." Next to the hotel there was a produce market place and a munitions plant.*

Ray Grist remembered life in the East River Houses as an extension of the tenement life in East Harlem. In addition, public housing fostered camaraderie and harmony.

Public housing then was an open experience. And your parents interacted with your neighbors. People could readily go in and out of each other's apartments. My next door neighbor was Italian and my parents asked them to care for us and my parents took care of their children. [In] public housing there was a lot of open space and not many cars. In public housing today, there is a lot of confinement and too much stress, which [dissuades] people from living there."

Ray reflects on his time in the East River Houses. He credits his formative years there as a wonderful cultural experience that shaped his life and the lives of many residents who lived there as well.

East River Houses was a very unique experience. All around us were people who I call cultural heroes, who lived within and became a part of the community. A natural part which, for me, the residents of East River Houses in essence became revolutionary heroes. Not revolutionary heroes like Malcolm X, Che Guevara, or Adam Clayton Powell, Jr. Revolution means change and these people would not likely be considered revolutionary, like Charlie Parker, Dizzy Gillespie, Duke Ellington, and Miles Davis. One of these revolutionary heroes was bandleader Chick Webb, who walked around the neighborhood and you saw him. He was short with a hump-

back but he was there. These people were available, like you and me. Unfortunately, today these people are unavailable. You can't know Wesley Snipes, You can't know Russell Simmons. You can know them by their celebrity, but you really can't get to know them personally. East River Houses being the first multiracial and multicultural housing project, we each synthesized one another. We shared each other's experiences and those experiences were shared by the children who grew up there. And those experiences affected our lives. It gave us a foundation to build a new world.

World War II

Five years would pass before the next housing projects were built in the neighborhood. The Japanese attack on Pearl Harbor on December 7, 1941, led the United States into World War II. As during World War I, housing material and scrap metal went to the war effort. East Harlemites recall the Pearl Harbor attack, its immediate aftermath and how the neighborhood rallied in support of the war.

Rose Savatelli: *Pearl Harbor was attacked on Sunday and we heard the news on the radio. President Roosevelt spoke the next day and asked Congress to declare war.*

Raquel Villegas: *I was eight years old and I remember the people coming out in the street screaming, "La guerra! La guerra! La guerra! [The war, the war, the war].*

James Bryant: *There was breaking news, a guy hawking newspapers came with the extra news edition and he said, "Extra, Extra! Japan declared war on the United States! Japan bombed Pearl Harbor!" My father was too old to get drafted into the war. He became an air raid warden and there were several air raid alerts that occurred in the neighborhood. As the air raid warden, you received a helmet, flashlight and an armband and you were part of the Civil Defense community. When an air raid warning happened, the sirens were heard and this meant all the lights in the neighborhood were turned off and everyone cleared the streets. Even after the war the air raids drills continued in case of a nuclear attack. I attended Patrick Henry Junior High School 171 and as students we were told to go into the subway or stay in the basement of St. Francis de Sales Church.*

Eugene Nardelli: *There were World War II drills and all the lights went out. War wardens wore white hats and they walked the streets. They had flashlights and yelled, "Put the lights out! Put the lights out!"*

Willie Lopez: *The blackouts were announced on the radio and they were held once a month. All the lights were turned off for twenty minutes, but some people got mugged and certain stores got robbed.*

Olga Quinones: *There were many blackouts and you walked around with*

2. The Great Depression and World War II (1930s–1940s)   53

a flashlight. All the lights in your apartment were turned off and at a certain times your windows were covered up. It was very popular to wear fluorescent earrings, bracelets, necklaces, and at night those items would shine. I had a ration book and on certain days you couldn't eat meat because of the rationing, and you received what the store provided and not what you wanted.

James Bryant: You had a ration book during the war and you only could get a certain amount of meats per family, and brown sugar. Or women couldn't get silk stockings because they used [silk] for parachutes. There were tremendous drives to salvage tin cans that were plied up in the streets for the war effort. People put flags in their windows for every son that went off to war and some people had four or five flags. But the average family had two sons in the armed services.

Raquel Villegas: I remember my mother worked at the defense plant during the war and our next door neighbor took care of me. Two of my uncles served in the war and if a parent or relative had a son that served in the war they placed flags in their windows. My grandmother had two flags because my two uncles were in the war. At school we brought war bonds and stamps to help the Red Cross.

Humberto Cintron: I remember parts of the war. You read it in the newspaper or you listened to the war reports on the radio, but mostly we hung around the radio. I had two cousins in the war and one cousin was stationed in Europe and the other one in the Pacific. My family went to the Heckscher Foundation on 105th Street and Fifth Avenue. The Heckscher Foundation was where we took our ration stamps to get food. The ration items provided were flour, sugar, oatmeal, cornmeal and chocolate candy with vitamins in them. Our family stood in line with the other families and it was so long it stretched around the corner.

Jim Arless: To support the war our neighborhood made large banners which were used to support the troops and the country. Different blocks had street banners and our block had a banner which depicted the battle of Pearl

Manny Diaz, Jr., also arrived from Puerto Rico on the *Cuoamo* as a child. Diaz served in World War II. His tour of duty included a memorable encounter with General George S. Patton. Diaz is seen in the living room of his apartment in 2003.

Harbor, and it spanned the whole street from one side to the other. We paraded through the streets and the banners were carried horizontally by a group of people. The neighborhood threw the money unto the flag or somebody picked up the money. People put up little flags in their windows as another form of support. Our block had approximately forty people from our neighborhood in the service. A blue star would designate a person in the service and a gold star meant a person was killed in the war and there were two gold stars in our block. We also had an honor roll for the men serving in the war. It was a board mounted on a fence listing the names of servicemen with a display of their pictures in the candy store.

Tom Brokaw's book *The Greatest Generation* celebrated the soldiers who fought in World War II. It is a tribute to those soldiers who fought to save democracy from Nazism, fascism and totalitarianism. America is forever indebted to these soldiers. But during World War II there were two Americas divided by race. All soldiers pledged their allegiance to defend the United States, but the soldiers of African descent fought two wars: one at home and one abroad. At home racism made them second-class citizens and the military was no different.

Because of their skin color, two Puerto Rican East Harlemites lived in different worlds during the war. Their contrasting experiences were typical of many black and white soldiers who served in World War II. Manny Diaz, Jr., whom we met earlier, is fair skinned and was accepted in the white unit. His military experience included meeting a famous general.

Manny Diaz, Jr.: *After I passed an aptitude test I got into the army. Because I could type I was placed in the signal corps unit assigned to General Eisenhower and worked on the radio. After a year in the army I rode in a jeep, but later I was assigned and became a delivery messenger. One time I was stationed in Normandy and I had to deliver a message to General George C. Patton who was in his big army trailer which also served as his office. He was sleeping, but the message was top secret so I had to get his signature. The corporal who guarded his trailer says, "You mean you want me to wake him up?" "Yes," I said. "That's an order." The corporal answered, "You wake him up!" I knocked once, twice and the third time the doors flung open and he's wearing his long johns, he's got his helmet on and he had two pearl-handled revolvers on his belt. He aims them both at me and I said babbling "General, General I, I, I got..." Finally he said, "Give me that!" He didn't sign it; he just drew a line across the paper. I don't know what was in the envelope, but Patton could curse. He was worse that George C. Scott, from the movie* Patton.

As a Puerto Rican, you never know who you will train with because it would be the black or white infantry camp. Despite my skin color I was placed in the white army infantry, but my cousin, who had blond hair and fair skin, trained with the black army, and he went to Mississippi.

2. The Great Depression and World War II (1930s–1940s) 55

As Manny Diaz, Jr., stated, Puerto Ricans of black, Taino and European heritage could train with the black or white troops. Raymond Rodriguez joined the army during the last months of World War II and remained in the service during the Korean conflict. He is also Puerto Rican, but of African descent and trained with a black infantry. He recounts the different standards the army used with respects to its black and white troops.

Raymond Rodriguez: *In World War II I went into a black segregated unit in Bainbridge, Maryland. I was assigned as a second mate and worked as a servant. The assignment was to serve the officers' food and clean their clothing, but I fought it. I said, I'm Puerto Rican." I went to the Catholic Church, but the church didn't help and they said, "you're black." I graduated from there and I volunteered for the submarine school in Connecticut. I remember the boot camp and at the camp the black soldiers trained with fake guns while the white soldiers trained with real guns. The training was the same for both groups of soldiers except the army command gave black soldiers fake guns. I got tired of serving people, and I was assigned to the USS Sea Robin, a submarine, and I was supposed to go on a tour to Australia. But two days before the ship was to sail, two white sailors said they wanted to go instead. Because of their request I and another black soldier were replaced by the white soldiers.*

Raymond Rodriguez (right), of Puerto Rican and African descent. Rodriguez's skin color placed him in the black infantry. He lived as a second class citizen, but despite this mistreatment, Rodriguez and the other black soldiers served America with distinction. Rodriguez poses with his cousin Victor Sanchez at the East River Drive (photograph courtesy Raymond Rodriguez).

Instead we went to Key West, Florida, by train, and as the train approached Washington, D.C., the army officials stopped the train and they said, "All you black sailors get off this car and go sit up front." We said, "Why? we like it here." This section is for white people only and the black people must ride in front." They replied. And why did we ride in the front? These were not steam engines, they were coal engines and the smoke came into the two front cars and hit the black soldiers in the face. The white people placed in the back were not affected by the smoke. We rode all the way down there in the two segregated cars and segregation remained the same when we wanted something to eat. The black soldiers waited for the white soldiers to eat first, and when the black soldiers ate we were ordered to eat in a separate section. We were in the same uniform, but that uniform meant nothing. This treatment continued as we arrived in Miami, Florida on a segregated bus, and segregation existed in the town as well. Blacks could not swim on the beach with the white soldiers, and black soldiers were sent to the other side to swim. When we went to the movies on the base the white soldiers got the front seats and the black soldiers were seated in the back if any remaining seats were available. Finally, when you went to the canteen concession to buy something to eat, you had to go into the black part of town to eat and this section was the run-down part of town. We didn't know what the white part of town looked like, for we never saw it.

War's End

Midway through 1945, the Allies knew that victory was within sight. However, President Franklin D. Roosevelt, who led America through the depression and World War II, died on April 12, 1945. East Harlemites reacted to his death and the end of World War II.

Raquel Villegas: *There was crying and screaming in the streets when FDR died because he was like the godfather of the people.*

James Bryant: *My mother cried when President Roosevelt died.*

Four months later, after the second atomic bomb fell on the city of Nagasaki, the Japanese government surrendered and World War II was officially over. East Harlemites, like most Americans, celebrated.

James Bryant: *People rejoiced in the streets when it was over. A parade of cars rode in the streets and horns were blaring off and the people celebrated by hanging out of their windows.*

Rose Savatelli: *When the war was over people were yelling and screaming, and really enjoying life. Don't forget it was four years. It was something I'll never forget.*

Efrain Marzan: *When the war ended, I will never forget this. It was nighttime and my father says, "Negro, Negro [negro is a term of endearment among*

2. The Great Depression and World War II (1930s–1940s)   57

Puerto Ricans] se acabo la guerra, se acabo la guerra." [The war is over, the war is over.] And he kissed me.

Raquel Villegas: *There were block parties to commemorate the soldiers that came back home and both my uncles came home back safely.*

George Arless: *People went to the roof and threw confetti or newspaper. There were block parties in the streets and lots of noise. Each time a person came back from the service the block or building had a big welcome home celebration. There were kegs of beer and foods.*

Next we learn the story of Vito Marcantonio. He first made a name for himself as La Guardia's protégé in the mid–1920s. He was elected to Congress in 1934, was defeated two years later, and regained his seat in 1938. He would dominate the political scene in East Harlem throughout the next decade.

3

Marc (Vito Marcantonio)

Vito Morcantonio has been gone from East Harlem and the political arena for more than half a century, but East Harlemites who remember him talk about his exploits as if were still alive today. He barely lived past his fiftieth birthday. Today when his name is mentioned it evokes praise and an unswerving loyalty from his admirers, who viewed him as a true friend of the working class. Some admirers have called him a saint. But among his detractors his memory brings scorn and derision. They think he was a demagogue who never should have been elected to political office.

Marc's parents were Sanario (later Americanized to Samuel) Marcantonio, a carpenter by trade, and Angelina de Dobitis, who married Sanario shortly after she arrived in America. Vito Anthony Marcantonio was born on December 10, 1902, on 112th Street between First and Second Avenue. His younger brother Frank joined the Marcantonio clan a few years later.[1] He began his education at Public School 85, located on 117th Street, where his leadership skills and intellect garnered him high grades. Marcantonio excelled in his history and public speaking classes, but he avoided athletics. Nevertheless, Marcantonio easily made friends and was the darling of his teachers. His younger brother, Frank, seemed likely to follow in his older brother's footsteps, but he suffered a mental disorder beginning in his adolescent years. Unknown to all but the closest friends the family, Frank lived in seclusion in the family's home until Marc's death. Afterwards, Frank spent the rest of his life in a mental hospital.[2]

Marcantonio's family was financially stable compared to other residents in East Harlem. This allowed the elder Marcantonio to buy a tricycle for his precocious son, who was one of the select few to own such a vehicle. The adolescent Marcantonio enjoyed swimming in the accommodating but garbage-strewn East River.[3] Sanarios' business also allowed Marcantonio to attend De Witt Clinton High School on 59th Street and 10th Avenue. This was a rare occurrence in Italian East Harlem at that time, for many of Marcantonio's peers worked to support their families. Not surprisingly, he was one of only two East Harlemites to enroll in high school. The other student who enrolled with Marcantonio eventually quit school.[4]

Marcantonio's family suffered a tragedy when a Third Avenue streetcar struck and killed his father. After Sanario's death, Vito's mother and grandmother did domestic work to supplement the family's income.[5] Despite his father's death, Marcantonio forged ahead. During his high school years his inclination for politics began. While his friends focused on their social life and sports, he developed an interest in politics, international affairs and labor issues. His classmates branded him a socialist, perhaps due to his activism in some of the school's socialist clubs, but he would not back down. On one occasion Marcantonio shot back and told his classmates one day someone would make money off of them when they sought employment and they should be aware of this.[6] Marcantonio learned about socialism as a student at De Witt Clinton High School. He was introduced to it by his history teacher, Abraham Lefkowitz.[7] Marcantonio's first involvement in community issues was during a tenants' strike in East Harlem. After World War I, many landlords throughout New York City augmented the rents on their apartments. These rent increases led to a number of evictions and the tenants sought to fight back. Instead of suing the landlord separately, the rent strikers sued as a group which in turn compelled many landlords to issue a countersue. But soon the court became inundated with countersuits.

Marcantonio, only seventeen, organized the East Harlem Tenants League. Its aim was to use the rent strike to promote a political solution to the problem. His activism continued as Marcantonio taught citizenship classes at La Casa del Popolo, an East Harlem adult education center.[8] Marcantonio also participated in international affairs when he sided with the Irish nationalists in their struggle for independence against British colonialism.

Another influential person in Marcantonio's life was Edward Covello. Two years before Marcantonio arrived at De Witt Clinton, Covello worked with Italian American high schoolers to discover their Italian heritage. And Covello instructed American students in southern Italian customs. This instruction focused on learning the Italian language and familiarity with Italy's history and culture. Marcantonio took full advantage of Covello's tutelage and he became proficient in Italian. This later paid dividends for Marcantonio in his political career.[9]

Marcantonio's political influence was guided by Fiorello La Guardia. La Guardia first met Marcantonio when Covello invited La Guardia as the guest speaker during an assembly at De Witt Clinton. Marcantonio, who was in his senior year in high school, gave a speech on old age pensions and Social Security. La Guardia, sitting on the dais, noted how eloquently Marcantonio spoke and after Marcantonio's speech ended he went up and gave him a slap on his shoulder. La Guardia would have the greatest impact on the life and career of Vito Marcantonio.[10]

After high school Marcantonio attended New York University Law School. He followed both his father's example and Americanized his first name, replacing Vito with Victor, but he shortly switched back to Vito. His law studies were much more rigorous than his high school curriculum, but Marcantonio still maintained his extracurricular activities. He worked during the evening hours at Haarlem House's adult education department. At Haarlem House Marcantonio met Miriam Sanders, a social worker, whose family hailed from an old New England family. It was a case of opposites attracting, for Sanders, eleven years his senior and five inches taller, was a Protestant who fell in love with the short, wiry Catholic Vito Marcantonio. They married in 1925, the same year he earned his law degree, but his grades were poor due to his extracurricular activities. His extracurricular activities forced him to earn forty-five credits to graduate.[11] One of Marcantonio's major distractions was politics. The previous year Marcantonio managed Congressman La Guardia's reelection campaign. With Marcantonio's help La Guardia defeated his opponent, Henry Frank, by more than three thousand votes.

La Guardia demonstrated his gratitude to Marcantonio by giving him a clerk position in his law firm. Marcantonio also received a crash course on politics working in La Guardia's congressional office while simultaneously overseeing the Fiorello H. La Guardia political club. La Guardia said publicly that he wanted to make Marcantonio his political heir. He soaked up every political opportunity available to him as Marcantonio helped La Guardia's constituents who needed legal assistance with immigration issues. He also kept the Little Flower abreast of the neighborhood's activities.[12]

There were striking similarities between the two men that could not be ignored. Both were short and of Italian descent (though La Guardia was half Jewish). Progressive, feisty, fiery in speech and sometimes in temperament, extraverts, fluent in Italian, they both loved people and fought for the lower class. Mentor and pupil developed a mutual respect for one another and Marcantonio became La Guardia's protégé, and he gained a surrogate father. And La Guardia looked upon Marcantonio like the son he never had.[13]

But La Guardia and Marcantonio had their differences. Once when Marcantonio was working as LaGuardia's clerk, he sent his mentor a memorandum regarding two cases. La Guardia replied that it was stupid to send the original papers. Marcantonio disagreed with La Guardia's assessment and wrote La Guardia a letter reminding him how busy he was.[14]

3. Marc (Vito Marcantonio)

Though La Guardia spoke brusquely to Marcantonio as he did to elected officials, the Little Flower never missed an opportunity to show his warm feelings toward his protégé. For example, La Guardia raised Marcantonio's salary. And dispensed more wisdom toward his energetic and hard-working protégé in a personal letter.

> You are young; you have a lot to learn and a long way to go before you will be a lawyer in the real sense of the word. I am fond of you and want to help you.

Progressive, fiery, controversial and unforgettable, Vito "Marc" Marcantonio represented East Harlem in Congress from 1934 to 1950. Despite his detractors, Marc had the allegiance of thousands of East Harlemites from all races, and ethnicities (Library of Congress, USZ62-73262).

> Were I not interested in you I would not have planned as I did looking far into the future. You have an opportunity presented to you such as very few boys have, other than those who can step into their own father's office and know that one day it will be theirs. That is what I am offering you. You must make up your mind to be fair with me. Are you going to be a politician, a social worker, or a lawyer? If you are satisfied, as I told you, to make a living from the Magistrate and Courts, with General Sessions as the possible limit, you can keep up your social and political activities. If you love your profession, want to be proficient in it and intend to follow it, then you have got to change your attitude and your whole mode of living. You have to cut out your evening appointments, your dances, your midnight philosophers, for the next five years and devote yourself to serious hard study of the law. Be careful in your personal appearance. Get a Gillette razor and keep yourself well groomed at all times. Be always respectful and courteous to all, the humble as well as the high and for goodness sake keep your ears and eyes open and keep your mouth closed for at least the next twenty years. Now my dear boy take this letter in the fatherly spirit that I am writing it.[15]

Marcantonio heeded his mentor's advice. Throughout the 1920s and early 1930s, Marcantonio either worked in La Guardia's congressional office or managed his campaigns. Learning about political machinations went a long way towards Marcantonio's political rise in East Harlem. The Little Flower again showed his gratitude to his protégé when he arranged for Marcantonio to become the United States Assistant Attorney General for the Southern District of New York.[16]

In 1932, a general election was held. Republicans in Congress lost many House seats as the country voted overwhelmingly for the Democrats. Though La Guardia was a progressive, he lost his seat to Democrat James J. Lanzetta. But La Guardia bounced back next year and won the city's mayoral election. With La Guardia in City Hall, Marcantonio was ready to run for office. After some infighting in the Republican Party, Marcantonio secured the GOP congressional nomination. Marcantonio's good fortune continued as Lanzetta hardly distinguished himself in Congress. His absenteeism became his first liability, but it was Lanzetta's position on housing issues that became his undoing. The issue involved mortgage indebtedness and Lanzetta backed the landlords and not the tenants in housing court. Many East Harlem tenants still fought their landlord in housing court and Lanzetta's stance was unpopular with working-class East Harlem.[17]

The 1934 midterm elections gave the Democrats overwhelming majorities in both houses of Congress. In East Harlem, running as a Republican, Marcantonio squeaked out a victory by some 250 votes out of 27,000 cast. He was one of only 103 Republicans elected to the Seventy-Fourth Congress. Upon taking office Marcantonio aligned himself with many progressives who retained a following during the depression.[18]

Marcantonio supported the New Deal immediately and though it was popular with many Americans some legislatures and legal experts questioned some of the New Deal's constitutionality—specifically Section 7A of the National Labor Relations Act (NLRA). The provision allowed workers the opportunity to seek redress and engage in collective bargaining to obtain better wages. Most observers speculated that if the case went to the Supreme Court, Section 7A would be found unconstitutional. The high court eventually ruled against Section 7A. Marcantonio voiced his opposition against any measure to strip Section 7A from NLRA and he upbraided his colleagues in the House and Roosevelt's administration for their lukewarm support. And he furthered argued that section 7A's defeat was linked to the administration's inability to fight for it.

Marc achieved success in another labor-related cause. The National Labor Relations Board was originally scheduled to operate independently, but some House members wanted to place the NLRB under the auspices of the Department of Labor. He successfully persuaded his House colleagues to establish an independent board free from the administration's control.[19]

In 1936, another election pitted Marcantonio against Lanzetta. Lanzetta rode FDR's coattails on the president's landslide reelection and defeated Marcantonio two years later, Marcantonio's again was assisted by La Guardia, who managed to have his protégé win the nomination of the newly formed American Labor Party (ALP), established two years earlier. Marcantonio had another trump card of his own and knew how to play it. The Republican Party needed La Guardia, and the GOP patched up their differences with Marcantonio and endorsed him.[20] Marcantonio's affiliation with the ALP made the difference as he garnered nearly 9,000 votes as its candidate to defeat Lanzetta, and returned to Congress.[21] Marcantonio entered the 1940s advocating for the political left and incurring the wrath of the state's political leadership and the press.

Annette T. Rubenstein met Marcantonio in 1934 and subsequently worked for him. She was an active member of the American Labor Party from 1936 until its demise in 1954.

Annette T. Rubenstein: *Marc in Washington was tremendously busy and not only on the floor of Congress, but rounding up support in the neighborhood. Usually when a person is in the [political] minority, that person just makes speeches. But Marc was so well known and so interesting and amusing that when he rose to speak in the House of Representatives even those in Congress who eventually voted against him rushed back to the chamber to hear what he had to say.*

Marcantonio's oratory skills were second to none, especially in Congress. During one House session, Marcantonio fought against a measure which would have barred all immigrants from seeking office as a union representative. In a brilliant and facetious retort Marcantonio commented. "I don't believe the amendment goes far enough. I believe we should restrict leadership of American unions to the descendants of those who came over on the Mayflower."[22] In East Harlem he was even better. Ernest Cuneo remembered how Marcantonio started his speeches very slowly. As he went on, Marcantonio would stomp his heel on the floor. This action produced a hollow noise which elicited a response from the audience. His voice rising as he repeatedly stomped his foot, he and the audience came alive. At the apex of the moment Marcantonio was shouting at full speed, and his foot stomping reminded many of dancing flamenco.[23]

Manny Diaz, Jr.: *The election eve rally was held on 116th Street and Lexington Avenue (the Lucky Corner). Five thousand people would be there and Marcantonio had an interesting way of orating. He would start very quiet and very slow and then, he would start getting excited. Next he raised his voice and end up screaming. Marcantonio knew how to turn that crowd up.*

Meyer Kukle: *Every politician went to the Lucky Corner on 116th Street and when Marcantonio spoke he did so with a very fiery voice. He presented his argument with factual statements and he'd spoke to the audience and told them the facts. He was powerful and he'd talk about change and as he talked he'd bounce up and down.*

In East Harlem Marcantonio always felt at ease. For example, many times when he returned from Washington, Marcantonio said he was glad to be back home in East Harlem. And his communion with East Harlemites that gave him the most pleasure.

Annette T. Rubenstein: *Marc really loved the people of East Harlem and it wasn't fake. Marc worked eighteen hours a day, seven days a week. Despite these long hours in East Harlem, he had the best attendance record in Congress, for he never missed a session. He did this while working in the neighborhood every weekend. Marc found time to do all this somehow and many times he didn't sleep. Marc would lug these position papers and for international affairs he was remarkably devoted. And he was honest and had tremendous energy, despite his diabetes, which is why he never drove because Marc was afraid he might black out.*

Lois Pascale Evans: *I walked with my father [Pete Pascale] from Haarlem House [now La Guardia House]. We walked down the street and I guess Marc lived down the next block. My father was so happy so see Marc and I would have to stand there while they both got lost in conversation. I thought they were going to talk forever.*

Marcantonio in Italian East Harlem was accorded with the respect he never enjoyed in the press. The newspapers constantly attacked Marcantonio for his progressive views. Though some in Italian East Harlem also disagreed with him, the community took umbrage as they saw an attack upon their congressman as an attack upon the neighborhood itself.[24] This was further evidenced in *Time* magazine, which wrote:

> The core of Manhattan's sprawling 18th Congressional District is a verminous, crime ridden slum called East Harlem. Its hordes of Italian, Puerto Ricans, Jews and Negroes have traditionally voted Republican. But in the last decade a new force came into power; the patchwork patronage machine of shrill, stooped, angry-eyed, pro–Communist Representative Vito Marcantonio. The little Padrone was the passionate 18th's new-style ward boss and idol. Taut, 43-year-old Vito Marcantonio was born in the congressional district he lives in and represents. To its gunmen, madams, policy and dope peddlers, he is "The Hon. Fritto Misto" (Mixed Fry), the man who began as a Republican with the blessing of East Harlem's Fiorello La Guardia, the man who ladles out jobs, pocket money, speeches—anything for votes.[25]

Many in Italian East Harlem ignored these attacks on Marcantonio and continued to support their favorite son in countless elections. As the article noted, Marcantonio's district included Italians, Puerto Ricans, Jews, and Negroes. Marcantonio had a tremendous following in Spanish Harlem (El Barrio) and he a sort of "quasi-congressman" of the Puerto Rican people. Throughout his entire congressional career he advocated for the independence of Puerto Rico and spoke at many progressive Puerto Rican organizations.[26]

In Spanish Harlem many Puerto Rican organizations and churches supported Marcantonio. Finally, Marcantonio traveled to Puerto Rico to represent Don Pedro Albizu Campos and seven other members of the island's Nationalist Party. Campos, along with the other Nationalist members, were charged with sedition. The men were convicted of the charges, however.

Marcantonio was successful in other areas when he managed to include Puerto Rico in the Social Security Act. Like Italian Americans in East Harlem, Puerto Ricans were the object of virulent sniping and subjected to callous and vile statements in the press. The conservative *Daily Mirror* wrote,

> During the last ten years and growing every year, there has descended upon Manhattan island like a locust plague an influx of Puerto Ricans. They are mostly crude farmers, subject to congenital tropical diseases, physically unfitted for the northern climate, unskilled, uneducated, non–English speaking and almost impossible to assimilate in an active city of stone and steel.
>
> A majority of these people were lured here deliberately because, as American citizens, they can vote. They are a power behind Congressman Vito Marcantonio.... Very few Puerto Ricans have or ever had $20.00 for the passage to New York City from Puerto Rico but the money seems to come from somewhere.... The callous exploitation of these weaklings is one of the dirtiest crimes in the long and shameful record of practical politics.

Marcantonio countered these statements and maintained that Puerto Ricans and other ethnic voters in his district were upstanding members of society. As Italian East Harlem shrank during his tenure in Congress, his Italian votes were replaced by the Puerto Rican vote.[27] Marcantonio continued to call for peace between Spanish and Italian East Harlem. Puerto Rican–born East Harlemite Piri Thomas remembers.

Piri Thomas: *Vito Marcantonio, I thought he was Puerto Rican because he helped everybody, all nationalities. The Puerto Ricans and Italians were always fighting and he was helping everybody out.*

East Harlem's multiracial neighborhood was not without its problems. Violence between African Americans and whites took place at Benjamin Franklin High School during the mid–1940s. To ameliorate the situation, Marcantonio contacted Mayor La Guardia to see if he could bring two celebrity representatives of both groups to East Harlem. La Guardia recruited Frank Sinatra and Joe Louis to help foster racial harmony. The Little Flower was partially successful as Sinatra came to Benjamin Franklin High School.[28] Marcantonio also arranged a multiracial unit to march in the Columbus Day parade that fall.

Marcantonio demonstrated his commitment to civil rights for African Americans. The attack on Pearl Harbor left two thousand Americans dead, beginning with African American Dorie Miller, the first mortally wounded American soldier. In recognition of Miller's heroism, Marcantonio rose in the House and paid tribute to the fallen hero.[29] He also tried to buttress the Fair Employment Practices Commission (FEPC). Through an Executive Order by President Roosevelt, the FEPC was designed to end employment discrimination. However, Marcantonio's congressional colleagues consistently voted to weaken FEPC. A decade after Marcantonio's death, through the Civil Rights Act, FEPC became law.[30]

Marcantonio also engineered the passage of a House bill which outlawed the poll tax. This method was strategically used to deny African Americans and poor whites the right to vote. Marcantonio worked to pass the law in the House on several occasions, but the Senate employed the filibuster to defeat the bill. As with the FEPC, a decade after his death, the Twenty-Fifth Amendment to the Constitution outlawed this practice. Finally, Marcantonio proposed a bill to outlaw lynching in the United States.[31] All of these measures were not lost on African Americans, as James Bryant recalls: *"People labeled him a communist, but he was the type of guy that if you had a problem with your relief checks he'd made sure you received them. He captivated the hearts of the East Harlem people and he had a following among blacks. People would say, 'You have a problem with rent or the landlord? Go to Marcantonio.'"*

Though many people identified Marcantonio as a communist, he was not a member of the Communist Party. Marcantonio, the practical politician, was at odds with the Communist Party and he disagreed with its theory. Plus, freedom from any organized association suited his needs, but he did believe in the party's right to free speech. Though Marcantonio was not a communist, he served as vice chairman of several communist organizations. And before Marcantonio returned to Congress in 1938, he was president of the International Labor Defense, an association which provided legal assistance and strategy to the Communist Party. In addition, Marcantonio's political success benefited from the Communist Party monetarily and organizationally as the party's dollars and foot soldiers were always at Marcantonio's disposal.[32] Thanks to these associations the communist label hounded Marcantonio throughout his political life. Here two East Harlemites deliver divergent opinions on Marcantonio.

Willie Lopez: *"He was supposed to be a communist and I shook hands with him, Marcantonio. I believed he was a propagandist and I think everybody liked him because he was a good propagandist. But a lot of people viewed him a negative way. Then came Senator Joseph McCarthy, but they didn't like him either."*

Meyer Kukle: *"Vito backed the Communist Party, but the Soviet Union wasn't perfect and he knew this. Bottom line, he was there for the people."*

Despite this perceived association with the Communist Party, Marcantonio managed to win reelection to Congress many times, but he still faced many problems. Infighting between the conservative and liberal factions in the ALP could not be ignored. The upstate conservative faction wanted to disassociate itself from those it identified as communists within the party. The conservatives in the ALP agreed with Roosevelt's foreign policy. Conversely, the liberal faction, located in New York City, desired to work with the communists and opposed FDR's foreign policy. This chasm in the ALP caused some ALP members to flee, like Luigi Antonini, a longtime friend of Marcantonio who broke with Marc and supported his rival for his Congress in the next congressional election.[33] Marcantonio was assured to win the Republican nomination, but the GOP gubernatorial candidate, William Bleakly, wanted no part of the progressive congressman and denied Marcantonio any monetary or organizational assistance. Even without Bleakly's support, Marcantonio ran as a Republican and the ALP candidate, facing James Lanzetta for a fourth and final time. Not even a national ticket headed by President Roosevelt could help Lanzetta this time as Marcantonio outdistanced him by over 10,000 votes.[34]

Another problem was World War II, which began in Europe in September 1939. In Congress, the House twice voted overwhelmingly to appropriate funds to strengthen America's military arsenal. Marcantonio twice disagreed with his House colleagues and twice voted against the legislation. But Marcantonio was not a pacifist, for he believed if war would preserve freedom for farmers or laborers then he would support such action. Instead Marcantonio advocated that Congress should use its powers to allocate funds towards all social and economic programs.

In the spring of 1941, Marcantonio again maintained his isolationist stance and again voted against Roosevelt's Lend-Lease Program. It should be noted that Marcantonio was not alone in his position, as millions of Americans wanted the United States to remain neutral. Then in September he reversed himself and urged America to assist the Soviet Union in any way possible. His attitude changed with Germany's attack on the Soviet Union. This stance angered some of Marcantonio's supporters, and the press was quick to jump on his perceived flip-flopping on the issue. Marc answered his critics by stating that if the Soviet Union fell into Germany's hands the United States would become more vulnerable.[35]

Annette T. Rubenstein: *The American Labor Party, like the Communist Party and other leftist parties was against America getting in World War II, as was the case when the American people were against World War I. Marc took an antiwar stand and won election as an antiwar candidate the previous year. When it became clear the Soviet Union was attacked and there was a real danger of Nazi victory, the left changed its position, and so did the ALP and Marcantonio. Though Marc* was elected on his promise to stay out of the war, what he was really going to do that summer was to campaign in his neighborhood and get a mandate. He explained to the people why he changed his stance in Congress. And Marc campaigned in East Harlem and Marc asked the people to write to him about the war and why the United States had to join it. His constituents wrote to him and this led him to change his stance in Congress in 1941.

Once America entered the war in December, Marcantonio wholeheartedly supported it and he encouraged young East Harlemites to join the navy. In 1942 there was another election and Marcantonio faced a new opponent as the Democrats chose Frank J. Ricca. On the Republican side Thomas J. Curran, the GOP leader, intensely disliked Marcantonio, whom he deemed a communist, and he backed Charles Mucciolo for the Republican nomination for Congress. Marcantonio even faced a primary challenge for the nomination of the American Labor Party. At that time New York State's election law allowed any candidate to run in all three primaries. Marcantonio seized this opportunity and won all three primaries, which insured his reelection in November.

Many outside East Harlem wondered how Marcantonio could endure constant sniping in the press and in the House and still win reelection to Congress. The answer lies in his indefatigable service to his constituents. Stories about Marcantonio's close relationship with his former constituents are legendary. When an East Harlem family was evicted, Marcantonio gave the family twenty dollars to stay at a nearby hotel. And during the holidays the congressman might purchase a turkey or Christmas basket.[36]

Ray Grist: *Marcantonio was a big hero and every Sunday he sponsored a block party or a little fair for the East River projects. There would be a stage and then an Italian band came and played music. Next, a big white sheet was set up and on the side of the building and movies would be shown on summer nights.*

Nicholasa Mohr: *We were indebted to him because we couldn't pay the rent and he kept my family from being evicted. We all campaigned for him and I remember distributing the flyers on his behalf.*

Ramon Ferreira: *He helped my mother when my father was a Merchant Marine. At that time money was hard [to get] and my father went to the Pacific and whatever money my mother made [went for] utilities. She went to many places for help and received welfare, but people have big mouths and word got back to the authorities. The City of New York came down on my mother. My mother went to Marcantonio and he said, "Don't worry about it," and Marcantonio helped her out and our financial problems were solved.*

Many of Marc's constituents received their services by visiting the congressman's office. From adolescents to the elderly, all would file into a long narrow hall. This procession continued until they reached Marcantonio, who was at his desk greeting his constituents. Marcantonio's office was staffed by lawyers and professionals who spoke many languages and were knowledgeable of the community's needs. These constituents had issues that ranged from divorce to juvenile delinquency to employment discrimination, income tax preparation and institutionalization. Marcantonio had two offices, one on 116th Street and, after 1945, a second office on 78th Street. Both of them dispensed legal and social services to the community.[37]

Annette T. Rubenstein: *Marcantonio came home on Friday nights and he left Sunday nights back to Washington. He came by train, for he hated flying unless it was an emergency. I worked at the 78th Street office on Saturdays and there was a big loft on top of the Woolworth store underneath. At one end there was a little railing on a slightly raised platform, not much raised and the rest of it was benches. When the people came in they got a number like you get in the bakery store and sat down on a bench. On this little raised platform was Marc's office which had a waisthigh store door, and there were volunteers and there were several lawyers and myself and a couple of other specialists, housing and so on. After a number was called people came up to Marc who acted as his own receptionist. He took three to five minutes to find out what the problem was, which could be housing, jobs, schools, or immigration issues. Marc would say here's so and so, or here's Dr. Rubenstein, she's a specialist on education and she'll take care of this.*

Marc actually saw each person who visited the office and this was good politics because everybody said, "Marc took care of everything," or "Marc took care of me personally." On the other hand if you wanted to meet all of the people it would drive you crazy. We were open from 10 A.M. to 9 P.M. and it didn't close until the last person was served. Sometimes it was so crowded we had to close at 5 or 6 P.M. to insure every constituent was serviced.

Eugene Nardelli: *Marcantonio tended to the community himself. You visited his office for any problem you had and he personally listened to you. I remember going with my father to his 116th Street office and you waited and then you saw him and he would refer you to a lawyer. One time our apartment went without water for months and he helped our family get the water running again. You either loved him or you hated him.*

Rev. Norman C. Eddy: *You walked in and he'd greet you and listen to your problem, then he would direct you to the person who knew about the situation. If it was housing, he would point you to the housing assistant, and if it was education, then he would appoint you to the education expert on his staff. Or if you needed a lawyer then a lawyer was there to assist you.*

Carlos De Jesus: *Vito Marcantonio was the precursor of Jesse Jackson's Rainbow Coalition and that was probably his undoing. The power structure in the* *city, they didn't want to see someone who had the allegiance of all these ethnic groups. But he did, he had Latinos, Italians, and blacks.*

It was the power structure that tried to undermine Marcantonio's political base. In 1944, the New York State Legislature redrew the congressional districts for each House member, and the 20th Congressional district that covered most of East Harlem was gone. East Harlem was now part of the 18th Congressional District which stretched down to East 59th Street. Marcantonio's new district included part of the wealthy and middle-class Upper East Side. But this new reapportionment did not prevent Marcantonio from winning his fifth term in Congress. With FDR again at the helm of the Democratic ticket, the Democrats nominated Martin J. Kennedy, a former state senator and congressman. Marcantonio again fought and won his party's nomination over a fractious ALP. This time the division among many members of A.L.P was irreparable and some ALP members left and formed the Liberal Party. The Republicans chose Lt. Robert C. Palmer, but he was on active duty and was virtually a non-candidate. Marcantonio again won all three nominations and was re-elected to Congress.[38]

World War II ended in 1945 and the country began to focus again on domestic issues. The Republican Party took control of both houses of Congress the next year, but this did not help Marcantonio, for the New York Republican Party bristled at the thought of nominating him and selected attorney Frederick Van Pelt Bryan, a colonel in the army Air Force. The Democrats chose Patrick H. Hannigan, a former naval officer and policeman. Marcantonio won his sixth congressional race as he edged out Hannigan in the Democratic primary, and with the ALP nomination, Marcantonio was able to win in November, despite losing the Republican nod to Bryan. However, there was one sad postscript to Marcantonio's victory that year. On election day, as East Harlemites went to the polls, Joseph Scottoriggio, a Republican district captain who supported Frederick Van Pelt Bryan, was savagely beaten and died nearly a week later.[39]

The press and Marcantonio's detractors immediately linked Scottoriggio's death to the East Harlem congressman or his associates. New York governor Thomas E. Dewey attributed the death to left-wingers in Marcantonio's district. The *Daily Mirror*, which always attacked Marcantonio, joined the fray and called the congressman's district the most criminally connected in the world. *Life* magazine became involved in the affair and ran a sinister portrait of Marcantonio, linking the congressman with gangsters. Monetary awards up to $13,500 were available to anyone with any knowledge of Scottoriggio's murder.[40] Finally, a grand jury's inquest involving crime in Marcantonio's district culminated with the congressman on the witness stand.

Marcantonio pointed out that he lived in the same district as some criminals, and he could not consciously deny anyone service no matter what their backgrounds were. Marcantonio also stated he never associated with gangsters, though he knew some of them lived in his district and he befriended everyone regardless of their occupation or class. Scottoriggio's murder went unresolved and the story remained in the paper for the next two years.[41]

The year 1947 was tough for Vito Marcantonio. The first blow came when his mentor, Fiorello La Guardia, passed away in September of that year. Second, the New York State Legislature passed the Wilson-Pakula Act, which limited a candidate to run only in the primary election of the party in which he/she was enrolled. This prevented him from running in the Democratic and Republican primaries. Now a candidate could only run on the party line with the endorsement from the party's committee. This law was designed with the sole purpose of defeating Vito Marcantonio.[42] But this law did not stop Marcantonio, who consistently put up a battle in Congress. This was nowhere more evident than the Taft-Hartley Act of that year. Proposed in the Senate by Robert F. Taft (son of the 27th president) and in the House by Congressman Fred Hartley, the law sought to stifle communist activities within the unions. Supporters of the law believed it was designed to halt any work stoppage that threatened the national interest.[43]

Marcantonio was vehemently opposed to any law that he perceived would limit the rights of labor. He was not alone, as President Harry S. Truman and some Democrats sided with him on this issue. Truman vetoed the law, but the Republican-controlled Congress, coupled with the assistance of many southern Democrats, overturned Truman's veto and the Taft-Hartley Act became law.[44]

The next year in the general election President Truman ran against what he called "the 80th Do Nothing Congress." Attacking the Republican presidential nominee, Governor Thomas E. Dewey, Truman criss-crossed the country on his train, the *Ferdinand Magellan*, and spoke extemporaneously at every whistle stop. Truman simply gave the Republican Party hell and shocked every political pundit who predicted his defeat by winning an upset election over Governor Dewey.[45]

Marcantonio did the same in East Harlem. Running as an ALP candidate he faced Democrat John P. Morrissey. As Morrissey spoke only three times during the campaign and this led some political pundits to believe there was a deal between the two parties. John Ellis, a veteran naval officer, was the Republican candidate and took on Marcantonio in an old-fashioned street fight. But there was a chink in Ellis' political armor as he was a stockbroker who lived in a fourteen-room apartment outside of the district. Marcantonio knew what to do, which was something he did for years: engage in class warfare. It was easy in the 18th Congressional District which was composed of middle-class voters and many lower-class residents. Ellis fought back with the usual charge that Marcantonio was a communist. The city's newspapers and notable Republican stalwarts endorsed Ellis'.[46]

Marcantonio appealed to his base, and his constituents rallied behind the leftist from East Harlem. He campaigned on street corners, school auditoriums, political clubs, or wherever an audience was available. Marcantonio met his detractors' charge of his alleged communist ties. Marcantonio stated that though he shared some opinions with the Communist Party, he was not a communist. He also believed that the people would support him in the future as they did in the past. Marcantonio went door to door as another means connecting with his constituents who couldn't come to his office. Finally, he also used what then were some radical techniques of communication by showing feature films during his congressional campaigns. Marcantonio emerged victorious as he defeated both Ellis and Morrissey.[47]

But times had changed, and though Marcantonio was consistent with his progressive views, he seemed out of touch with many Americans. Many progressive members of Congress who served with him during his first years in Congress were gone. And many Americans believed America should take an active role in world affairs. The Soviet Union, America's ally during the war, now was America's enemy. Besides former Vice President Henry Wallace, who advocated an accommodationist stance with the Soviet Union, there existed no other high-profile politician who took this position.[48] Perhaps the most revealing of the times was the widespread fear of communism in the country. This fear led to the renewal of the House Un-American Activities Committee and the political opportunism of Senator Joseph McCarthy. Both the committee and McCarthy would destroy many American lives.

Still Marcantonio stuck to his beliefs and opposed the Marshall Plan and the Truman Doctrine, both designed to prevent Soviet expansion. He also voted against aid to Turkey and Greece as he felt the appropriations should be used for the American people.[49] The next year Marcantonio ran for mayor, where he gained only fifteen percent of the vote, losing badly in a three-way race. In the 1949 elections, Assemblyman Earl Brown with the support of the Democratic, Republican and Liberal Parties defeated the communist candidate for City Council, Benjamin Davis. After that election, columnist Frank Conniff of the *Journal American* suggested the three parties replicate the same strategy to defeat Marcantonio in the upcoming congressional election. Moreover, ALP enrollment which had been slightly less than 100,000 was only now half that number.[50]

Back in the House, there was no stopping him as he again remained the maverick congressman who differed with many of his House colleagues. Marcantonio spoke out against giving aid to Chiang Kai-Shek in China. In June

3. Marc (Vito Marcantonio) 73

1950, after the North Koreans crossed the 38th Parallel and attacked South Korea, the United Nations responded, bringing coalition forces into battle against the North Koreans. Many American soldiers fought in what President Truman called a "police action"—the Korean War. Marcantonio became the lone dissenter to vote against the use of military force in Korea.[51] Meanwhile in New York City, animosity and political hatred against Marcantonio was palpable, especially in the press. James Donovan, Harvard educated and a Columbia Law School graduate, was Marcantonio's opponent in 1950. This time all three political parties heeded Coniff's advice and gave their nominations to Donovan. Though Marcantonio outpolled Donovan individually, the combination of the three parties gave Donovan a plurality of 14,000 votes.[52] The third time proved to be a charm for Marcantonio's enemies, and though he was out of office, Marcantonio continued to serve East Harlemites as if he were still in Congress.

Efrain and Eva Marzan. Efrain was part of the first generation of Puerto Ricans to arrive in America via the airplane. Mr. Marzan remembers the neighborhood before it disappeared and was remodeled through public housing.

Annette T. Rubenstein: *He kept his former district offices open after he lost his seat. And the people still called him the congressman, because he was still helping people and he still had a lot of clout downtown.*

Marcantonio spent idle weekends in Danbury, Connecticut, where his wife, Miriam, had inherited a house from her brother, but the sedentary life bored him. In 1953, Marcantonio did the unthinkable when he left the ALP. In early June 1954, Marcantonio sent word to his supporters of his impending return to politics. This time he would run again as an independent for his old House seat. His chances of mounting a political comeback looked promising, but on the morning of August 9, as rain fell on New York City, Marcantonio was running to his office when he suffered a fatal heart attack. The first stack of petitions was on his desk ready to be inspected.⁵³ Even in death, Marcantonio could not escape controversy: he was denied a Catholic burial. His funeral was held at Giordano's Funeral home on 115th Street and First Avenue.⁵⁴

Father Al DinCeccio: *When Marcantonio died he was carrying his rosary beads. As a priest, when you find someone in that condition, a person who is not faithful to the church wouldn't carry those things. The fact that you are not going to church with the rosary and you still have those beads means you still have some affiliation. Mass was given by Father Anastasia. I was at the funeral, and my mother was holding my hand. Afterwards, if anybody said anything negative about Marcantonio my father would counter it.*

He was buried in Woodlawn Cemetery in the Bronx, right next to his mentor Fiorello La Guardia. His life ended in the summer of 1954, but he has not been forgotten. In December 2002, nearly two hundred people gathered in the auditorium of Museum of the City of New York to celebrate his centennial birth. A film of Marcantonio's 1948 congressional race was shown. Seeing him on the screen brought back memories to many of Marcantonio's followers. A number of speakers, including Annette T. Rubenstein, spoke movingly of Marcantonio.

4
Planting Roots II (1945–1950)

During Marcantonio's last years in office and shortly before his death, East Harlem's ethnic population changed again. This time an unprecedented wave of Puerto Ricans and African Americans came to East Harlem. This chapter looks at this transformation.

Throughout World War II Puerto Rican immigration to New York City was small as the presence of German submarines prevented many ships from entering American waters. But some Puerto Ricans managed to travel to New York City, like Francesa Santiago, who arrived in the city in 1944 and worked in the garment industry. After her arrival, she met her future husband Fundador and raised four children in El Barrio.[1] After the war, Puerto Rican immigration to America rose sharply. From 1941 to 1950 the average number of Puerto Rican immigrants was 18,794, but this average doubled to 41,212 from 1951 to 1960.[2] Several factors contributed to the increase in Puerto Rican immigration. As it had before, employment opportunity became the main inducement to leave the island for New York City.[3] Some Puerto Ricans still arrived in New York on passenger ships, but air travel superseded sea and truncated the travel time from the island to the United States. Three Puerto Ricans recall their journeys from the island to El Barrio after the war using both the passenger ship and the airplane.

Pablo Figueroa: *My mother, my older brother and I came from Puerto Rico to New York on the ship called the* **Marine Tiger***. This is before the airplane became the standard way of travel. On the boat I was called Master Figueroa and I remember running up and down the ship. And during the trip we encountered many storms and when we passed Cape Hatteras the ship was engulfed in a powerful storm. But despite the storm I was so excited about traveling to New York that I seemed to ignore what was happening. Instead I looked through one of the portholes and it was an incredible thing to see. The storm seemed to be twenty stories higher than the boat and it looked like the boat would hit rock bottom then, suddenly it came up. I remember this for as we were about to go to dinner and every passenger on the* **Marine Tiger** *became sick. Because the ship moved so violently all of the dishes fell off the table. It took four or five days to travel from Puerto Rico to New York and my family* and I arrived in New York during the winter months. We rode in a car and after we ascended from the dark tunnels I saw these tall grey buildings. It was like God erased the colors from the earth because back in Puerto Rico the island was so colorful and now I arrived to a place that had tall buildings without any color.

Efrain Marzan, who we met earlier, and Josephina Rosario both recalled how modern transportation changed the way many Puerto Ricans immigrated to the city.

Efrain Marzan: *I was born in Isla Grande, Puerto Rico, and my family and I took a DC-37 airplane to the United States. We arrived in New York City on April 10, 1945, and came to East Harlem, but we took many routes to get to the neighborhood. We first boarded the plane from Puerto Rico [and went] to Santo Domingo (Cuidad Trujillo) in the Dominican Republic; the next stop was Port-au-Prince, Haiti, then to Santiago de Cuba and the final stop was in Miami, Florida, and from there we took the train to New York.*

Josephina Rosario: *I was born in Mananti, a small town in northern Puerto Rico, and I arrived in New York on June 14th, 1953, which was Flag Day. The day was celebrated back then and I remember seeing many American flags in the city. My brother also left Puerto Rico but he went to the Korean War. As for myself my aunt sent for me and the trip cost sixty-four dollars. It took eight hours to travel from Puerto Rico to New York and we came on an airplane called the Constellation. After my arrival, I lived with my aunt, her daughter, my cousin and her husband in a five-story tenement on 127 East 109th Street between Park and Lexington Avenue. The building was later demolished to build the De Witt Clinton Houses. When I moved to East Harlem I was excited because many Puerto Ricans lived in the building. Except for our Canadian landlord who lived above us with his wife and son, mostly everyone was Puerto Rican and I felt as if I were back in Puerto Rico. I arrived from Puerto Rico on Saturday and by Monday I went to work with my aunt at the Consolidated Laundry on 62nd Street and Second Avenue. The laundry establishment washed all of the laundry for many of the city's hotels.*

The last factor was "Operation Bootstrap," a policy initiated by the United States to industrialize Puerto Rico.[4] This initiative led thousands of Puerto Rican farm laborers to New York City. Operation Bootstrap's legacy is a mixed one; nevertheless, many Puerto Ricans looked for economic opportunity that existed on paper in both New York City and Puerto Rico.

Responding to the massive influx of Puerto Ricans to New York City, the Puerto Rican government created the Bureau of Employment and Migration, which later became the Migration Division under the United States Department of Labor. This office kept statistics on Puerto Ricans who immigrated to New York and other parts of America. Also known as the Commonwealth Office, the Migration Division established this center to help Puerto Rican migrants find employment and acclimate themselves to the United States.[5] East Harlemite Joseph Monseratt worked for the office from 1951 to 1960. He became its director in 1952.

Joe Monseratt: *After I was discharged from the army I learned the government of Puerto Rico was conducting studies on Puerto Ricans living in New York. The government allocated $50,000 to Columbia University to do the study. Clarence Senior and C. Wright Mills were both major players in this study. In fact Senior was the director of the research bureau at the University of Puerto Rico. And based on this scenario I called Mr. Senior and introduced myself because I was interested in the development of Puerto Ricans in New York City. We met and became acquainted with each other and at that time he worked for the office of the Commonwealth of the Puerto Rican migration and I was hired as a consultant. The office reorganized the Division and Senior became its chief and he invited me to become director of the New York office. The secretary of Puerto Rico, Fernando Garcia, recommended me to Luis Muñoz Marin (the first elected governor of Puerto Rico, serving 1948–1962]. That's how I was appointed and later became director of the office in 1952. When I became the director of the office I insisted that I first be oriented about all things Puerto Rican. Myself, Tony Vega, the director of the Chicago office and another gentleman, whose name escapes me, made arrangements to visit the entire island of Puerto Rico.*

When I arrived in Puerto Rico we went to see Luis Muñoz Marin, the governor, and spent a number of hours with him. And from this meeting we developed a plan to help Puerto Ricans acclimate themselves upon their arrival to New York City.

Mr. Monseratt explains the commonwealth's office functions.

Joseph Monseratt: *The office had seven functions. (1) It tried to help Puerto Ricans find employment. (2) The office implemented a social program to assist Puerto Ricans dealing with their personal problems. (3) An educational program to help Puerto Ricans enroll in school or adjust to a new school. (4) An identification program to deal with many documents requested by the American government. (5) Farm labor programs to assist Puerto Ricans living in the rural areas. The last two functions were an information and research program to provide Puerto Ricans with the knowledge of key city services.*

Later, it developed an identical program in Puerto Rico and, contrary to what people think, the Commonwealth Office was concerned about Puerto Ricans immigrating to the States, especially if they didn't know what they were doing. We had an office at two airports, one in Puerto Rico and the other at Idlewild [now John F. Kennedy International Airport].

Community in El Barrio After World War II

The previous generation of Puerto Rican immigrants who arrived in New York during the early twentieth century brought the island's music with them.[6] Traditional Puerto Rican sounds such as *bomba* and *plena* were just some of the music played on the streets of El Barrio. Postwar Puerto Rican musicians continued this tradition and many Latin bands played in El Barrio. Latin music giants such as Machito (Frank Grillo, Tito Puente and Tito Rodriguez lived and played in El Barrio, the Bronx or the legendary Palladium ballroom on Broadway and 53rd Street. Several dance halls existed in El Barrio during this period. For instance El Teatro Triboro, headquartered on 123rd Street and Third Avenue, featured Arsenio Rodriguez. Other locations in El Barrio include the Park Palace/Plaza located on 110th Street and Fifth Avenue near the end of Central Park[7] and the social club on 102nd Street and Madison Avenue.

Efrain Marzan: *The concerts took place in Central Park on Tuesdays or Wednesdays.... Many people rented rowboats and we would row to where the bandstand had set up. Tito Puente, Machito or Tito Rodriguez and other musicians played there in Central Park in the summertime. And if you lived in on the tenements near Central Park on Fifth or Madison Avenues you went up to the roof to hear the music. The musicians played so many hours that some people slept in the park or on the roof to hear the music.*

Angel Rene, raised on 111th Street between Fifth and Madison Avenues, is a drummer who has played with Eartha Kitt, Charlie Palmieri, Bobby Darin, Paul Anka, and Sammy Davis, Jr. One of Angel's most cherished memories as a musician happened when he performed with Tito Rodriguez at the White House. The occasion took place before an audience which included former president Richard Nixon. Angel also details his experiences with the great Latin musicians named above.

Angel Rene: *Machito's specialty was Afro-Cuban music. He was a big man who traveled and worked in some of the biggest jazz clubs in New York like Birdland, the Village Gate, the Vanguard and the Blue Note.... I worked with Charlie Palmieri for about five years and he was one of the best piano players that I've ever seen. His brother, Eddie, is a great musician as well, but Charlie was something else. He was like Oscar Peterson, who was another great pianist.... Tito Puente was a very nice man who had many talents and there will never be another talent like that ever again. He played all instruments and he read, arranged and composed music. Tito Puente was called "El Rey"—The King of Latin Music—and today you can go all over the world and everybody [knows] who Tito Puente was. As for Tito Rodriguez he was the Perry Como for the Puerto Ricans. And every time Tito Rodriguez was hired and did a performance he sent you a thank you note.*

Angel Rene explains that a rivalry between the two Titos existed until Tito Rodriguez passed away; however, the men respected one another.

Angel Rene: *There was a competitive streak between both men because they both came up in the same era and both performed at the Palladium. But Tito Puente was a musician and a drummer whereas Tito Rodriguez was a singer and entertainer, and a singer normally sells more records than a drummer. Tito Rodriguez's record sales were great. And when I played with him, we sold fifty thousand records a month. Tito Puente sold a lot of records, but during the early years he did not sell as much like Tito Rodriguez.*

Tito Rodriguez always said despite our competition Tito Puente is the best musician who ever lived. Tito Rodriguez admired Tito Puente because of his musicianship. They never became close friends because of the competition. Still, Tito Rodriguez respected him. Right before Tito Rodriguez died he said, "Listen, I don't want Tito Puente at my funeral because he is going to come and try to get in, but I want you to stop him." And after Tito Rodriguez died, Tito Puente went to the funeral parlor at Frank E. Campbell's funeral home on 81st and Madison Avenue and he asked for me. Tito Puente said to the attendant, "Can I see Angel Rene?" And I went outside and Tito Puente says, "Angel, can I please see Tito Rodriguez?" And I let him in. But Tito Rodriguez's wife told me, "Remember what Tito [Rodriguez] told you, that he didn't want Tito Puente at his funeral." I replied, "Mrs. Rodriguez, I know and I will deal with it after I die and face Tito Rodriguez." But I couldn't say no to Tito Puente, because he wanted to go to see him [Rodriguez] for the last time. When Tito Puente saw Tito Rodriguez in his casket, Tito Puente began to cry. I saw the tears stream from Tito Puente's eyes.

In 1940, blacks accounted for only 20 percent of East Harlem's population, but after the war the black population rose in East Harlem.[8] Black migration from the southern states coupled with new residents in many of East Harlem's burgeoning public housing projects contributed to this population surge.[9] This chapter looks at two distinct black neighborhoods in East Harlem.

The first neighborhood no longer exists for it was demolished to make way for the Hospital for Joint Diseases. But in its heyday this community, like other communities in East Harlem, sustained itself through its close relationship with its neighbors. The other black neighborhood profiled in this chapter comprised public housing. Finally, we will look at Langston Hughes' time in East Harlem. Mahmoudah Young is the mother of actor Malik Yoba, who was born in Columbia Presbyterian Hospital. Her first recollections as a child occurred during the late 1940s when she lived in East Harlem on 120th Street between Madison and Park Avenues. Mahmoudah Young moved with her family to Atlantic City, New Jersey at age six, but returned to East Harlem five years later to live in the same neighborhood.

Mahmoudah Young: *I lived at 77 East 120th Street between Madison and Park Avenues. My block was filled with many brownstones and tenements which were five story walkups, all railroad flats. Your block was your whole world and you didn't go to another block. If you lived on 120th Street, you didn't go to 121st Street. If you went past the New York Harlem Railroad [sic] on Park Avenue (today Metro-North) it was another world. Many mothers spent their time shopping or visiting their friends and the children played games. Boys played stickball or the girls played jacks, hopscotch or double-dutch on the sidewalks. And there were some fathers on my block, but the majority of the residents were women and children and you sensed your block culture.*

There were some junkies and they needed to be watched because they would steal your mother's clothes. Unfortunately many men were junkies, but it was contained, and there was no proliferation. Also, we had bars and the people drank a lot and there were lots of alcoholism due to the southern experience of racism. Gays and lesbians also lived on my block and they were fully integrated in the community and nothing negative was said about their lifestyle. There may have been whispers, but nothing political or shameful.

Like East Harlem itself, blacks in this community were composed of different ethnicities and classes and pockets of other races and ethnicities worked or lived within this block.

Mahmoudah Young: *The ethnic makeup, you had black Cubans who spoke Spanish, and I was amazed that people of African descent spoke Spanish. We also had West Indian blacks, Southern blacks, New York blacks. The West Indians were the entrepreneurs and they had a fish and chips concession stand, and another West Indian operated the cleaners. And non-African Americans were part of this neighborhood too. Artie, who was Irish, owned the newspaper stand under the New York and Harlem railroad at 121st Street and Park Avenue. And Eli, who was Jewish owned a plumbing store on the same block. The other ethnic groups were the Gonzalezes who owned a grocery store on 120th and Park Avenue. Then you had an Italian man who owned a meat and vegetable market and a laundromat run by the Chinese. There was also the Chinese restaurant upstairs, and when you entered the restaurant you felt like you were in another world. The room was dark and the curtains came down and the waiters were all elegantly dressed and they poured the tea. Finally, on Madison Avenue between 118th and 119th Streets was a santería temple which I briefly attended.*

Vickie Beckford lived on 129th Street and Madison Avenue but spent her formative years on 130th Street and remembers when people held rent parties to raise money. She also recalled when many black men worked as day laborers, handymen or painters, and how black East Harlemites ventured to Harlem and attended the Apollo Theatre.

4. Planting Roots II (1945–1950) 81

Vickie Beckford: *If you had money you went to Count Basie's Jazz club on 132nd Street and Eighth Avenue [new Adam Clayton Powell, Jr. Boulevard] or Wells which was next door.*

Then, you had Connie's Ballroom on 129th Street and Lenox Avenue [now Malcolm X Boulevard] and Thursday night was ladies' night. I remember when my girlfriend and I went to the Apollo to see Nina Simone and that day we left school early and we didn't even take our books. We sat in the audience, heard them shout their request songs to Nina Simone, but Nina replied "You paid to see me and I'll sing what I want." Many artists didn't do that, but Nina did. We saw many live performances at the Apollo because back then it wasn't expensive to see live entertainment at the Apollo.

When public housing arrived in East Harlem (see Chapter 6) many African Americans who lived in nearby Harlem or throughout New York City moved into the neighborhood. After the public housing boom, blacks resided in all of East Harlem's housing projects. In one housing project alone, three-fourths of its residents were black.[10] While blacks resided in East Harlem, many blacks still retained a close attachment to West Harlem. Marilyn Goodman, originally from West Harlem, was part of one of the first black families to live in the James Weldon Johnson Houses Projects. She describes how her family spent time in both East and West Harlem.

Marilyn Goodman: *We went to the movies on the West Side in Harlem, for my life was still there because many blacks in East Harlem attended church in Harlem. Back then when you went to church the men wore a hat, white shirts, tie and a blazer. And even if you didn't attend church, whenever you went out, especially with your parents, you dressed properly.*

Langston Hughes, the poet laureate of Harlem, spent the last third of this life in East Harlem on 127th Street between Fifth and Madison Avenue. His residence was landmarked in 1976. Hughes' time is East Harlem was eventful as he continued to publish many books. He also appeared before the House of Un-American Activities Committee during the 1950s. There Hughes deftly answered questions before Senator Joseph McCarthy and his assistant Roy Cohn. The time is the 1950s (photographer unknown, courtesy Schomburg Center for Research in Black Culture New York Public Library).

Katherine Miles-Brockington, born in Harlem Hospital, first lived in a brownstone on 127th Street between Lenox and Fifth Avenues. When the building became unstable, Brockington's family moved to the Johnson Houses on 112th Street and Third Avenue. Both of her parents hailed from South Carolina. Her father worked first as a merchant seaman on a navy ship and her mother worked as a domestic.

Katherine Miles-Brockington: *When my family first moved into East Harlem, I spent my early years in West Harlem because my mother's friends were still on 127th Street. I attended Sunday school at Mount Moriah Baptist Church close by [126th–127th Street and Fifth Avenue] on weekends because I really didn't stay in East Harlem except on the school days. It was like back and forth, but after I was ten or eleven and became older, I made my own decisions and where I wanted to go. And this included spending more time in East Harlem.*

Langston Hughes joined other African Americans who moved into East Harlem during this period. Dubbed "the poet laureate of Harlem," Hughes spent nearly the last third of his life in East Harlem. Born on February 1, 1902, James Langston Hughes, the son of Carrie and James Hughes, overcame a fractured childhood to become a successful writer. His parents separated shortly after his birth and he was reared by his grandmother until her death in 1915. Afterwards, Hughes lived with his mother and stepfather first in Cleveland, Ohio and later in Lincoln, Illinois. Hughes briefly reunited with his father, but this reunification proved disheartening and throughout their brief acquaintance, Hughes never developed a warm relationship with the elder Hughes. But his father supported his son's ambition to attend Columbia University. Meanwhile, Hughes began his writing career and some of first work appeared in *The Crises,* a periodical edited by W.E.B. Dubois.[11]

In the early 1920s, Hughes landed in New York City and fell in love with Harlem. Hughes became part of a group of artists, writers and intellectuals during the Harlem Renaissance, but he left Columbia University and traveled abroad to Africa and Europe. After he returned in 1926 *The Weary Blues,* his first poetry book, was published. That same year, Hughes returned to college, this time at Lincoln University, from which he graduated in 1929. Before he graduated Hughes traveled around the country and gave recitals. One of Hughes' poems from this period was "Goodbye Christ" and many believed the poem was an attack against Christianity. "Goodbye Christ" would hound Hughes for the rest of his life.[12]

Hughes returned to Europe and covered the war in Spain and while he was there he befriended such literary icons as Earnest Hemingway and Federico García Lorca. Hughes continued to write and one of the books was *The Big Sea,* his autobiography published in 1940. But after he returned from

Europe, he felt the negative affects of his poem "Goodbye Christ." At this time Hughes was financially spent and very ill.[13] He spent the early 1940s convalescing in California before he returned to New York. During the mid–1940s, Hughes collaborated on the play *Street Scene* which proved profitable and netted Hughes $30,000. After numerous published works, he finally acquired enough money to buy a home. In 1948 Hughes moved from a rented room in Central Harlem to a brownstone in East Harlem on 20 East 127th Street between Fifth and Madison Avenues. He shared the brownstone with Emerson and Toy Harper, whom Hughes had met in the 1920s. It was Mrs. Harper who added decorations and gave the brownstone a certain elegance and warmth. Also, it was decided that the extra rooms would be rented to several boarders. This agreement allowed the brownstone to pay for itself.[14]

Raoul Abdul hails from Canada and like Hughes, spent his early years in Cleveland, Ohio. He struck up a friendship with Hughes when the two met in the Buckeye State. Upon arriving in New York City, Abdul reunited with Hughes who began his daily routine when he rose at noon. After he drank his coffee, showered and shaved, Hughes went down to the kitchen and ate breakfast prepared by Mrs. Harper, whom Hughes affectionately called "Aunt Toy."[15] Raoul Abdul recalls.

I understand that Mrs. Harper became his adopted aunt. She was Langston's mother's best friend and Langston admired her and Mrs. Harper was just the perfect person in his life. She was a strong-willed woman who fiercely defended him and protected him from all harm.

If time permitted, Hughes would attend to his correspondence, delivered to him by Nate White, Hughes' first secretary until Abdul took over.[16] When this period ended, Hughes tended to his appointments. However, if he had no appointments, he received guests. But visitors first had to pass Toy Harper before she allowed anyone to see Hughes.[17] Still her work was not done as Mrs. Harper also took great pains to insure the preparation of the meals were served on the most elegant kitchenware, even if this meant delaying her own dinner. Raoul Abdul remembers Mrs. Harper's diligence in preparing the meals.

Langston always went down to dinner, but I was never invited for a long time until he managed to have me invited to dine with the Harpers. Mrs. Harper cooked first and it was good southern food, which was not greasy. And we ate our own meals on sterling silver, but ironically Mrs. Harper ate her food on an aluminum square plate. I asked her, "Why eat on these square plates?" Mrs. Harper replied, "While serving everyone else, I can preserve my food and keep it hot."

The Harpers also served Hughes on another level and this time it was Emerson, Mrs. Harper's husband, whose personality inspired Hughes to develop his fictitious character Jesse B. Semple. Hughes later shortened it to Simple. Simple did not possess wealth, fame, or intelligence, but made more sense than the smartest person in government or academics, which the average person could relate to.[18] Abdul gives an insight to this character:

Langston said Simple was based on someone else, but Simple was a composite. The few years I worked as Langston's secretary and spent time with him and ate with the Harpers, Mr. Harper made these statements that would later appear in the Jesse B. Semple cartoon. Langston and Mr. Harper had many arguments on current events or any mundane discussions and if these discussions were any good, you soon read it in the newspaper. Basically Emerson Harper was Jesse B. Semple.

Hughes ventured outside to Harlem during the evening hours and returned home early the next day when most of the tenants were asleep. Hughes took advantage of this solitude to write. After his writing was done, Hughes went out and purchased the papers and then slept as the neighborhood awoke.[19]

Raoul Abdul: *When I arrived at noon, he'd say, "Uh, oh," which meant he wanted attention. And I would say, "Langston I know you're awake. "And he'd say, "Abdul, just heat some water up, I want a cup of tea and two Alka-Seltzers." He wasn't drunk, but he'd sip it slowly because he didn't drink until after dinner which was Seagram's mixed with ginger beer. And he'd sip, sip, sip. But Langston didn't write until I was gone and this usually took place after midnight and I never saw him write, unless he had a deadline.*

Abdul first worked for him part-time. When Abdul became his full-time secretary, Hughes discovered that Abdul could type, spell, make corrections, and compose in Hughes' style. Abdul proved indispensable, especially when Hughes could not be reached to finish his work. But he trusted Abdul to polish it up, and as Hughes' confidant he became more than just a secretary. Abdul also assisted Hughes by sharing his thoughts on Hughes' work.[20]

Raoul Abdul: *With his poetry, I was critical or shall I say analytical with his style. If it was not up to par, I'd say, "Langston, this is a piece of shit and it should not go out under your name." He'd say, "Abdul, I would never say that to you." But he knew what I meant, that his work could be better and then he revised it. I tried to be honest, because I liked him and I knew his writing style. I'm just a simple mind and if I saw something beneath Langston's level then I knew others would notice it and comment. We had a very special relationship where I could criticize his work in person, but never in front of anybody.*

Hughes had to deal with more than Abdul's critique because during the late 1940s and early 1950s America's fear of communism and McCarthyism engulfed the country. Suspicion replaced proof even among friends and the fear of McCarthyism ruined many careers and lives. If Langston was not care-

4. Planting Roots II (1945–1950)

ful, he too might become a victim and his livelihood might end. This became evident as his poem, "Goodbye Christ," continued to hound him as never before.[21] He flatly denied communist affiliation, but the issue remained alive and his detractors still believed that Hughes was a communist. Hughes was subpoenaed to testify before the House Un-American Activities Committee, chaired by Senator Joseph McCarthy of Wisconsin. Appearing before the committee, Hughes explained that his early poetry explored a wide variety of social problems and the poem did not refer to Hughes himself. Hughes told the committee that certain titles from his poems did not reflect his true sentiments. For example, "Shakespeare in Harlem," a poem about a Ku Klux Klansman, would obviously not reflect Hughes' personal views about that organization. Hughes explained that "Goodbye Christ" was reprinted without his authorization by groups who were bent on stirring up racial and social animosity. He firmly stated he was not an atheist or a communist and stressed harmony for everyone regardless of race, color or creed. Hughes then answered questions from Senator McCarthy's lead counsel, Roy Cohn. In this exchange Hughes insisted that he sympathized with some aspects of the Soviet ideology during and after the depression. Also, he said he recognized the former Soviet Union when the communist country and America were allies during World War II, but those sentiments ended by the late 1940s.

Hughes maintained that he believed in the American form of government and disagreed with the lack of free speech in the former Soviet Union. Finally, Hughes pointed to the better race relations between blacks and whites during the postwar period. After Hughes answered several more questions from Roy Cohn, he again faced Senator McCarthy. The Wisconsin senator commended Hughes on his straightforward answers and said that though he did not completely agree with some of his statements, he acknowledged that many of Hughes books were obtained by communist sympathizers. Hughes answered that "Goodbye Christ," was "a very young, awkward poem." Senator McCarthy thanked Hughes for his appearance before the committee and Hughes reciprocated by acknowledging the cordiality he received from Senator McCarthy and his staff. Many years later, it was revealed that Senator McCarthy winked in a gesture to convey a sense that both sides achieved their goals.[22]

Raoul Abdul: *Langston knew what to say and he never intimidated anyone and never gave away anybody else's name. Langston manipulated his appearance before the House Un-American Activities Committee perfectly and he came out of it without getting anybody else involved.*

Hughes' appearance before the committee gave him some modicum of relief. And he resumed his life as a writer and lecturer to support himself financially, but he continued to just get by.

Raoul Abdul: *Langston was always on the edge, but somehow he always came through. He never took out a loan and he was self-sufficient, but he had to take on a lot of responsibilities. He had to work, because the most he made one year was $35,000 from the play* Street Scene. *And from that success he really thought he hit the jackpot. But, he never made much money, for Langston only had only $5,000 in his bank account.*

During Hughes' years in East Harlem, many of his contemporaries, like Richard Wright, Countee Cullen and others from the Harlem Renaissance, passed away. By default and deserved recognition, he became the elder statesman of African American writers. This list included Ralph Ellison, James Baldwin, Leroi Jones [now Amiri Baraka] and later Alice Walker.[23] Raoul Abdul recalls what Hughes thought of these writers.

Raoul Abdul: *Langston called him Ralphie. Ralph Ellison briefly served as Langston's secretary.... Langston never understood why* Invisible Man *became the high mark of black literature. Langston felt Ralphie was too intellectual and Langston liked writing so that everyone could understand it.*

On James Baldwin, who in his youth also lived in East Harlem and attended Public School 24, right across the street from Hughes' brownstone:

Raul Abdul: *He admired James Baldwin, who was super talented, but he wasn't perfect.... The problem with Jimmy and Langston took place when Jimmy wrote a review of Langston's poems. The article said that Langston Hughes was a lazy genius who never fulfilled the promise. But this is what Jimmy did to another mentor, Richard Wright. Jimmy, like many young and coming artists chose to destroy your idol, by attacking your idol. Then after this is done you would come back to the fold.*

Abdul remembers that he and Hughes were dining in a restaurant

Calliope Gravanis, who hailed from Salonika (Thessaloniki), Greece, immigrated to East Harlem in 1946. Upon her arrival she enrolled in high school and lived on 117th Street between First and Pleasant Avenue. Mrs. Gravanis is shown here in 2005 at the former location of Dimitrios Garden Center.

when Baldwin "came back to the fold." Upon his return from Europe, Baldwin sauntered over to the table where both men were sitting and gave Hughes a European kiss. This gesture was the rapprochement which in public ended the strife between both men.[24] However, Hughes would not sit by and forgive Baldwin so easily for his transgression and got his revenge.

Raoul Abdul: *Langston wasn't so forgiving and he was very vindictive in his own cute way. Many people invited Langston to give readings and maybe twenty-five to forty schoolchildren invited him to speak at their school. But this was to be done for free and Langston couldn't afford to do the freebees. Mary McLeod Bethune told him to take every invitation, but for a fee. This is how he got even. Jimmy Baldwin had an apartment on Horatio Street and when I received the invites, I typed on his stationery like this: "Mr. Hughes is currently on a lecture tour and he cannot come to your school, but Mr. James Baldwin who lives at 11 Horatio Street might consider." And all of these invitations were sent to Jimmy. Years later, when I got to know Jimmy, I wanted to tell him, but I didn't because other people were around. I think Jimmy would have been amused [to learn] why he got all of those letters.*

Hughes' stay in East Harlem also coincided in the early days of the Civil Rights movement. Some in the movement thought Hughes was not radical enough. Raoul Abdul offers different perspectives regarding Hughes' feeling towards the Civil Rights movement.

Raoul Abdul: *He was very left bent, for he held progressive views. Langston also believed in confronting white injustice, but in moderation. Because he was afraid the tide would turn against civil rights, because for every action, there is a reaction. If one pushed too hard, the situation would get nasty and Langston was right. He was not a conservative in any way, but he was an artist and he knew how to survive.*

Hughes demonstrated his racial consciousness through his writing. He was in the forefront on writing about the African diaspora. He published a book called *First Book of Africa* which was targeted towards young blacks. And for the adults, Hughes published *An African Treasury*, a collection of articles, essays, stories, and poems written by Black Africans. Its importance was demonstrated when apartheid South Africa banned it. Hughes insisted on a moral code of conduct for many African American writers, whom he felt should refrain from depicting the black race in any negative way.[25] Hughes was not shy about speaking his mind.

Raoul Abdul: *Once in a while, Langston used the "N" word. He would say it when black people did terrible things, or there was a riot or something he felt black people did that was unbecoming, because he had a wonderful consciousness of race pride. He'd say, "Uh, uh, no more niggers, no more culture, let's go downtown," where we'd seek out some lovely French culture.*

But even in cosmopolitan downtown New York City, Hughes was still a black man. Though he was a renowned poet and writer, he was still subjected to the mundane questions regarding his blackness.

Raoul Abdul: *He admonished those people for inviting him to dinner and then the first thing mentioned at the table was the Negro problem. He said, "I don't want to be someone else's problem and when I am invited socially, we should laugh and talk about every thing that every other human being talks about because I am not the spokesman for the Negro race."*

Artists from all over the world visited Hughes' brownstone even though the neighborhood had deteriorated during his years there. David Givens, whose great-grandparents settled in East Harlem in 1926, lived on the same block as Langston Hughes. Givens remembers.

At that time yellow cabs came to his East Harlem brownstone. Langston worked either very early in the morning or very late in the evening. I met Langston Hughes at aged eight, but he was sick for about two years. He wouldn't get up until one or two in the afternoon only to realize he didn't have any milk or orange juice at the time. Whoever was on the block at the time, he would lean out the window and say what he wanted. I went to the store for him a couple of times and I would run errands for him.

Langston Hughes never married; however, he adopted a son, Sunday Osuya, from Nigeria and visited the youth of East Harlem.

David Givens: *Langston visited our assembly school programs at the old P.S. 24 between Madison and Fifth Avenues at 128th Street. And Langston spoke and he told us to stay in school and he read one of his poems. Of course we were just children and we didn't give a hoot and we didn't want to hear that. We didn't really know who Langston Hughes was. But when I went to high school then I realized the significance of Langston Hughes during my English Literature class.*

Hughes would remain a presence in the East Harlem until his death in 1967.

Other ethnic groups arrived in East Harlem after World War II like the Greeks. Calliope Gravanis emigrated from Greece to East Harlem. Upon her arrival she resided in a small Greek enclave in the neighborhood. Calliope Gravanis was nicknamed Yiayia, which means "grandmother" in Greek. But Calliope's father, Eleftherios, was an American citizen who worked on the railroad to avoid conscription in the Turkish army while Greece was occupied by Turkey. He returned to Greece during the depression and married Themelina Kanakaris.

Calliope Gravanis: *My father's friends hailed from Crete ... and he was born in Theopolese which is close to Istanbul. When many Greek boys reached the age of fifteen they secretly immigrated to the United States so they wouldn't get*

4. Planting Roots II (1945–1950) 89

drafted into the Turkish army. Both my father and uncle traveled to Alaska, then to New York, where they both became United States citizens at fifteen.

Calliope Gravanis recounts her own voyage to East Harlem.

Calliope Gravanis: *I was born in Salonika [Thessaloniki] in the northern part of Greece and we left Salonika on January 30, 1946. We arrived in America on February 20, 1946. Many Americans who lived in Europe during the war traveled on the same boat. When we arrived in America the Red Cross and the Salvation Army both gave us some coffee and donuts. Next, we took a taxi to a Greek hotel on 47th Street and Ninth Avenue and lived there for one month. Interestingly, my mother came to America with a Greek passport. My father didn't need one because he was American, so I used his passport, because I was under eighteen.*

We moved to East Harlem and lived on 117th Street between First and Pleasant Avenues. Back then Italians and Greeks both shared the same neighborhood and our building number was 446 East 117th Street. I attended night school before I went to Benjamin Franklin High School in 1947. I remember going to an Associated Market which started out as a grocery store on 117th Street ran by a guy named Catsimatides. There were a lot of Greek restaurants in the neighborhood and not surprisingly my father became an entrepreneur. He owned a candy store which he brought from a Greek man on 124th Street and Lexington Avenue.

There were several Greek communities in East Harlem. Greek families lived on 107th Street and Second Avenue, 117th–118th Street between First and Pleasant Avenue, and 124th and Lexington Avenue. As with Italian East Harlem, Greek East Harlemites from different towns lived in separate streets throughout the neighborhood.

Calliope Gravanis: *Several Greek families who lived on 118th Street were from Crete, while other Greek families that lived on 117th Street hailed from Sparta. In my five-story tenement building, three floors of Greek families hailed from Sparta, while the other two floors had families that hailed from Theopolis.*

Italians and Greeks living in the same neighborhood sometime married, but as Calliope explains, such arrangements were not always easy.

Calliope Gravanis: *My brother met his Italian wife who lived in the same neighborhood. He didn't tell my mother and instead went to my husband regarding his marriage plans. He says, "I don't know, what I am gonna do? I'm gonna get married, but I won't tell my mother. I'll say that I'm living in a friends' house with girls." My husband said, "If you don't inform your mother and she finds out from somebody else, this information will devastate her." Instead my brother decided to let me tell my mother about his marriage plans. Well, I started talking about other people who were living with us, then my father said, "Why are you telling us this story?" Then I said that my brother is in love and my mother almost caught a heart attack. She said, "I* *want him to come and look at me in my eyes and tell me that." I told him, "You look at my mother." And he did. Then my father said "Do you love her?" My brother said "Yes." Then my father said "I'm gonna give you my blessing." They got married and when they had a baby, the baby was put in the water and I became the godmother.*

Calliope recounts how she acclimated herself to a new country, but family traditions are not easily forgotten. On holidays and birthdays Greek traditions continued in East Harlem. Finally, Calliope reflects on her East Harlem experience.

Calliope Gravanis: *Not all Greek people break plates because it is only the lower-class Greeks that do this, whereas the upper-class Greeks don't do this. Instead of celebrating someone's birthday, we celebrate what we call the name day. For example St. George is on April the 1st and there would be different names on different days. On Greek Independence Day there is a Greek parade on the 25th of March on Fifth Avenue. And on Good Friday, Greek people would go around at night for the funeral for Jesus Christ. According to the Greek tradition on Thursday afternoon Christ was nailed on the cross. And Friday after he is taken down off the cross his body is placed in the box and everybody goes in the street carrying the box. And this is exactly like a funeral. The parade was popular and much bigger when I first arrived in East Harlem.*

The neighborhood was something very special and good. When I came here with my parents we were a close family, but even with my parents after I came here I felt like I was an orphan, because I immigrated here. But after one year you get used to it and you feel you were always here. You learned the customs and especially in New York City which has so many cultures. Also I went to work and to school and I mixed with other people. This began when I started out in the garment industry and after I got married, I helped out my husband in the flower shop.

In 2002, movie goers flocked to see the surprise hit movie *My Big Fat Greek Wedding.* As with Calliope's family, this was the story of a woman who lived with her tight-knit Greek family who eventually falls in love and marries outside of her culture. Calliope describes how the movie was indicative of her Greek family in East Harlem.

Calliope Gravanis: *I thought the movie was a drama because it was similar to what many Greek families have gone through, my family included. We are all afraid to meet [people] outside our culture and I remember when my mother sent my sister and me to Greece to get married. And I got married in the American Embassy in Greece, but I still renewed my vows in a Greek church because all the Greeks are traditionalists. For example, my family attended a Greek church to meet Greek people or eat Greek food. All the Greeks did this and we thought this is customary. My family will sing Greek songs, and learned the Greek dances and maintained the Greek language. I kept the tradition by sending my children to a Greek American school and they learned how to read and write Greek grammar and learn Greek history.*

5
Community and Diversity

> Doors were open and they were never locked. My mother's door
> was always open and there was never a problem.— Miriam Correa

After World War II East Harlem was still a vibrant, sustainable and functioning community with stores, and local entrepreneurs that allowed East Harlemites to enjoy their neighborhood. But within fifteen years the neighborhood that East Harlemites knew would disappear. We first begin with the neighborhood's movie theaters, parks and stickball games.

Piri Thomas: *I lived in the movies. It was my world and I saw characters like Jack LaRue and Bob Steal. There were no Puerto Rican movies and instead we saw the Mexican films. I spent so much time in the Eagle Theater on 102nd-103rd Streets and Third Avenue that it became [like] a nursery. My mother put me there in the morning and picked me up at night. Customers saw five cartoons and three major pictures for only seven cents. I also went to the Fox Star on 107th Street and Lexington Avenue and the Cosmo on 116th Street between Lexington and Third Avenues.*

Hortencio Morales: *Everyone you knew in the neighborhood went to the Cosmo Theater, which was very cheap and you saw two movies for fifty cents. Then the owners raised the price to one dollar, but still the price was affordable. The first movie was an outdated one and a second movie was new. I also remember going with my father to the Azteca Theater but that theater played movies that were entirely in Spanish. One movie I remember was called* Three Dedos *it was about a cowboy with three fingers.*

Raquel Villegas: *We'd go the Regan on 116th Street Fifth Avenue and the Spanish Theater called the Latino, which gave live performances on 110th Street and Fifth Avenue. This was right next to the Park Plaza, which was a famous dancing place but is a church now. The Municipal movie theater was on 113th Street and Madison Avenue, but it had a different name, El Meaito which means "pissing pot," for the Theater smelled like urine. We saw shows like* Shazam *or the* Three Stooges, *and plenty of movies and sometimes we didn't pay the movies any mind.*

Andrew Perez: *At the Municipal theater the attendants sprayed perfume to get rid of the smell.*

Isidro (Ted) Velez: *The Fox Star became the Boricua Theater in the early 1950s. And at that theater you saw action movies in the daytime and during the evening hours the dramas were shown. You saw movie stars like Marilyn Monroe or Frank Sinatra.*

Willie Lopez: *If you arrived at the movie theaters on Saturday mornings before 10 A.M. you got an outdated comic book. They were Marvel Comics, Action Comics and Classic Comics.*

Efrain Marzan: *The Madison movie theater, which later became the Azteca movie theater, played the newsreel called* The World News *throughout the day. And if you came to the theater on Saturdays at 12 P.M. you didn't leave until 6 P.M. because you got your money's worth. You saw twenty-two cartoons, three movies—a western, a regular movie and a comedy. It might be the Three Stooges, and then you saw the Shadow chapters one or two, or it was Superman and the cost for a movie was only seven or eight cents. The matron escorted you to your seat and she knew almost every customer because the same people went to the same theater so often. It was like babysitting and you received the comic books. But the Azteca Theater also had ladies' day and all the women who came received got a cup, and the next week, you received a saucer, and by the end of the month you had a set of dishes.*

Different types of entertainment and recreation were also part of the neighborhood. Some people listened to the radio, took in a show, or invented new games. Stickball games took over the streets of East Harlem and in warm weather, every block had its own fountain (fire hydrant).

Hortencio Morales: *You had the fire hydrant, or the water pump which we called la pumpa. The water pump was always open on every block in East Harlem. Someone in the neighborhood would get this big wrench to turn the water on. Next, you found an empty can and scraped both sides of the can until both lids came off. With the water coming out of the hydrant at full blast, you placed the can in front of the nozzle and you had a powerful force of water just gushing out. The person who held the can controlled the water and made it turn it left or right. The water almost covered the whole block and my friend Panchita said, "Chencho," my nickname, "Come, the pump is open." I took turns and jumped in the water to cool off or I took one of the girls and held her and we both became wet.*

The funny thing happened when the water was on and you drove by with your car. If you were respectful then your car wouldn't get wet. But if you said, "You better not wet my car or else," then the car got wet. I remember one of the guys would wait until the car was halfway down the block. Suddenly he picked up the can and sprayed the car. You saw the driver rushing to close his window to avoid getting his car seat wet, but the car owner got a free car wash minus the soap. The water pump was open all night and I wondered how much water was wasted. Many people claimed they hated getting wet, but later on they appreciated it because back then summers were hotter and winters were colder.

Rose Savatelli: *I listened to the radio and heard the classic stories such as the Shadow, the Lone Ranger and Baby Slopes. During the winter months our family sat around the radio and kept warm.*

Willie Lopez: *There were stickball games on every block and we'd play the other team on their block or their team came and played on our block. Our team was called the Devils and the Irish stickball team we played against was called the Dukes. We also played softball, but the guys called it a girl's game.*

Now, every second Sunday in July on 111th Street from Madison to Lenox Avenues the Annual Old-Timers stickball reunion convenes in East Harlem. Here many former East Harlemites return and mingle with old friends. Charlie Candelario, who heads the event, explains the rules of stickball:

You pitched or bounced the ball once on the street and you have one swing. The batter runs in to the ball and, hopefully, you hit a hard line drive down the street. If you hit it on the roof, that's an out, but when you played on the block, you always had cars and fire escapes. Your goal was to hit the fire escapes or the wall because, if it bounced down off the wall, that's how you could get an extra run. Or if the ball hit a parked car it was still in fair territory and you could run many bases.

Plus, if the ball hit the fire escape and goes down into the basement, that's a double. But if the ball bounced off the car and you caught it that's an out. In addition, if the ball hit a fire escape and it came down and you caught it that's also an out. The fire escape had its advantages and disadvantages.

Stickball players knew the game's rules; however, the game was not an exact science, for who knew where the ball would go once it left the stickball bat.

Charlie Candelario: *There were broken windows, oh yeah, because if the ball bounced off the fire escape and broke the window, we never knew who broke it (laughing) because nobody ever told. Our main concern was the police, for they didn't like stickball games or playing in the streets. If the police caught you, they would take your stickball bat and put it in a manhole cover in the center hole and pull the stick down like pulling a lever and break the stickball bat. To counter this we hid our stickball bats by throwing them under the parked cars. Our team was called the Dandies and our uniforms were dark blue and yellow. We had jackets and jerseys and our design was a tuxedo shirt, a hat with the cane and a wavy D. Every stickball team had a different color jacket but there were no championships like stickball world series because our team played for money. The team could book a game between the black stickball team known as the Miltons in Harlem or the Italians in Italian East Harlem. Each player put in three or four dollars a game.*

Mike Lentini organizes the Father-Son Stickball Game, which convenes every second Sunday in September. This league is composed of many former Italian East Harlemites and many generations. As with the Old Timers Stickball reunion in El Barrio, many return to East Harlem to participate in this tournament.

Michael Lentini: *My social club was called the Bisons and we were located on 119th Street and Pleasant Avenue. We played stickball at the park down at the East River Drive where the Benjamin Franklin High School is located. Every neighborhood had a gang and every neighborhood had a sports team and every Sunday there would be big-money games, two hundred dollars a game or even sometimes two thousand a game. People in the neighborhood bet on games and sometimes the big shots as well. Or our stickball team would travel to downtown Manhattan, Mulberry Street, and play the Italians who lived there. It was the battle of the neighborhoods and you always wanted to beat the stickball team from the other block or neighborhood, the black stickball team from Harlem or the Puerto Ricans stickball team here in East Harlem.*

As Lentini says, black East Harlemites also played stickball. The neighborhood served as a backdrop to these contests.

Jesse Hamilton: *Our team competed against the guys on 100th Street or another stickball team on 106th Street. Your team told the other team, "We'll play you on Sunday," and everybody gathered on the fire escapes or you closed down the block until the police came. The audience sat on the fire escapes or outside with their folded chairs like it was a stadium. And you hit the ball from one end of the block to the other end. Cars were there, but the street was a nice size for stickball because it was not too small.*

As the stickball teams utilized the tenements to advance an extra base, many East Harlemites advanced to these same tenement roofs to fly kites.

Isidro (Ted) Velez: *I liked flying kites, which we called diamonds, and I ventured to the roof on 102nd and Madison Avenue and flew kites. If you saw another person flying a kite you challenged them to a duel or kite fight by fighting them with your cord. To do this, you crushed a piece of glass into a powdered ball and mixed it with glue. Then you put the glass on the cord and you would encounter another kite in the air some hundred yards away and cut their kite in the process.*

One of the city's pleasures was Central Park, and many East Harlemites took the opportunity to escape the tenement life and enjoy the trees, shrubs and green grass.

Nicholasa Mohr: *My family and I visited Central Park where my mother would take a blanket and spread it out. And on the way to Central Park, I would take some empty jars and punch holes in the lid. And once in Central Park I would* fill them with fireflies. Late at night it looked like a lantern and it blinked and shined [sic] in the quiet darkness, but this happened in the middle of the city in Central Park.

There were many mom-and-pop stores in the neighborhood.

Dr. Alvin Poussaint: Back then candy was literally a penny and sometimes you got two pieces for one cent. Candy stores were on every block and you visited the soda fountain stores where you could get more candy or buy a fountain soda or seltzer. And it only cost two cents back then. The drugstores in the neighborhood sold candy and certain stores served french-fried potatoes. They'd cook them in the restaurant fresh, which only cost a nickel for one bag and that was one of our major little snacks besides potato chips.

Jesse Hamilton: A Jewish proprietor owned the candy store on our block and my friends and I brought our candy, seltzer and the egg cream and we loved our egg cream. The owner was a nice guy who really catered to the children in the community. He knew everybody's name and he was a part of the community and you didn't mess around with that store.

Ramon Ferreira: I lived on 101st Street between First and Second Avenues and on our block the drugstore was on the corner. We also had a regular grocery store and a butcher shop. When my family moved to 109th Street between Second and Third Avenues, next to the old Public School 83 was a public bath. In my old apartment the tubs were in the kitchen, and the bathroom was down the hallway. To flush the toilet you pulled the chain, which was connected to the box that was above you. My family moved again to 170 East 110th street, and the building owners were Kirby—Kirby's clothing store.

James Bryant: Back then in East Harlem you had a sense of community. Today I live in a twenty-six floor co-op on the Upper West Side and I hardly know the names of ten people in that building. I see them and we say hello in the elevator, but that's it. When I grew up in East Harlem, people kept their doors open because in those days, no one had an air conditioner. The open door provided a cool draft, which is why we kept our doors open. And it was normal to see children visit your neighbor's apartment and all the children played in the hallway. There was a cohesiveness that existed in each building, and each block and each community.

Andrew Perez: Everybody knew everyone and if a new neighbor moved in, almost the whole neighborhood asked for your mother's or father's name. The block also asked what town you're from.

Morton Ross: When I was a kid, we threw away the key because we didn't lock our doors in East Harlem. It was a "whose a dare" [who's there] system and if anyone came in the building there was a superintendent or a janitor. And if someone came by your building that didn't belong there, or if a person banged on the door, our Italian janitor said "whose a dare" and that trespasser ran like hell.

Carlos De Jesus: *People looked out for one another by keeping their doors open. This allowed people to come and express their concerns or share any joyous news and when people said "hello," they meant it. Just by getting together and not being isolated in little pockets because it was an open community.*

Michael Lentini: *Growing up in East Harlem we didn't have window bars. And if your neighbor needed a cup of coffee, they knocked on the door and took whatever they wanted and they would say, "I took a bottle of milk and I owe you a bottle of milk." And people trusted each other in those days. We were not poor, but we were rich in our own way and each family had the same thing, and everyone had a lot and a little. What each family had, we all shared and it was very family oriented. Every family was like your own family and that's the way it was back then.*

Manny Segarra: *Most of the people my building knew everybody on the block on 104th Street. Whenever somebody from another block came in and started trouble, everybody knew they weren't from that block. If I did something wrong and my next-door neighbor saw me I was in trouble. Everyone looked after everybody's child and they became unofficial guardians.*

Efrain Marzan: *I remember the police in my neighborhood. They'd come by and if we were hanging out and talking bullshit, the police would come by and say, "It's almost nine o'clock, I don't want to see you hanging out." Then at nine the cop would speed up and he'd say "Where do you live?" We'd say 109th or 111th Street and the cop replied, "Go home!" Many police officers were Irish and we gave them nicknames. For instance there were two policemen who patrolled our block and one officer was small and the other one was tall and we called them Mutt and Jeff from the cartoon, or "La Hara." (The Spanish slang for many policemen was O'Hara.) Back in those days, the police walked in the neighborhood and you could have a conversation with them. The police could say to you, "If you don't behave, I'll tell your father," or "You better go upstairs." Try that now.*

Johnny Colon: *If you were outside the worst word you could say then was shit. And if someone heard that word you got slapped in the back of the head. Curse words were not to be spoken in the presence of a lady or a child, because it was total disrespect.*

Dr. Alvin Poussaint: *When I was nine or ten, I had a very bad case of rheumatic fever. I spent three months convalescing in Mount Sinai Hospital and another three months at home. I received strict orders for I was on bed rest and I couldn't do anything to stress my heart, and I bided my time reading books. I read so many books and I think I got smart, for my academic and language ability improved remarkably. I couldn't play any games like stickball, kick-the-can, or ring-a-levio and my friends were very supportive of me, because they knew I couldn't run around and they didn't let me. And my friends sometimes carried me up the flight of stairs so I wouldn't have to walk to my family's fourth-floor apartment.*

5. Community and Diversity 97

The icebox, the forerunner to the refrigerator, kept food fresh. And to dispose of garbage you placed it in the dumbwaiter.

James Bryant: *The icebox was a compartmentalized unit that kept the food refrigerated. The top of the box was where you placed the block of ice and the food was placed in the bottom section. Our iceman was an old Italian gentleman and he came by in a wagon and you called downstairs and asked him for a piece of ice which cost twenty-five cents. And he used these tongs to pick up the ice and he would deliver it to your door. The icebox had a pipe which went down the floor and you placed a pan on the floor to catch the water. Once the water filled the pan up, you emptied it and started all over again.*

Dr. Alvin Poussaint: *Sometimes children like myself worked for the iceman and carried the ice. The ice was placed on your shoulder with a cloth so the ice wouldn't dig too hard in your shoulder. Then, you would put the other hand to hold the ice and you carry it upstairs. I think I got two cents or a few pennies, which was money back then.*

Jesus "Papoleto" Melendez: *There was a horse stable on 111th Street and Second Avenue right across the street from the firehouse. A blacksmith was in there and that's where they kept the ice wagon. He came down the street and there was a bell above where the driver sat and you heard the huffs and the horse had visors on and [it work] bells which made this cacophony. The frankfurter man and the piragua [snow cone] man would store his cart in there. And this piragua man looked liked Santa Claus, he had this mustache and he was a roly poly type. And in the summer he would sell the best piraguas. They were a nickel and the big one was a dime. And when I said it was a big cone, it was a big cone.*

Vickie Beckford: *You placed your garbage in the dumbwaiter, which began at the top floor. The super would say fifth floor, he would literally pull a big brown rope and pull it all the way up to the fifth floor. When it got to the fifth floor, you opened it like a little tray. The dumbwaiter was also used in private homes or in the service quarters to bring your dinner or other meal. You closed the dumbwaiter and the super would lower the garbage and take the garbage down, and this was repeated on each floor.*

Diversity

If you couldn't distinguish a foreign name you were called a greenhorn. — Morton Ross

In his book *The Heart Is the Teacher* Leonard Covello noted that East Harlem was once home to thirty-four different ethnicities and twenty-seven different languages.[1] In essence East Harlem was a mixed neighborhood in a mixed city. Entrepreneur David Blake, who is Jewish, owned Blake's Pharmacy on 103rd Street and Third Avenue for over forty-four years. He recalls his years in East Harlem and how he acclimated to the neighborhood's changing demographics and became a successful businessman.

I found out through a mutual friend about a pharmacy in East Harlem that was available and I bought the store from Joseph Freilich. When I ran the pharmacy it was open until 11:00 P.M. at night and customers came to the store until 10:55 P.M. This led me to extend the store hours until midnight on Saturdays. The first few years were a struggle and a challenge because I competed against Nelson's Pharmacy, which was also in East Harlem. After awhile I slowly gained the confidence of the customers. At first, I sold Italian Christmas cards because Italians still lived in the neighborhood, but when East Harlem became predominantly Puerto Rican I sold Christmas cards in Spanish. I found conversing in Spanish very helpful which quickly increased the customers to the store. The years quickly went by and I prospered as the owner and I didn't have to roll down a gate or use a burglar alarm, because crime was very minimal in this part of the neighborhood. Then in the 1960s or early 1970s I had to buy the roll-down gate and installed cameras in the store.

Piri Thomas: *The neighbors were Latinos, blacks and on Third Avenue were the Italians. By seeing each nationality you learned their mannerisms. "Hey, paisan," from the Italians, the blacks would say, "What's up, brother," and Puerto Ricans said "Que dice."*

But diversity also brought some problems in East Harlem and non–Italians were warned not to walk east of Third or Second Avenue. Conversely, Italians did not walk west of Third or Lexington Avenue. Leaving your territory risked trouble. Some Italians and Puerto Ricans fought in East Harlem, however, for two men who were combatants in their youth, but years later a meaningful friendship blossomed.

Manny Diaz, Jr.: *If you wanted to use Jefferson Pool on 114th Street and First Avenue, you risked getting into a fight, but our group, composed mainly of Puerto Ricans, developed a strategy. Half of the group would start a fight with the Italians and the other half would scoot around to 116th Street and use the pool. The next day we switched roles and the guys who fought yesterday got to swim that day while the other group who swam at Jefferson Pool the day before fought the Italians.*

Many years later, I was an adult running an agency at Union Settlement in East Harlem, and I hired an insurance agent to work on our insurance matters. He happened to be Italian, who lived on 114th Street between Second and Third Avenues. We began talking and we realized we were the same age and that we fought each other right across Third Avenue. This was tongue in cheek, and the insurance man's name was Frank. I asked him, "Frank, how come you wouldn't let us use the swim-

ming pool?" And what he said was classic. Frank replied, "Because you guys always left a ring around the pool." We laughed and we became good friends.

Robert Deleon also fought his way into Italian East Harlem, only partially successful.

If you walked past the Italian block, you'd get beat up. I remember going to Jefferson Pool, but you could not go to the pool without getting your ass kicked. I lived on 113th Street and I didn't know any better and I thought I would go to the pool in the morning when it was free. On my way there I'd got my ass kicked, but I wanted to go swimming and I went back to the pool, but every time I left to go home I got my ass kicked again. It happened so many times that the Italians who lived there recognized me, and they said, "Oh, it's him." And they only kicked my ass once. Instead I went to Highbridge Pool in the Bronx, it was a better pool, less fighting and there were more girls.

Efrain Marzan: *I went to P.S. 170 between Lenox and Fifth Avenue and I was told to watch out for the blacks [who] would beat you. After school, I ran home with my books flying all over the place until I reached Fifth Avenue which was the boundary line where Spanish Harlem began. But I got tired and one day I stopped and I fought back and earned their respect, which allowed me to go back and forth to school without any trouble. But when I graduated and I went to Galvani Junior High School 83 on the Italian side, on 109th Street between Second and Third Avenues, the Italians beat the hell out of you. We [Puerto Ricans] were in the middle.*

For Italian East Harlemites, Peter Gallo echoed these sentiments from the other side.

As far as crossing over Lexington Avenue, that was not our territory and I only went to Park Avenue with my mother when she shopped at 116th Street Market. The only other reason to cross Lexington Avenue took place when we went to school, at St. Paul's Church, which is located on 117th Street between Park and Lexington Avenues. Otherwise we never hung out west of Lexington Avenue.

Felipe Luciano has a different take on the ethnic issues in East Harlem.

Felipe Luciano: *Remember each immigrant culture likes to think of themselves as the only victims in the world. They like to say all of its scholars, poets, or even drunks are unique.*

Not all Puerto Ricans who ventured into Italian East Harlem met such resistance. Gladys Rivera lived in Italian East Harlem on 306 East 113th Street between Second and Third Avenue.

If you lived in the same building [as Italians] you didn't have any problems. Only the boys like my brother who attended Benjamin Franklin High School had some problems, but not the girls. However, if you lived on Park Avenue or Lexington

Avenue and crossed Third Avenue on your way to Jefferson Park near First Avenue you had some problems.

Joe Monseratt, also Puerto Rican, shared his experience of life between Spanish and Italian Harlem.

Joe Monserrat: *Benjamin Franklin High School was one of the outstanding high schools in New York City. It was created by Pop [Leonard] Covello, because at that time East Harlem had a large Italian neighborhood. He believed Italians should have rights, and African Americans and Puerto Ricans should have rights too. Despite the tensions and fights between the groups, Pop Covello was one of the first to recognize Puerto Ricans in the school and in the community. The school was a community center and it was a very nice place.*

Though Robert DeLeon fought to enter Italian East Harlem, he and other East Harlemites fondly remember the diversity in the neighborhood.

When I lived on 102nd Street, it was a mixed block; Italian, Irish, European Jews, and southern blacks were the supers of the building and everyone got along well.... Back then you knew the Irish, you knew Italians. During the 1930s, we were not identified as Puerto Ricans—they called us Spanish.

Pablo Figueroa, a Puerto Rican, experienced the camaraderie between Puerto Ricans and blacks living in East Harlem.

On 116th Street near Madison Avenue were working-class black people. The men were chauffeurs who drove a Buick, but they only used it for working. Today on the corner of 116th Street is Mount Zion, a Baptist church; then it was the Hispano Theater. Every Sunday, you had a parade of black women in hats and all of my closest friends were black. It was the first time I discovered gospel singing and heard Baptist music. My friend invited me to a storefront church and the singing was incredible. We sat in the last row and we didn't want to leave when the singing was over.

Dylcia Pagan has a humorous story about her neighbors.

My father was part of Los Hijos de Yago (sons of Yago.) We lived in a two-family house at 1662 Madison Avenue (near 111th Street), today it is the Schomburg Plaza. Back then it was the only little house in the middle of the block. The Gallways, a black couple, were the only other residents who lived in that house. He was an electrician in East Harlem with his wife Annie. And Mr. Gallway's office was on 111th Street and Fifth Avenue and I remember when I was taking dance classes, Annie, his wife, came upstairs and knocked on the door and told my mother "Dylcie, you dancing too much." "But Miz Annie," I replied, "I have to dance." "OK, Dylcie, then you have to do that," Miz Annie answered. Before I had never met her husband, and I remember I must have been four. One day I came up with my dad, and Mr. Gallway opened the door, and I'll never forget that moment, for when the door opened I said, "Hi, you son of a bitch." My father smacked me in the butt. Because sometimes

5. Community and Diversity

A harbinger of things to come in East Harlem, the construction of the James Weldon Johnson Houses: 112th–115th Streets between Lexington and Third Avenue. The tenements and brownstones that once adorned this area were destroyed and replaced by the "super block." This scene was repeated many times throughout East Harlem.

my father would call someone he didn't like a son of a bitch. But my Gallway was laughing, "Oh, she called me a son of a bitch." That's how he and I became buddies, and having them as my neighbors I never saw them as anything different than as Miz Annie and her husband.

Felipe Luciano: *The interchange was incredible between the two Harlems. Cab Calloway, Duke Ellington—my father hung out with these hipsters. The differences between the two Harlems were not as great as it is now, To listen to jazz you went to the Cotton Club or to the Savoy to listen to Duke Ellington and Count Basie, Fletcher Henderson, Chick Webb, or the Palladium or the Park Plaza. When you crossed Fifth Avenue to 110th Street and entered Spanish Harlem and you listened to Machito, Tito Puente, Tito Rodriguez, Maximo Guerra, Jose Timbello, the interchange was incredible and you could hear it in the music. Black folks were listening to Latin music and vice versa. Mario Buazá told me he was the one who introduced Chano Pozo to Dizzy Gillespie and that's how Dizzy introduced a new form of music called cubop. And finally, it was Mario Buazá who introduced Ella Fitzgerald to Chick Webb.*

Finally, Eugene Nardelli recalls his diverse neighborhood how its environs helped his father adjust to his new country.

This is the finished product of the exact location of the previous photograph. The James Weldon Johnson Houses has been around since 1947.

Eugene Nardelli: *There were blacks, Jewish and Italian people. Our black neighbors and customers taught my father English. Some black men worked as chauffeurs and the black women wore blue dresses. There was a synagogue on 10th Street between First and Second Avenue and another one on 102nd between Second and Third Avenue when Jews still lived in East Harlem. I remember Ronald Smellowitz and his father owned a big plumbing company and his family went to the country on weekends. After they moved out, a kid from Puerto Rico named Robert Rodriguez, whom I studied with, helped me with my English as the blacks helped my father. It was a unique neighborhood.*

6
1950s — Three Strikes: Public Warehousing, Drugs, Tribalism of Gangs

Public Warehousing

This next chapter is told in three parts. During the 1950s the neighborhood underwent a tremendous change through the creation of public housing projects. The controversy surrounding public housing, especially in East Harlem, has been debated for over half a century. A decade which saw the emergence of the Civil Rights movement and the suburbs saw heartbreak and devastation in East Harlem. Bulldozers rampaged throughout the neighborhood and replaced its tenements with public housing projects. Through eminent domain, East Harlem's cohesiveness, lifestyle, camaraderie and sustenance ended. Its diversity, homes, apartments, and businesses were destroyed. East Harlemites and other city residents who protested these actions were ignored as their rights were nullified. To this day the neighborhood has not recovered from this period.

Public housing proponents believed these edifices would erase the urban blight that existed in East Harlem, but they were wrong. It was also predicted that many public housing residents would uplift themselves and thereby one day leave public housing. Some East Harlemites eventually moved away, but many residents have spent their entire lives in public housing. However, credit must be given to those residents who were reared in public housing and led outstanding lives, such as Associate Supreme Court Justice Sonia Sotomayor. And public housing has remained affordable for many New Yorkers. When public housing began in East Harlem in 1941 the neighborhood was mostly intact. East Harlem possessed many tenement buildings and mom-and-pop stores on every block, which allowed a family or their neighbors to interact with one another. This interaction also helped East Harlemites to develop support systems, which were helpful in this working-class neighborhood.

Jane Jacobs whose famous works included *The Death and Life of Great American Cities* examines public housing and how it changed East Harlem. Jacobs believed that public housing was anathema to urban life and characterized it as another form of slums. Jane Jacobs also stated that after the World War II, East Harlem was a prime candidate for "unslumming," which is done when residents and entrepreneurs are encouraged to stay and work in their communities.[1] Sound economic plans and proper rehabilitation initiatives to uplift East Harlem were needed. But by 1940, the neighborhood was redlined by the banking industry as an unprofitable investment.[2] Jacobs also points to Le Corbusier, a European architect whose concept of the "Radiant City" was adopted by New York City's reformers. This idea involved skyscrapers and enabled the population to expand vertically instead of horizontally. The result, it was believed, left the ground free of traffic and with plenty of open space.[3] But Jacobs pointed out that this vertical model left the streets and the sidewalks devoid of stores and other businesses. A proponent of LeCorbusier's Radiant City was Robert Moses, who is also important to this story.

Born in New Haven, Connecticut, and reared in New York City, Robert Moses hailed from an upper-class family of German Jewish New Yorkers. He attended Yale and Oxford universities and earned a Ph.D. from Columbia University. Moses, an idealist, sought to reform city government and worked for the reform mayor John P. Mitchell. After Mitchell was defeated, Moses worked in several reform organizations. He returned to public service after Al Smith became governor of New York in 1924, but Moses' appetite for the reform movement changed under Smith. Moses still wanted to work for the public, and he got his chance when Smith appointed him Long Island parks Commissioner. He created this office for himself, and he repeatedly used this technique to shield him from the elected officials and the public.[4] During the 1920s and 1930s, Moses' reputation grew as he built parks and other public works, such as Jones Beach on Long Island. Moses' career in city government began when Mayor Fiorello La Guardia asked the state legislature to waive the restriction which allowed Moses to serve simultaneously in both city and state governments. The state legislature complied and Moses became New York City Parks Commissioner. Before long, he refurbished the Central Park Zoo and earned a reputation as a man who could get things done. He was never elected to public office, though he ran unsuccessfully for New York State governor. But he still wielded enormous power, holding twelve city and state positions at one time.

After World War II, Moses, who up to now had only constructed parks and bridges mostly outside of the five boroughs, would build in the city. In late 1948, Moses became aware of a new law called Title I. According to Title I the government would financially support private developers to rebuild poor

6. 1950s — Three Strikes

and urban areas. As before, Moses drafted legislation which allowed him to create the position of construction coordinator. As the construction coordinator, he became the sole liaison between the federal government and the city and all monies flowed through him. More importantly, Moses controlled the city Housing Authority. Moses went further and convinced the city to create a slum clearance commission — with, not surprisingly, Robert Moses as its chairman. This power allowed Moses to decide where each public housing project would be built. Moses also belonged to the city's planning commission.[5]

There was some merit to replace the tenements which after decades of decay needed rehabilitation. They were also constructed on landfills where once were marshes near the East River.[6] And finally, many tenements were destroyed by fire and left an empty lot.[7] East Harlemites recall the harsh conditions of their tenements.

James Bryant: *The tenements were constructed of plaster and poorly maintained because the buildings were nearly one hundred years old. If a pipe broke in*

A policeman is directing traffic on 104th Street and Madison Avenue, May 1950. This photograph describes the East Harlem many residents remember before the advent of public housing. Brownstones and tenements are shown. There are many storefront businesses and residents knew one another (photograph courtesy New York City Housing Authority).

the wall then it leaked.... And if a rat or another rodent died inside the wall, a smell emanated and stayed there for three or four days until it dried out.

Carlos De Jesus: *The tenements were mostly railroad flats and small rooms. Some buildings were infested with roaches and the rats were big as cats. But not all the buildings were poorly structured, and there were many absentee landlords who did not make the needed repairs. The ceilings could fall apart and there was a lot of moisture in the bathroom. I remember the moisture led to poison mushrooms [sic] that grew on the wall.*

Public housing construction ceased during World War II but commenced immediately afterward. It became heavily concentrated in East Harlem. Here we will read personal accounts from several current and former East Harlemites who were affected by public housing. These oral histories will convey how each housing project rose and changed the neighborhood. The Mayor's Committee on City Planning recommended remodeling the neighborhood by constructing public housing projects. However, the Manhattan Development Committee published a document called "A Realistic Approach to Private Investment in Urban Development." This committee, composed of architects, planners, and bank and insurance executives recommended that most of the neighborhood's housing stock be demolished but the schools, churches and health services spared. All public housing towers would range from seven to thirteen stories high. The committee hoped this idea would appeal to any prospective tenants in the low, middle and upper income levels.[8] But the advice contained in the 1939 mayor's report to construct six-story housing projects was ignored.

James Weldon Johnson Houses was the next public housing project to be built in East Harlem. Named after the great African American writer and lyricist, the Johnson Houses stretched from 112th to 115th Street between Park and Third Avenue. When the East River Houses was built, only four families were relocated from their neighborhood. In contrast, nearly 1,000 families were relocated when the Johnson Houses were constructed and the cross streets on 113th and 114th stretching from Park to Third Avenues were eliminated. Louis Rosaly recalls those former tenements.

Before the Johnson Projects were built, on that block were five-story tenement buildings. I went to the old P.S. 57 near 115th Street and Third Avenue, and next to the school you had three-story walkups with the stoops in the front.

The first part of the Johnson housing projects was finished two days before Christmas of 1947. James Weldon Johnson's widow and Robert Moses both welcomed John and Annie Ewart and their five children into the East Harlem's second housing project.[9] All told, 1,310 new apartments were now available, but it would take another year until all of the Johnson Houses were

6. 1950s — Three Strikes

Exact location fifty years later. The beautiful brownstones and tenements and small stores were demolished and replaced by the George Washington Carver Houses. Except for a few cosmetic changes, the block has remained the same since it was constructed in 1958.

finished and fully tenanted. For some residents the Johnson Projects represented an improvement in their lives.

Arnie Segarra, a former deputy assistant comptroller to Bill Thompson who lived in the Johnson Houses at 1840 Lexington Avenue, remembers:

Housing projects were luxury housing back then and it was the first time anyone rode in an elevator and had a maintenance crew.

The future of public housing was evident as the majority of the James Weldon Johnson Houses were constructed at 15 stories. In contrast to our old tenement apartments, the projects had plenty of heat and hot water. The rest of the buildings were six stories. The same day the Johnson Houses opened, the Abraham Lincoln Houses, located on 132nd to 135th Streets between Fifth and Park Avenue, also opened. A majority of these buildings stood fifteen stories. They contained 1,286 units, which replaced dozens of tenements. In 1950, the Lexington Houses, East Harlem's fourth housing project, located on 98 to 99th Streets, between Park and Third Avenue, replaced the former 99th Street IRT garage. Upon completion in 1951, 448 units were available and no residents were relocated. This project was consistent with the other new projects as they were fifteen stories. The Johnson and Lincoln Houses projects added to East Harlem's population. The first four public housing projects were scattered throughout the neighborhood. The next three housing projects would destroy communities in East Harlem.

In January 1951, the New York City Housing Authority (NYCHA) requested the city Board of Estimate (formerly composed of the mayor, city comptroller, city council president, and five borough presidents, who voted on the city's budget) to condemn 159 acres of land for nine public housing developments throughout the city. The following housing projects were sited in East Harlem: the George Washington Carver Houses from 99th to 106th Street between Madison and Park Avenue; the George Washington Houses which covered 97th to 104th Street, Second to Third Avenue; and the Thomas Jefferson Houses, which covered 112th to 115th Street, First to Third Avenue.[10]

East Harlemites noticed that after their tenements were razed and replaced by public housing, their lives were disrupted. These residents fled the neighborhood like refugees as families became separated from their neighbors and community. Generations who grew up in East Harlem suddenly vanished. After the buildings were destroyed and the debris was cleared, several East Harlem blocks became one giant vacant lot. The empty acres symbolized an eerie feeling of helplessness that pervaded East Harlem. Later, neighborhood blocks that once teemed with East Harlemites patronizing local businesses would emerged as one "super-block." Under construction, an empty stretch of three blocks was melded together to welcome the construction crews, who were the only ones there. The construction company would install a small office trailer and construction of the next housing project would begin. The support beams were embedded in the ground and then the projects began to rise. James Bryant, Ted Velez, George Espada, Johnny Colon and Manny Segarra all lived in or near the tenements before the George Washington Carver Houses were constructed.

James Bryant: *I lived on 99th Street between Madison and Park Avenues when the Carver Houses were built. I had relatives and knew families who lived across the street where the projects began. And those tenants had to move for [the old] apartments were soon demolished. I'll tell you how the buildings were demolished. Demolition was done by hand and the beams were knocked out and the fire escapes were cut with a torch. What I remember were the rats that moved to our side of the street, in addition to our own rats. Then the shell for the bottom of the housing project of what would become 55 East 99th Street was built. And President Eisenhower was in the newspaper looking over a railing into the housing construction. Every day you saw moving trucks, for those people stayed in their apartments for thirty years. You didn't move because rents were cheap and plenty of apartments were available. When the city knocked the tenements down, they created the relocation office to find dislocated tenants a new apartment. If you found your own housing you received got $300 and if the city found it for you, you received $150.*

George Espada: *My family lived in a brownstone between 104th and 105th*

Streets on Park Avenue behind the grocery store. And I remember the barrels of mackerel fish that were displayed out in front because it was a lot of trusting in those days and nothing was stolen. And the newspaper, milk, food, and soda were delivered to the door. When the tenements were destroyed we were relocated to 113th Street and Madison Avenue to a railroad flat. I went back after that happened and saw the hole in the building on 104th Street. After the projects were built I saw some of my old neighbors who lived with me but they now lived in the projects because they had bought their apartments under the table.

Ted Velez, who founded the East Harlem Tenants League in the early 1960s, remembered how the creation of the super-block eliminated his street and business.

Isidro (Ted) Velez: *On 103rd Street from Park to Madison Avenues was a row of tenement buildings that went straight through the block. But because of the housing projects you can't walk through the streets or drive through there anymore. There was a newsstand near the northeast corner on 103rd Street and Madison Avenue and I would buy fifty or sixty papers, the* Daily News *or* Daily Mirror *and sell them, but after the Carver Houses were built the newsstand was gone.*

Johnny Colon, the famed bandleader who founded the East Harlem Music School, remembers:

"*My family lived on 180 East 106th Street between Madison and Park Avenues and the apartment was pre–World War II. [The building] was square, and it went up the stairs and it also had a courtyard. There were four apartments in every corner on each floor and all of them were very well built. I remember the*

Lifelong East Harlem resident Clemente Flores and his son Malvin. Mr. Flores, an accomplished painter, lived in the tenements prior to the construction of the Robert Taft Houses. He, like many East Harlemites, was relocated from a tenement building to public housing.

awnings on the stairs and the decorative sill ornaments. And they were made of mahogany wood and from upstairs you could look down and see all of the floors. In our apartment you walked into the hallways on the right and there was a large enough kitchen to cook and have a dining table. By the window facing the courtyard between the buildings stood our refrigerator, the ice box. And during the fall or when the weather turned cold, you bought tin cans from your local store and you put your milk, eggs, meat in the can and placed it on the fire escape and nothing spoiled in the winter. In the summer, you had your ice-box and placed your food in there.

Also inside the apartment was a nice big sink and you walked further and you had a bathroom with a small tub. Next you kept moving down you had a nice size living room and right next to that room was a small bedroom where my uncle slept. It was beautiful and very narrow and the room also had nice built-in closets. Followed by my parents' bedroom, and then grandmother's bedroom where she slept with my sister. When I was a baby, I slept in a crib by my parents. The smaller buildings allowed more people to know each other. Years later a study was done that concluded that people did well when they lived in smaller buildings and people did poorly who lived in high rise buildings. In 1951, we were told we had to leave for the city condemned all of the buildings through eminent domain. My neighbors and I received our notices and we left in 1952 and this was done to poor and to blue-collar people.

We had three selections to choose our housing project and we moved to the Patterson projects, 2645 Third Avenue on 143rd Street in the Bronx. My mother selected that project because of its diversity and there were some Puerto Ricans, Italians, Irish and Jews and plenty of African Americans. There were political motives and it was the worst thing that happened to my eight-member family because the tenements were a wonderful opportunity for people to know each other. Don Miguel, a light-skinned Cuban black man looked out for us. Relocation ripped a major [hole in] my life for I was dislocated and taken away from my friends and acquaintances. Most importantly, I was taken away from my neighborhood with all its support systems. Later, I saw my old building which was already half destroyed, but I never saw my friends again.

In the Bronx, people did not look out for each other because like my family, the people were relocated from other neighborhoods and placed in these projects. And we were all still in shock over the move and tried to maintain some sense of normalcy. But you couldn't walk next door and talk to a neighbor, or ask for a cup of sugar.

In late January 1955, the *New York Times* reported that an elderly couple happily became the first tenants of Carver Houses. The apartment was lauded in the press for its amenities: larger floor radiators which allowed more heat, ceramic tiles in the bathroom floor, and each room provided more sunlight.[11] Carver Houses was expected to be fully tenanted by June 1956, but this prediction was inaccurate and by October 1955 twenty-nine families still lived in nine tenements on Madison Avenue and 102nd Street. Eventually those residents would be relocated,[12] but it wasn't until 1958 that the Carver Houses was fully tenanted. Meanwhile, some East Harlemites like Manny Segarra had the unenviable task of watching the tenements bulldozed right before his eyes. He realized that relocation was imminent and his building too would soon be demolished.

Manny Segarra: *My family still lived on 67 East 104th Street between Park and Madison Avenues. From 99th Street on down they demolished all of those buildings and we saw the projects coming towards us. And the city started tearing down 102nd and 103rd Streets and the whole area looked like Berlin at the end of World War II. Scores of tenements were destroyed, which left empty lots and this practice was commonplace throughout the city. I was ten years old and I kept thinking that this was a nightmare and I went to bed thinking the next day I would wake up and everything would be OK. But I went downstairs and saw the empty buildings. And my neighbors who lived in my building started moving out and people across the street and down the block also moved out. After my family was relocated the tenements stood there until the city tore them down and my family moved to the projects in lower Manhattan. I came back one last time after the building was vacant and it was strange because nobody was there and the whole place was empty. I went to my neighbor's apartment and my friend's sister was an artist and she had drawn something on the wall. And that was the last time I saw my old tenement. Years later I came back to where my building once stood, but it was replaced by the Carver projects.*

We move to Italian East Harlem prior to the construction of the Thomas Jefferson Houses. Al Loungo, realtor and head of the Mt. Carmel Festival, lived in the neighborhood before it was demolished and replaced by the Jefferson Houses.

Al Loungo: *I was fourteenth of sixteen children and there were so many rules to follow. But we played in the streets, with the cardboard box and kick the can and there was a lot of innocence. Back then the area was predominantly Italian and I was not allowed to go past 120th Street. I remember there were many markets at the time and there were all of these tenements on 115th Street. My dad was a florist and he had a business on that street and he worked for the expenses of having sixteen children. We lived above the store, and there were three different apartment buildings on the same block and the same landlord cleaned each building. I remember they were 2234 Second Avenue and 402 and 404 East 115th Streets. Jimmy Durante's cousin lived there on 2234 Second Avenue and when Durante visited his cousin, many tenants stuck their heads out of the window to see him. He doffed his cap and said, "Cha, cha, cha, Mrs. Calabash," and the neighborhood got a kick out of that.*

I remember my first phone call at a drugstore on the corner on 115th Street. My mom allowed me to walk across the street to call a relative and this was a big deal for me, for I was a child. It was around 1951 and you had the receiver and you told the operator the number and then you put in a nickel. There were plenty of stores. You had pizzerias on the same block and other Italian stores that existed and sold Italian cheeses, Italian bakeries, where you could eat fresh bread and fresh coffee. And there were all these mom-and-pop Italian stores.

Though Al was young boy and could not fully grasp the situation, he nevertheless recalls what happened and was affected by relocation.

I was only six, so my comprehension wasn't fully aware of what was going on, but all these stores started to close and the buildings wore torn down. Then the city started to put up these planks and the barriers were put up for protection because of the construction of the projects. And many people left the neighborhood and moved away so they could get housing and thousands of people, mostly Italians, moved out. My family brought a house and moved to Allerton Avenue in the Bronx, but we didn't want to move and leave the neighborhood.

Rent control was the one of main theories on why the tenements fell apart. Phil Mancino, head of Metropolis [TV] Studios, further delves into this theory.

Rent control was one of the reasons why the neighborhood deteriorated. Though it is popular with the people because the city can't raise your rent and you think it is ok. If the government were to say to the landlord we also won't allow you to raise your rent, and we'll never increase the cost of fuel, maintenance and insurance. And we won't charge any more taxes than we did, say, in 1950, then rent control would have worked. But this didn't happen and the landlords couldn't make the payments on their mortgages and they abandoned the buildings. When that happened in East Harlem the city took over the buildings, which by then had deteriorated.

Public housing construction continued in East Harlem as massive demolition and relocation transpired along 120th to 124th Street, First to Third Avenue. This location became the Robert F. Wagner Houses, named in honor of the late senator and father of Mayor Wagner of New York City. Many residents were Italian–East Harlemites. And this working-class community was transforming itself into a stable neighborhood and would have "unslummed" itself if it had not been replaced by the Wagner Houses.[13]

We travel a few blocks South to the East River Houses Extension, which later became the Woodrow Wilson Houses, located 105th to 106th Street between First Avenue and the FDR Drive. The Benjamin Franklin Houses was the next housing project scheduled to rise in East Harlem, at 106th to 109th Street, First to Third Avenue, but this site became the Franklin Plaza Cooperative. Nevertheless, Willie Lopez and Wally Lambert were both relocated before the cooperative was built.

William Lopez: *We lived in a tenement apartment on 107th–108th Streets and Second Avenue. It was a five-story walkup with a bar downstairs and you had marble floors that were kept clean, but the building deteriorated after 1951. Because of rent control the landlord was unable to raise the rents. He bought the materials to fix the apartments, but he couldn't recoup all of the expenses he paid to upkeep the buildings and naturally they deteriorated. Two years before my family was forced to move, the city bought the building from the owner for $16,000 and assumed authority. But the city never told us that they were going to build a housing project. My family received a letter from the city which instructed us to pay our rent at the Casita Maria, then on 107th Street and Madison Avenue. Because my parents and siblings all worked, our combined salaries were over the pay scale and we couldn't qualify for the housing projects. This happened to many people in my neighborhood, and we bought a wood frame house in the Bronx. The only good thing about building the housing projects, it got rid of the many bars that existed in East Harlem.*

Wally Lambert's family lived on 108th Street between Second and Third Avenue. Unlike Willie Lopez and other East Harlemites, Lambert's family was able to return to the same location. However, their return was a stark contrast to their previous accommodations.

Wally Lambert: *My family resided in a tenement on the second floor and I think we lived with my grandmother. But one day we found out that we had to vacate our apartment and I never understood why because those apartments built at the turn of the twentieth century were good tenements. After the city took her apartment, I don't know where she lived for that period of time. Later, I found out that my family left because the city was going to build the projects. I remember the old apartment on 108th Street and [in] the closet was a toilet bowl and the sink was the bathtub. There was also a wood-burning stove which I remember some of best spaghetti was made on that stove. When you came into the apartment, you had the kitchen and the dining area and to the left was a bedroom, and to the left of that was another bedroom, and to the left of that was a living room.*

Later when my grandmother moved back to East Harlem in Franklin Plaza it was a small one-bedroom apartment. You could place a small table in the tiny kitchen, a living room and in the back was a bedroom and that's it.

In addition to the neighborhood's physical transformation, its economic status changed as well. As Willie Lopez stated, only low-income East Harlemites could live in public housing and these residents were forced to move if their salaries rose and exceeded the pay scale. This fact was clear: a plethora of housing projects in East Harlem insured that East Harlem remained a low-income neighborhood.

Wally Lambert: *Low-income people moved into East Harlem and the neighborhood's income levels changed. The Italians who did construction or sanitation* *made money and the Jews who had plenty of the small candy, carpet or hardware stores were gone. Public housing construction forced many people to move to the Bronx or other places.*

Carlos De Jesus was one of the lucky East Harlemites whose tenement apartment was not demolished for public housing. Carlos succinctly details what happens to the properties in and near the adjoining tenements.

Carlos De Jesus: *I was not relocated, but on 115th Street between Fifth and Madison Avenue those tenements were razed after I left. In order to build housing projects you have to raze everything to the ground and nothing is left.*

Housing construction continued into the late 1950s and early 1960s. The Robert F. Taft Houses, located on 112th to 115th Street Fifth to Park Avenue, was named in honor of Robert Moses' friend. The late Ohio senator and son of President William Howard Taft, who died in 1953, was known as Mr. Republican. He spearheaded Title 1 back in 1949.

Clemente Flores, a painter whose works have appeared in the *Quarterly Black Review* and on the cover of *Boricuas*, a book edited by Roberto Santiago, grew up in the neighborhood before the Taft Houses.

Clemente Flores: *I lived on 1694 Madison Avenue on 112th Street in Apartment 5N. The building number still exists today, but a housing project has replaced my old tenement building. It wasn't a private building and my apartment was a railroad flat and everybody knew each other. My apartment had five big rooms and my mother rented the living room to a local musician named Kako, who needed a place to hold his house parties. My block was a very lively block and we played stickball and when you were a child you felt safe to play because everybody looked after you in addition to your parents. And there was one store we loved to hang out because the store owner, Don Eusabio, would let you buy on credit if you didn't have the money and we liked him. Because there was another store owner, whom we called him El Viejo Cheape, Old Cheap Man, because he always tried to overcharge you by five cents. For example back then comic books cost ten cents and he tried to gyp his customers by charging you fifteen cents and we didn't like him.*

Then there was a store called Gray Ruder located on the corner of Madison Avenue which sold nice clothes. Followed by Leoncio Barber's Shop and this place was where you went to hear the latest gossip. You heard whose wife was having an affair and most of the neighborhood's news came out of that barber shop. The next store was Lu Lu's Candy Store, and she was the aunt of the vibraphone player for Joe Cuba. The other stores were Raymond's Bazaar, a shoe store, and Almacenes Hernandez, a furniture store, followed by a television repair shop and Murray's Pharmacy on 113th Street. Then across the street were San Miguel's grocery store, a linoleum and carpet store, a candy store, and then a bakery and above the bakery was a poolroom where the bookies hung out. We also had the beat cop who walked the neighborhood, and we nicknamed him Red because his skin color was practically red along with his red hair. And he dressed sloppy but he didn't care, and he knew everyone on that block. Finally, you had the old-timers who set up a card table and played dominoes on the street.

I lived in my apartment until 1959 or 1960, when it began to deteriorate. My family and I were uprooted and relocated to the Stephen A. Foster Houses two blocks away on Lenox Avenue. Occasionally, I visited my old block because my friends were still there, but it wasn't the same, for all the buildings were gone after the city knocked them down. Also, public housing broke up our singing group, the Verdicts, because the lead singer moved to Long Island and the other member moved to Brooklyn. The Taft projects also killed our neighborhood and the city started warehousing people in the housing projects. And this was painful for you sensed your loss. My whole family and I never liked living in public housing because we went to from living in a small building to a big building. And neighborhoods were neighborhoods then, but that's not the case now.

Louis Rosaly also remembers the neighborhood before the Taft Houses were constructed. However, not every place in East Harlem was wholesome and inviting.

Louis Rosaly: *On 115th Street between Madison and Park Avenue were the following businesses: Rosenfield's Hardware Store, which was a major hardware store in New York City, stood on the corner end of Madison Avenue. And going towards Park Avenue there were two major oil distributors and on the southwest corner of Madison Avenue was a plumbing supply house and a carpet business. On Fifth Avenue from 110th to 112th Street you had open prostitution and before drugs came into the neighborhood, prostitution and bootleg liquor were the problems. And one time a person died making wood alcohol, which we called it Mata Rata or Dana, and he sold it as regular alcohol and nineteen or twenty people died.*

After the Taft Houses were completed 112th to 115th Street, First to Fifth Avenue, was solidly filled with public housing.[14] This housing construction eliminated twenty-four blocks that once had cross streets and stores that provided life and commerce in the neighborhood. The tenement carnage and relocation continued with the development of the Gaylord S. White Houses on 104th Street and Second Avenue, comprising 248 units, and the Herbert H. Lehman Village Houses, 107th to 110th Street, Madison to Park Avenue and the DeWitt Clinton Houses were built in two sections. This incongruity began with the first section at 104th–105th Streets near Park Avenue, while the second section covered 108th–110th Streets, Park and Lexington Avenue.[15] Humberto Cintron lived in the area before it became the Clinton Houses.

Humberto Cintron: *I lived on 133 East 109th Street and our apartment had three rooms, ... each room led into the other room. In my block, there existed four-story* tenements and on the right corner of Lexington Avenue was a grocery store. Across the street was a pharmacy and then on the other part of the corner there was a delicatessen. Then there was Felipito's Barber Shop which was an institution because all the musicians from Puerto Rico or Cuba had their hair cut there. And they sang songs, played guitar sober or drunk, and right under the barber shop we used the basement and made it our first clubhouse and the members played checkers and other games and we paid dues. The clubhouse had a jukebox which played music and allowed us to hold dances. The police came and tried to say our clubhouse was illegal, but we put up an American flag and obtained a charter and placed it on the wall and the police left us alone. I went into the military on January 19, 1955, for the GI Bill was about to expire on February 1st and if you wanted to get all of the benefits such as money for college, or a home, you had to sign up before the expiration date. When I returned from the service in December 1958, the city was relocating people and my family became the last residents to be relocated. By then the junkies had entered all the abandoned buildings and vandalized it and sold the copper pipes. Our building protested this [relocation] because we felt that redevelopment was harmful and instead of rebuilding existing apartments and moving people back into their buildings, the city moved the people out and scattered them all over the city. This is a shame for every block was a community and every community was a small town. You had developed relationships on that block and even though my block was gone, I would not trade growing up in El Barrio for anywhere in the world.

The neighborhood's population decreased through public housing construction. This table details the number of apartments in East Harlem before and after the public housing was constructed.

	Before	After
Carver Houses	2,000+	1,246
Franklin Houses	2,092	1,400
Jefferson Houses	2,621	1,495
Taft Houses	2,534	1,440
Wagner Houses	2,740	2,158
Washington Houses	2,150	1,515

As the oral histories have stated, public housing also eliminated East Harlem's entrepreneurship as many stores and other businesses vanished. The situation became so dire that on January 16, 1956, the East Harlem Small Business Survey & Planning Committee (EHSBS) presented a startling report which yielded ominous signs for East Harlem's future. The report concluded that East Harlem's housing was outdated and warranted replacement. But, the banks, insurance and realtors chose not to invest in East Harlem. The EHSBS looked to the city to spearhead the revitalization of East Harlem, which included housing but also schools, public institutions, small businesses, churches, and political and social clubs. After World War II, many changes came to East Harlem, but the EHSBS felt the New York City Housing Authority and the city Planning Commission never truly worked with the neighborhood[16]—unlike before when Leonard Covello and the East Harlem community worked with Congressman Vito Marcantonio and Mayor Fiorello La Guardia to bring the East River Houses to the neighborhood. The EHSBS believed that real improvement was defined as maintaining the neighborhood's best houses and the businesses located on those premises. It also believed that many racial or ethnic groups should remain in East Harlem, but East Harlem was becoming a segregated neighborhood. It concluded by saying real improvement exists when residents continue residing in the community, but public housing eliminated all of these ideas. The figure below details how the housing projects led to the loss of blocks, stores and how both of them were not replaced.

Project	Units	No. of Blocks	Store Losses	New Stores
Carver	1246	7	200	0
East River	1140	3	4	0
Franklin	1200	5	169	*
Jefferson	1495	6	170	0
J.W. Johnson	1310	6	175	0
Lexington	448	2	0	0
Madison (Lehman)	500	3	140	0
Taft	1440	6	170	*
Wagner	2158	9	225	0
Washington	1515	7	200	0
Wilson	398	2	120	0

All total, 1573 businesses employing over 4,500 people were gone. And the property owners received only modest compensation for their land or entrepreneurship in East Harlem. Here were the kinds of the businesses that vanished after the tenements were demolished for the Franklin Houses on 106th to 109th Streets First to Third Avenues: Appliances, Baby Carriage, Bars, Barber Shops, Bakery and Pastry Shops, Beauty Shops, Bicycle and Candy Stores, Carpenters, Cleaners, Clothing–Dry Goods, Contractor–Electrician–Construction, Cheese–dairy, Drug, Egg, and Fruit stores, Funeral Parlors, Furniture and Rugs, Fortune Telling, and Garage and Parking Grocery stores, Hardware-Houseware, Jewelry and Laundry stores, Law Office, Liquor, Loan, Luggage and Mattress Store, manufacturing and wholesale stores, Meat Markets, Moving-Storage, Novelty and Paint Store, Paper, Pet Shop, Plumber Poultry, Printer and Radio and TV Repair store, Real Estate–Insurance, Restaurants, Shoe Store and Repairs, Toy Stores and Travel Agencies and Union Offices, Churches, Social and Political clubs.

In sum, nearly 170 stores employing over five hundred people disappeared for good. Six months later the East Harlem Merchants Association (EHMA) met for a testimonial dinner for City Councilman John Merli and issued its progress report. The EHMA praised the steps taken by the city administration and NYCHA to provide adequate space for 30 additional stores in the Franklin, Taft and East River Extension (Wilson) Houses. This step was an improvement, but the owners were compensated for non-transferable fixtures at minimum value and they received no compensation for moving expenses. Nevertheless, the committee achieved these concessions:

1. NYCHA would construct and oversee the new stores at the Franklin and Taft Houses and protect the displaced businesses.

2. The displaced businessmen received an opportunity to open their businesses in both housing projects.

3. To protect the commercial strip along Third Avenue and 106th Street, future housing projects would have shopping facilities and more parking spaces, which had disappeared with the creation of the super-blocks. However, these additional parking spaces would be sited at the project and available only to public housing residents.

The City and NYCHA were to discuss all future plans with the East Harlem community. While these initiatives were an improvement, it was too late to save the thousands of East Harlemites who lost their residences and businesses. The EHMA knew that East Harlem would change, but the EHMA felt that East Harlemites should be consulted.[17] On February 28, 1957, the EHMA issued additional information on the aftereffects of public housing in East Harlem. This time it reported on the lack of business activity near the new housing developments along First, Second, Lexington and Madison Avenues.[18] When the Taft Houses and Franklin Plaza were constructed, these developments provided modest accommodations for local business. However, the Wilson and Clinton Houses did not.

Title I failed to live up to its intended goal: the city was supposed to use eminent domain so that private developers would construct decent housing for low-income residents. No Title I projects were completed in East Harlem or anywhere in New York City for low-income residents. But Title I was successful for the real estate developers and landowners who were not obligated to build new apartments for low-income residents.[19]

Thanks to the construction of public housing the city's most vulnerable residents and entrepreneurs in East Harlem and elsewhere lost their apartments and businesses. Most East Harlemites who remained in the neighborhood and moved into public housing saw their neighborhood become de facto segregated, as the majority of East Harlemites were now African American or Puerto Rican. Most remaining whites who lived in East Harlem were Italians, and later many of them moved out.[20]

Margaret McCants: *Public housing began to segregate people because when you filled out an application at the housing office they knew where they wanted to send you. This was done to separate you and I remember when I left the Johnson projects because I was told my family needed more space. I wanted to go to Lehman projects in East Harlem on 108th Street and Madison Avenue, but my application was sent to the Drew projects on the West Side. The housing assistant said, "That's where the blacks are and I thought you wanted go there." I said, "No, I don't want to go to the West Side," ... but since my husband worked for the housing authority my family was able to move into the Lehman Village houses.*

East Harlem's public housing edifices were dully uniform and devoid of any individuality.

Piri Thomas: *Housing projects are like institutions, all built the same way. And these are the same type of rooms, same type of entrances, same type of exits and the same type of courtyards. Basically the same type of projects on every street corner.*

In the housing projects, East Harlemites found that even daily deliveries suffered. Efrain Marzan who eventually moved in the Taft Houses explains.

In the Taft Houses the newspaper and the milk was delivered to our door every day. But both items were stolen and even the milkman who tried to bring our milk was held up. And many of the delivery men who serviced our building stopped coming.

When the projects were constructed, many looked upon public housing as an improvement over tenements, but today public housing is reviled by many urban planners. The housing authority enforced strict rules for residents at first, but over the years these rules were relaxed. However, recently the housing authority returned to strict rule enforcement.

Josephine Carson: *When I lived in public housing, there was a chain around the grass which prevented you from walking on it. If your child walked on the grass you got a fine and if your child got in trouble with drugs, knives, or guns or any criminal activity you were evicted from your apartment. These rules allowed you to have a real hold on the children.*

Public housing's answer to curbing the trespassing on the lawn was to replace the chain with metal bars. However, this only exacerbated the situation.

Robert Espier: *When my grandmother moved into her apartment at 1830 Lexington Avenue, in the James Weldon Johnson Houses, public housing was an open and neighborly experience. And hardly any family ever felt a need to lock their doors,* *and you entered your neighbor's apartment freely and unannounced. Children would run out front to play without their parents fearing for their safety, because neighbors would keep an eye on each others' children—scold or smack them if necessary. But today in James Weldon Johnson you have containment fences everywhere. Someone must have gotten the idea that they were going to improve the immediate environment by putting railings around everything, protecting the lawns from playing children. It is an attempt to control behavior by controlling movement. What it does create is an image of corralling cattle.*

When the DeWitt Clinton Houses were completed in 1965, 14,000–15,000 units of public housing were created. East Harlem held the distinction as one of the most public housing in a neighborhood city. All told, 75,000 East Harlemites lived in public housing which cost the government some $330,107,000.[21] Despite the abundance of these projects, many of the neighborhood's problems persist, such as poverty and poor health. And many East Harlemites felt their neighborhood was violated: too many changes too quickly. East Harlem barely had time to catch its breath.[22] Though the neighborhood would see other high-rise developments in the future, public housing singlehandedly disfigured the face of East Harlem. Families and neighbors from the same country, town, or province were scattered. People who once told stories from about life in the mother country disappeared. And the stores, movie theaters and other businesses that brought life and vitality to East Harlem faded into history. The people who once traveled to the corner store for a newspaper, comic book, or magazine, or ascended to the roof to have a cookout or fly kites were gone. Now the only thing left were the memories. From *New York: A Documentary Film*:

Robert A. M. Stern: *Sometimes, I think the United States embarked on urban renewal as out of some kind of elaborate guilt trip over bombing so many places out on the course of the Second World War in Europe. Because, we saw that by clearing these sites, suddenly, the bombs made it possible for new kinds of development and a way to modernize cities, how to tackle the problem here, we really used the same technique.*

After some kind of study of declining demographics, we declared whole areas, susceptible to demolition; just simply moved people out. It became incredibly disruptive to people lives. You scattered neighborhoods which might have been very, very poor, but still had a very dense network of associations. And you began through urban renewal in a city like New York, but it's true in Chicago and elsewhere, that process which we are still reeling under of wrenching communities apart and then families collapsing, the whole support system of the less well advantage in our society collapses and we wonder why they then become increasing unable to function in a society as a whole.[23]

One can look at Franklin Plaza as a model of mixed-income residents living in a poor neighborhood. It was constructed over fifty years ago, when East Harlemites demanded the chance to own their cooperative. Also small stores were included in this development.[24] Franklin plaza is not perfect, but a little ingenuity and proper planning can lead to better results.

The End of Italian East Harlem

The anti-immigration statutes also curtailed the population of Italian East Harlem, which never rose above 80,000. During the depression some Italians left the neighborhood and returned to Italy. And by the 1940s, Italians abandoned East Harlem in large numbers. Italian East Harlem further declined with the construction of the George Washington, Thomas Jefferson and Robert Wagner public housing projects. The remaining Italian East Harlemites reluctantly moved into the housing projects with its high floors and elevators.[25]

George Di Martino: *You didn't have an option and if your house was brought for $3,000 it could have been worth $20,000. And people sold their properties. Those Italians that could afford to move left East Harlem and this happened block after block and this led to the decline of the housing stock in East Harlem.*

Audrey Berghaus: *My family tried to fight it, but we were the little people and we didn't have any money. The city promised everybody in my building that we would be relocated to a nice area, and my grandmother, being an old-fashioned person who barely spoke English, said, "I am never going to leave this area." But my family moved when the city found us an apartment in the Soundview Houses, in the Bronx, but she said no way. Then the city found her an apartment in the Jefferson Houses. And she accepted the offer. My family left in July 1956 when the area was completely cleaned out, but it was devastating for the whole neighborhood. Many people moved to Pelham Bay, Gun Hill Road and Throggs Neck: all parts of the Bronx. Some diehards remained but the neighborhood was never the same again.*

Lois Pascale Evans: *I remember 119th Street in the summertime when people played and cooled off in front of the hydrant near the tenements. And those blocks would be teeming with people. The neighborhood changed when the city demolished the buildings and built the projects. And many Italians moved out, but before that happened East Harlem was a bigger Italian neighborhood than the one that exists today in Little Italy.*

By the late 1960s the population of Italian East Harlem declined rapidly to about 11,000.[26] Today, approximately 600 to 1,000 Italians reside in East Harlem. Along with the Italian East Harlem, the small enclave of Greek East

Harlemites where Calliope Gravanis once resided also vanished. She still returns to the neighborhood to visit the Greek church.

Calliope Gravanis: *We moved to Astoria in 1954 because of [East Harlem] started to get bad. Also, we were on the fifth floor and there weren't any elevators and it was a little hard. We moved to Astoria because of the nice rents, but we still came to East Harlem be close to the St. Demetrios church.*

Drugs

Drugs anesthetized not only East Harlemites individually but also the whole East Harlem neighborhood. Like public housing, these substances, especially heroin, became a major problem during 1950s. During the early 1950s New York State Assemblyman Hulan Jack, who represented both East and West Harlem, and Representative Adam Clayton Powell, Jr., both tried to get the state legislature and Congress to pass legislation that provided treatment for drug addicts. Both measures were defeated. Years later, Jack in his autobiography wrote that, if the state legislature had heeded his warning perhaps many neighborhoods could have controlled drug abuse before it spread.

Meanwhile drugs elicited the attention of the press and in the early 1950s the *New York Times* published several articles involving the arrests for possession and selling of heroin throughout East Harlem.[27]

Bob Deleon: *We called drugs or marijuana or a person who took them a moto which meant you were a low-life. And people who sold drugs hid their stuff under the stairwells in the tenements. But we were curious and one time we found it either on the ground floor or in the backyard.*

Carlos De Jesus: *Marijuana could be seen in the neighborhood, but I saw heroin affect my community during my adolescent years. By the time I was twenty, for every five guys on the block, maybe one was addicted to heroin.*

Louis Rosaly: *Drugs started in the late 1940s, but it was a very small group selling it, until it exploded. And then every block had three or four junkies. At first only men used it, but by the middle 1950s, the women used heroin and it became the curse of the neighborhood.*

Ray Rodriguez remembers his childhood friends before some of them became hooked on drugs and died. And Ray was fortunate because a stern parental warning steered him away from drugs and maybe saved his life.

Ray Rodriguez: *Heroin became the common drug used in East Harlem as cocaine was used by rich people. I remember seeing heroin when I was twelve or thirteen. My father said, "If you use drugs you might as well die because I will kill you." I remember the guys who I hung out with on my block who were affected by drugs.*

6. 1950s — Three Strikes

Everybody had a nickname. Fiqui was short for Figueroa. Then, you had Boston Blackie who was a dark-skinned Puerto Rican with straight hair. The name came from a character in the movie, but he also got hooked on drugs. Another guy, Harry Smith, was a Panamanian Indian and back then movies showed cowboys and Indians (Native Americans). And in the movie the Indian was called Mala, so we called Harry Smith, who looked like the Indian in the film, Mala. Mala in Spanish means bad, but he was a good guy and he too became hooked on drugs. Henny, who was Polish, and my friends went to his room and did drugs and his mother was oblivious to this. I found out by walking into his room one day and saw all of them shoot up. They said come in, but I refused as I remembered my father's warning. I only hung out with friends who didn't do drugs, and they were Johnny Sabatel and Ramiro Palmer.

The three of us are only ones alive from that neighborhood today. The other people from the group, Mala and Boston Blackie, they overdosed, all died. Another friend of mine, Butch Rosado, and his whole family used drugs and all died. And about twenty friends of mine died in the streets or in the buildings.

Two more residents detail how drugs affected their lives. One, James Bryant, used drugs, while the latter abstained but suffered because his sibling did drugs. James Bryant's earlier East Harlem memories reflected a caring neighborhood, but his memories included some dark times as well. Here Bryant details his own drug use and how he overcame it.

I think I first noticed drugs in our community in 1949 because you saw guys nodding on the street. Heroin may have been sold in the neighborhood before, but it was low-key then and drug dealers sold reefer or heroin. First, only my friends took drugs, but then my family members began using it and eventually I started using drugs. I first used drugs in 1952 in a high school bathroom, and I went from smoking reefer to snorting and shooting heroin. This led to my arrest, and after I was arrested I voluntarily went to Lexington, Kentucky, for rehabilitation. And I [stood] there for two weeks, then I had a relapse during my rehabilitation stint. But I became an addict again and I struggled for four or five years to break my habit. And I continued to use drugs and one time I did drugs on tenement rooftops. Presently, the 23rd Precinct is located on 102nd and Third Avenue, but back then it was located on 104th Street between Lexington and Third Avenues. I always said the police never saw I did drugs because during the course of one of the arrests in 1959, I secreted a hypodermic needle in my mouth. I was arrested [and] later, I went to a local hospital and was X-rayed and the needle was still in my stomach. The doctors told me to eat plenty of bread and to take a laxative and this would extricate the needle from your stomach. And it worked, for I was X-rayed again and the needle did not appear. I was incarcerated and given six months and sent to jail at Rikers Island for the drug paraphernalia. My friend asked me to attend a Pentecostal church and this helped me to kick my drug habit. There were no drug treatment programs back then and the church said if you received the gift of the Holy Ghost it will give you power and you will beat drugs. When I came out I worked at a Brooklyn factory for five years, and I started going to night school. Afterwards I went to New York Community College, which is now called New York Technical College in Brooklyn, and obtained my associate's degree in accounting. I furthered my education by obtaining my bachelor's degree and MBA. I was called to the ministry and became an ordained minister and I attended New York Theological Seminary and received a second master's in theology. In 2008, I received my doctorate in ministry from Drew University in Madison, New Jersey.

After surviving rheumatic fever, Dr. Alvin Poussaint attended Patrick Henry Junior High School 171 and Stuyvesant High School. For college Dr. Poussaint chose Columbia University over Yale University because Columbia was near his apartment. But this choice meant living in his neighborhood which now infested with drugs. Though Alvin didn't use drugs, Poussaint's brother Kenny, whom James Bryant knew, did. His brother's drug use and unpredictability interrupted Dr. Poussaint's studies while he attended Columbia University.

Dr. Alvin Poussaint: *I was hesitant about attending Columbia University for I knew I would live at home with my older brother Kenny. And he was my roommate and was also a junkie with a bad heroin habit. During my time at Columbia University I lived in East Harlem. And the advantage of living in the neighborhood was that I had all my friends in New York City. Also, I didn't have to adjust to a new place being a commuter student. But it was a real challenge for me because while studying at Columbia, I routinely did my homework during the late hours. But sometimes when I returned home my things were a mess, for my brother sometimes smoked in bed. Or Kenny would burn the bed or he would fall off the bed and hit the floor. If I had an exam the next day he might return at two o' clock in the morning and bang things around and it was really a strain. But despite these distractions I did okay. Afterwards, I wanted to go to Cornell Medical School in the city, but the same issue came up if I attended Cornell, for I would have to confront the same problems I had with my brother all over again.*

To make matters worse he started disappearing, because at various times he was in jail or in various mental hospitals. I considered applying to Harvard Medical School, but the advisor called me and said, "I thought you wanted to attend Cornell." I explained to the advisor the situation with my brother. He said, "Let me call you back on Monday." That day he called and said if Cornell gave you a scholarship and room and board, would you withdraw your application from Harvard Medical School? I said yes. And I received the scholarship and I went to Cornell Medical School and lived in the dormitory. This was quite a salvation, to be out of there because I was in a depressing environment because there were drugs all around my community.

Alvin Poussaint escaped his brother's drug habit, and graduated from Columbia University and later Cornell Medical School and became a successful psychiatrist. Today, James Bryant is a retired administrator of the Addicts Rehabilitation Center in East Harlem. Unfortunately, Kenny Poussaint lost his battle against drugs.

James Bryant: *Kenny and I were both addicts and spent time together in Rikers Island in 1959. I was released on March 11, 1960, and I think he was released right after me. He entered a drug treatment program once, but he didn't stay for its duration. Shortly afterwards, I heard that he died.*

Dr. Alvin Poussaint and James Bryant's recollection on drug abuse in East Harlem is a tiny fraction of this story. Sadly, this story is still pertinent today.

The Tribalism of Gangs

Gangs became another problem for East Harlem during the 1950s. That was when this problem reached a boiling point and led to one of the most sensational murders in the city's history. Several contributing factors led to the creation of East Harlem's gangs during this period. In his book *Vampires, Dragons and Egyptian Kings*, sociologist Eric Schneider opined that a lack of employment led some teenagers to join the gangs. In the early twentieth century, much of New York City's economy was predicated on the garment, printing and construction industries, while laborers found work on the docks. Jobs disappeared with the depression and many laborers were left unemployed. World War II brought a temporary reprieve to this problem and New Yorkers worked in the munitions factories. Many teenagers took advantage of this opportunity and also worked, but these jobs ended after the war. In addition, over 100,000 blue-collar jobs in retail and manufacturing industries were lost through relocation.[28] Defense contractors took their businesses to Long Island and to the southern and midwestern United States. New York City's workforce reconstituted itself during the late 1940s to the mid–1960s through the financial industry, in legal, insurance and banking jobs. Government and civil service jobs were available to Irish Americans, while garment and retail jobs were held by Jewish New Yorkers.[29] Unemployed black and Puerto Rican youth were prime candidates for gang membership. Another factor was the absence of adult supervision during and after the war. As many men served in the war and the women worked in defense plants, the phrase latchkey children became part of the American lexicon. After the war, drugs and lack of employment opportunities led to the breakup of the stable family.³⁰ Some teenagers used gangs as surrogate families to offset their broken homes. Mike Rivera, a former Dragon, recalls his experience as a gang member. Mike grew up on 103rd Street between Madison and Fifth Avenue. Later, he moved to the George Washington Carver Houses on 60 East 104th street.

Mike Rivera: *I got into the gang at fourteen or fifteen and the gang was like a family, but you mostly join the gangs for protection. Because if you walk from 103rd Street to 104th Street there's another gang located there on that block. Only Central Park was a neutral zone.*

The turf was very important as different gangs controlled certain blocks of East Harlem.

Manny Segarra: *There were gangs all over the place. On 102nd Street the gang was called the Demons; [the] 103rd Street gangs were the Dragons, and also the Copians (Copasetics) patrolled that area. No gangs existed on 104th Street until we started our gang, the Condemners. The Viceroys' turf was on 110th Street and sometimes they came to 103rd Street to fight the Dragons. On 105th Street was the Corsicans territory and on 106th Street the Colts ran that area. At 107th Street and Madison Avenue you dealt with the Turbans, and finally from 109th to 111th Street were the Untouchables and the Viceroys.*

Racial hostility was another factor in the creation of gangs. Many gangs composed of the same racial or ethnic group fought other gangs of different races and ethnicities. Puerto Ricans, blacks and Italians each formed gangs to protect their territory from outsiders.³¹

Bob Montesi (Puerto Rican): *I was in the Viceroys and I joined the Enchanters later. It was about protecting your turf and you did whatever was necessary to protect your turf. It you had to kill, you killed. Myself and many members in my gang carried pistols. When I was in the Viceroys we fought the Dragons. It was a war and I remember one time we went to the roof and waited on the Dragons to throw bricks at them.*

From the 1930s up to the late 1950s Spanish Harlem/El Barrio coexisted with Italian East Harlem, and both neighborhoods established gangs. In Spanish Harlem, the two most prominent gangs were the Viceroys and the Dragons. Race played a role in both gangs. The Dragons were mostly light-skinned Puerto Ricans whereas members of the Viceroys were mostly dark-skinned.³²

Louis Rosaly (member of the Viceroys): *The Dragons' position was that the Viceroys didn't like them because they were light-skinned Puerto Ricans. This is odd, for I went to grammar school with these same Dragons at P.S. 57 and spent time in their apartments. Later I went to junior high school, at the old James Fenimore*

Cooper School, on 116th Street. And these same friends, I was now fighting them because they were Dragons.

As the Puerto Rican population grew during this period, inter-ethnic clashes between Italian East Harlem and Spanish Harlem mirrored the fighting between Irish and Jewish East Harlemites years before. The line that divided Spanish and Italian Harlem was the Third Avenue El. Pablo Figueroa remembers when the Third Avenue El separated these communities.

Pablo Figueroa: *The Third Avenue El became the demarcation line or demilitarized zone between Italians and the Puerto Ricans. On the platform you looked at them [Italians] and they looked at you [Puerto Ricans].*

Peter Gallo: *For some reasons the Italian gangs may have felt threatened that their territory might be taken away from them. And they organized gangs to hold that territory. The Italian gangs, you had the Red Wings at Jefferson Park, 112 to 115th Streets and First Avenue, and the Italian Dukes on 114th Street and Second Avenue, or the Crusaders on 118th Street between Second and Third Avenue and Billy Grasse from 120th Street through 124th Streets and Second Avenue. I was not a member of any gangs; however, I went to school with many of them, for instance on my block on 118th Street between Second and Third Avenues [they] had a gang there. And many people joined the gangs because they felt safe because they knew if there were any problems they had a crew that would back them up. I had this problem growing up in East Harlem because I could beat some guy in a fight, but I wouldn't do it, because if I fought one member I would have to fight the entire crew.*

The most respected and feared gang in Italian East Harlem was the Red Wings.

After World War II Manny Diaz, Jr., graduated from City College and earned his master's degree at Columbia University. His first job was at the Union Settlement Community Center located on 104th Street between Second and Third Avenue. Coincidentally the Red Wings frequented the Union Settlement center, but the gang broke some of the center's rules. But the Red Wings still wanted to use the center and the gang announced they were going to kill the blacks and Puerto Ricans. Diaz took exception and barred the Red Wings for two weeks. Sensing that he would have trouble, Diaz went to the police to defuse the situation. The police stated they would send an officer the next morning, but they did not. When the center opened, the Red Wings' leader appeared along with twenty gang members. The leader wanted Diaz to admit his members back into Union Settlement, but Diaz refused.

The Red Wings' leader knew Diaz' address and threatened his family. Diaz, who grew up in East Harlem and once ran with a gang called the Dukes, abandoned his professional demeanor and reverted back to his street ways. He promised to harm the Red Wings' leader if anything happened to his family. After the leader saw that Manny was serious, he backed down. Diaz held his ground and the Red Wings did not enter Union Settlement for two weeks. For Diaz, his past gang life helped him. However, the Red Wings remained a strong presence in the neighborhood. Part of their strength was their alleged access to organized crime, and some Red Wing members were said to eventually become members of the Mafia.

But the Mafia refrained from association with the Red Wings if that association would elicit unwanted attention from the police or interrupted their operations. The Red Wings like many Italians gangs, were instructed to use action only for defensive purposes.[33] But fights continued.

Louis Rosaly: *We used to go after the Italians too and we used to light them up. And the gangs were Red Wings and the Italian Dukes. We went to the Boys Club and they [the gangs] did a number on us and then we went to Jefferson Park and they did a number on us again because the Italians fought in groups. One time we fought this guy on 113th Street and Third Avenue and he just took it. He was light-skinned and we thought he was Italian until he spoke in Spanish, that's how we learned he was Puerto Rican. We apologized to him and he said, "The Italians are beating me and now the Puerto Ricans are beating me up."*

Prior to the war, the public, press and the police tried to ignore the gangs. But with the aid of many returning soldiers, gangs procured advanced forms of weaponry and developed strategies to counter other gangs. For instance, ex-soldiers instructed gang members in hand-to-hand combat. After the war, gang violence compelled both the police and the public to admit that the gangs were a serious problem.[34] James Bryant and Louis Rosaly recall how the gangs' weapons progressed from zip guns to actual firearms. And Rev. Normam C. Eddy became astonished at how gang violence all but exceeded his wartime experiences.

James Bryant: *the zip gun was a little wooden gun and to make the gun, you took an antenna from a car and turned it into a little pipe. Next you used an old heavy rubber band and next you placed the bullet in the latch and then you pulled the rubber band back and it would go off, but it was unreliable. Because many times the pipe blew off the gun or the latch hit your finger and the zip gun would go off, but you were a big dude with the zip guns.*

Louis Rosaly: *It went from fists, to bats, to homemade zip guns or you brought a real gun. I had a German Luger, a forty-five which had fourteen rounds. And all the guns we obtained came from the soldiers. Back then guns cost $15, $20 and $35, which was a lot of money in those days.*

Rev. Norman C. Eddy: *We just lived with the gangs all over the place, even on our block. I remember one time when, suddenly, we heard shooting in the neighborhood and my wife Peg and I were caught in the crossfire. And we had no place* to go, so we leapt into our car and crouched into the dashboard. But the shooting continued as the bullets flew over our heads. Finally, the shooting went away and I was so astonished because I just went through three and a half years of World War II, and seen a lot of fighting in the war, and I thought I was used to a lot of gang fighting and I became concerned. I was so afraid for Peg, who was right next to me, her shoulder against my shoulder, and I looked over and she just said, "Hey, that was exciting."

Not surprisingly, the procurement of guns increased the murder rate among young people during this period.[35] But some East Harlem gangs were nonviolent and operated as social organizations.[36]

Bob Deleon: *I was in a social club called the Gay Robins and back then gay meant happy. We played stickball and softball and hung out on 114th Street between Park and Madison Avenue and threw parties.*

Dr. Alvin Poussaint: *I belonged to the Cherokees and we were a nonfighting gang and we tried to be neutral with the Copians.*

Ray Grist: *Our gang was called the Diplomats and we had parties and dances at the church of the Ascension. We printed the tickets and sold them, but we were in the gang for protection.*

Carlos De Jesus: *I was a member of the Junior Social Gents and that's a name in itself. The gang fighting was not our thing. We were about socializing and having parties or stickball. We had a few weapons to protect ourselves, a zip gun, or gun in case people came to our turf.*

Certain individuals were off limits to the gangs: religious and spiritual persons and long-time residents who operated as community leaders. Usually, nongang members or adults were spared any confrontation by the gangs. If fighting commenced, it usually took place after school or before bedtime.[37] But nonfighting gangs could not always remain neutral.

Dr. Alvin Poussaint: *I stayed out of the way, but sometimes you couldn't avoid it. One time a gang member who was bigger than me wanted to fight. He didn't want to leave me alone so I smashed a bottle and cut his arm and the guy wound up getting stitches in that arm, but he never bothered me again.*

Machismo was another part of the gang culture. Gangs demonstrated their machismo in several ways, such as through violence which was felt to neutralize the stigma associated with poverty and gave the member the feeling of being powerful.[38] Metaphorically, gang members painted their reputation on their turfs and used the streets as their canvases. As Eric C. Schneider wrote, "Membership in a gang provided a boy with pride and respect, which the legitimate world could not supply." A gang member's reputation was a source of respect among his contemporaries. This reputation separated the men from the boys. To maintain this reputation, the gang member was not adverse to employing violence. This reputation helped instill fear, which became an essential part of his personality.[39]

Some East Harlemites through divine intervention or courage vowed not to let gang violence overcome them.

Bob Montesi: *Norman Eddy was the minister of the 100th Church Street of the East Harlem Protestant Parish. And the church held many dances for the teenagers in our neighborhood. But the dances could turn violent and many fights occurred. I remember shooting broke out in the streets and then everybody would scatter and the lights were turned off, but after the shooting Norman Eddy was there turning the lights back on.*

Rev. Norman C. Eddy remembers another dance that started out as a peaceful and fun; however, the scene quickly turned violent.

Rev. Norman C. Eddy: *The Jewish Synagogue on 317 East 100th Street ended. And our church's youth group rented the ground floor for seventy-five dollars. We remodeled it and the boys and girls agreed to run a dance. And this was a lot because then most rooms were thirty-five dollars to fifty dollars a month. The group had nice teen-age boys at the door and the church charged twenty-five cents to pay the rental. Many children from all over East Harlem went to the dance and instead of fighting, people were dancing. At the center I didn't know [that] the fighting gangs also attended the dance, until one day when I was with my wife Peg in our upstairs apartment when I heard shooting. Then I realized it was coming from the family center. And I ran downstairs and one of the gangs had come in. Eddie Suarez, a gang member, had been wounded. I said "Eddie, you better get to the hospital." At first he didn't want to go, but later on he agreed to enter the hospital. And until that night the family center had been a neutral zone.*

The gangs also differentiated themselves from mainstream society through various styles and customs: speech, walking, clothing, attitude or music. Certain gangs transformed themselves into singing groups.[40] Some gang members went to dances or parties to meet girls. Gang members often wore jackets or sweaters bearing an emblem or symbols.[41]

Charles Faulkner: *My gang liked to hang out on the streets and we listened to rock and roll music back then. This is today's equivalent of children listening to rap music. We came together and practiced singing doo-wop under the street lamp. And sometimes we became juvenile delinquents. You didn't go to school, for you had your girl or get laid. If you wanted to see a new girl, this meant going to new territory and dealing with a rival gang. Also, during the week you talked about which dance hall you wanted to visit, for many gangs visited the dance halls and this gang will be here and that gang will be there. When the gangs arrived you were not to mess with that person's girl because what usually started the fight was a girl.*

Gangs then wore sweaters, but you don't see that today. In those days, gangs were Ivy League and clean cut. The cleaner you were, the more prestige you had as a gang. Today's gangs will have a handkerchief as their color or symbol, but back then it was the sweater. My gang was called the Lanterns and our colors were green and white. The sweaters were a dignifying symbol with the stripes on your sleeve and the big logos up front because your power in the gang was on your sleeve. One stripe meant you were the head leader and two stripes you were the war Lord and three stripes meant you were a regular member.

Dr. Alvin Poussaint: *The Cherokees' colors were gray and maroon; we had jackets—sweaters, we had a C in front and Cherokee written somewhere.*

Ray Grist: *Our gang was the Diplomats and we wore a blue and white sweater with the word* Diplomats.

Mike Rivera: *The Dragons' colors were green and gold.*

Each gang member proudly wore these outfits, but sometimes their clothing brought unwanted attention from another gang.

Efrain Marzan: *I was in a stickball gang called the Demon Juniors and I also played for the Gordon Knights. And it was playing stickball where I met my wife Eva. Later I played for the Turban Midgets. I used to go to P.S. 83, and I wore my jersey, and all of a sudden I got surrounded. The black guys from the West Side, the Copians, said, "You're a midget. I said, Yeah, but I play ball," but it made no difference and they kicked the shit out of me. Then he said, "If you are gonna be around, never wear that again," and I never wore it again.*

A gang's name was also important. Some gangs chose a certain name that reflected the group's outlook. There were the regal Viceroys, Dukes or Young Lords. (Two gangs named the Young Lords existed during this period, the former on the West Side of Manhattan and latter in the Bronx. This gang shouldn't be confused with the East Harlem organization of the late 1960s and early 1970s.) Other names were chosen to suggest strength, such as the Dragons or Comanches. A name like the Social Gents projected a nice image.

Though the gangs' activities sometimes hinged on incivility, there were moments of discipline. Rules of engagement were used to declare the time and place of a fight or to make peace. If a fight occurred, the war counselor or warlord from one gang would contact the other gang official of the same rank, and they would work out the logistics such as which arms were allowed.[42]

Charles Faulkner: *Let's say a dispute erupted between two rival gangs and the president and the war counselor would sit down. Our gang would get together and arbitrate and tell what happened and he would talk about it. Now if it called for action then me, being the war counselor, would contact the other gang's war counselor and say, "You know what, you fucked up and let's rumble." The war counselor decides if you go to war. Today, people in gangs just shoot and don't meet. Back then we met.*

However, though the rules were agreed upon, rules also were made to be broken. Mike Rivera was on his turf when he and his gang used weapons.

Mike Rivera: *I befriended two brothers who practically became brothers to me. They were Bobby and Georgie Lemus. And if anything was done to them it affected me. One night the Viceroys came to the Casita Maria and said they were looking for Georgie. One of the five members of the Viceroys was named Huskie Willie, and he was a crazy dude. They asked me, "Is Georgie here?" I said, "What do you want with him?" Then I thought something is going to happen, because I knew Georgie and Bobby. I tried to stall the Viceroys, but then Georgie opened the door, and a Viceroy responded by shoving Georgie. And then Georgie shoved the Viceroy back. Then a shoving match ensued between both gangs, but when the Viceroy comes into the Dragons territory, I know they are armed. Though Georgie managed to escape the melee, I knew he went to retrieve the guns that the Dragons had stolen from the Viceroys.*

Then I said, "Listen, why don't we sober up?" and I tried to be the peacemaker. I said, "You guys are high, and I know Georgie ain't gonna take no shit." But the Viceroys didn't want to leave and we're over here arguing and we had only a few Dragons in there, because the Viceroys caught us by surprise. All of a sudden I hear Bobby and Georgie slam the door and they drew their guns and fired two shots in the air. I got in the middle between Bobby and Georgie, and the Viceroys backed up when they saw the guns. But, Huskie Willie was so messed up that he opened up his leather coat, and he went to reach for his gun which was shining. And I said watch out, then boom, boom, boom! Georgie and Bobby both emptied their guns on Huskie Willie. And he got shot with a thirty-eight special and a twenty-two baretta. But Huskie Willie was seriously injured and was on the ground. Our gang took the guns and dumped them in the river. But Chino from Viceroy witnessed the shooting of Huskie Willie and Bobby went to jail.

Most gangs and non–gang members knew which boundaries to cross to avoid trouble. East Harlemites oblivious to those boundaries suffered serious consequences.

Dr. Alvin Poussaint: *We wouldn't go to Jefferson Park because if you went to the Italian neighborhood, they would throw bricks from the roof. And if you went to St. Francis de Sales, the Catholic church located on 96th Street between Lexington and Park Avenue, then the Irish would jump you. The Irish community was still there on 98th Street and Park, Lexington and Third Avenues. Bigotry was the rule of the day.*

Peter Gallo: *Some people may have joined a gang because their friends were members. Others just have hate, racial, ethnic hate. The hate is almost always from the older people who pass it down to the young. The Red Wings owned Jefferson Park and any non white would be putting their lives in their hands by entering the park. A few people were killed.*

This was further evidenced on June 1, 1958, when four members of the Red Wings were arrested and charged with the death of Julio Ramos. Ramos, a Cuban immigrant, was mistaken for a Puerto Rican, but he was a Latino and in enemy territory. Though Italian East Harlem was reduced through the construction of the housing projects by this time, the remaining Italian gangs still ruled the area. Simply put, Ramos was at the wrong place at the wrong time. As Ramos sat with his girlfriend on a bench in Jefferson Park he was confronted by the Red Wings. He tried to run away, but he tripped and fell and was immediately attacked by the gang. The Red Wings assaulted Ramos with bench slats, a wire trash basket, and a water jug, which broke Ramos' head. The Dragons responded by sending threatening letters to the families of the four men charged with Ramos' murder.[43] Eventually all four Red Wings were convicted of Ramos' death. In response to the murder of Julio Ramos, Puerto Ricans and Italian East Harlemites banded together and formed the East Harlem Italian–Puerto Rican Good Neighbor Committee, chaired by Dr. Leonard Covello.[44] The committee's aim was to foster understanding between both ethnicities. Two years later, the committee, with the aid of the Puerto Rican government, sponsored a trip to Puerto Rico for seven Italian East Harlemites.[45]

Inevitably all things must end. There are several reasons why the gangs declined during the late 1950s and early 1960s. Gangs primarily composed of teenagers and young adults realized they couldn't maintain the gang lifestyle forever. Leaving the gangs wasn't easy, but standing on the corner and growing old while the world passed them was a frightening thought even among the gang members. The Enchanters abandoned the gang lifestyle and went "social," or they quit. They renounced violence and discarded their weapons. With the assistance of the East Harlem Protestant Parish, they opened a storefront club. The gang went so far to reform its image that the group dropped the name Enchanters and became the Conservatives.[46] And mediation played an important role in this transformation.

Bob Montesi: *You realize there is a better life and there are more important things to do than kill over turf or for a girl. The gangs that congregated on 100th Street were the Viceroys, the Dragons and the Enchanters. It was there where I met Eddie Suarez, and he was the Dragon's war counselor, and Ramon Diaz worked with Norman Eddy. The gangs met and we decided to give up the gang lifestyle. We changed our name to the Conservatives and went social, or became a social gang, and the fighting subsided. Also we were growing up, for we weren't children anymore. You had to find work, but some of my friends fell back into the gang life and got back into fighting.*

Rev. Norman C. Eddy: *I became acquainted with the gang members* on 100th Street, They were the Dragons, the Viceroys and I also had some contacts with the Red Wings. And I earned the respect of the gangs and because I wasn't pro-Enchanter or pro-this gang or pro-that gang. This is one of the very important things about mediators. They have to be trusted by all of the sides during the mediation. The gangs may not agree and everything, but at least they trusted the mediator. I remember mediating between the Enchanters and the Dragons. There were flare-ups and gang wars and people were shot and I managed to bring three or four gang leaders to sit at the table. And we talked for a while and they brought out their grievances about [someone] looking disrespectfully at one of the girlfriends. But there were honest disagreements and the gangs realized that the fighting was going nowhere. And they finally agreed to stop the fighting. Then one gang leader said to the other leader, "The shit's off," and the other leader reached across the table and replied, "Yeah, the shit's off." And they shook hands, and the gang wars stopped for a few months.

This transition was not easy. After the Dragons heard about the Enchanters' decision to go social, one member of the Dragons decided to take advantage of the Enchanters. As the Dragons arrived at the location formerly held by Enchanters on 100th Street, fearing attack an ex–Enchanter reverted to his gang persona. He went up to the roof and threw rocks and fired several shots at the Dragons, but the police arrived just in time to thwart any further violence. An ex-member of the Enchanters went to prison for his actions, but the Enchanters remained social and the peace between both groups endured.[47]

Several other factors prompted the decision to leave the gangs: violence, temporary or permanent injury or jail.[48] Monetarily, the gang members knew that their parents could not take care of them forever. And some members tried and were successful at finding work while others struggled.

John Torres was another gang member who knew when it was time to quit. He was caught with a gun by the authorities and spent four years in a reform school. John credited this incident as a wake-up call. With the help of the New York City Youth Board, John was able to leave the Viceroys.[49] Later, he founded the Cadet Corps in East Harlem.

John Torres: *I was with an organization called the American Friends Service Committee. And they were located on 111th Street between Park and Madison Avenue. All Quakers who wanted people to do something with their lives. And I saw the Cadet Corps coming down the block and the children in the American Friends program wanted to be a part of the Cadet Corps, which is learning about the military. The marching and the uniformity impressed me. And I found myself trying to get these children to join the cadets which they did. Those children who were in the Cadet Corps moved on, I kept the cadets going. In the Cadet Corps they learn discipline and the real thing about cadetting is to keep them involved until they get* big enough to make something of themselves. Because when I was an adolescent, I didn't feel like I had a choice in life. Today, you have to make children feel there is a choice in life.

Other gang members turned to religion, which became their saving grace and helped them leave the gangs. Then there were the gang members who found a nice girl and decided to settle down, and marry. Other gang members joined the armed forces. Some gang members fought in the Korean War and a decade later in Vietnam.[50] Mike Rivera was one of these ex-gang members who joined the armed forces for several reasons.

Mike Rivera: *My friends got locked up and I had quit high school and got a girl pregnant and I joined the navy. After I came out of boot camp I got married.*

Heroin helped to end the gangs. Drugs provided a seeming escape from obligation, pressure or possible failure, eventually the gang member no longer cared.[51]

Bob Montesi: *It started in the late 1950s. Many gang members became hooked on drugs and that gradually ended some of the gangs and decreased the gang violence.*

Finally, many social service and youth agencies helped to steer the gang members and encouraged the transition from gang life. Gangs reemerged in the 1960s and 1970s.[52] In the 1980 and 1990s and into the 21st century many gangs throughout New York City became involved with drug dealing.

The Group Ministry

Public housing, drugs and gangs brought relocation, addiction and rounds of ammunition. Public housing separated and later compartmentalized people and eliminated many of the neighborhood's businesses. Drugs meant a lengthy struggle — or death — for some drug users. Gangs fighting for territory brought fear and violence. East Harlem seemed to coming apart during this period. East Harlem was without a progressive spokesperson to advocate for the neighborhood. Marcantonio's defeat in 1950 had left the neighborhood without a leader, and his successor, James Donovan, practically ignored the neighborhood's needs. He was defeated in 1956 by Alfred Santangelo, who took a more active role in his congressional district than his predecessor had. But without the Democratic Party's assistance with its access to jobs and other city services, many East Harlemites were left in a vacuum.[53]

Social workers and the clergy filled the void during the post–Marcantonio era. Union Settlement and Haarlem House (later La Guardia Memorial House) were staffed with professionals, and some of these multi-service organizations in East Harlem served the neighborhood as Marcantonio's office once did. Another agency that served the neighborhood was the East Harlem Council, composed of community leaders, civic organizations and social workers. But many members of these organizations lived outside East Harlem.[54] The East Harlem Protestant Parish (EHPP) was an exception, as its members lived in the neighborhood while advocating for the rights of East Harlemites.

The East Harlem Protestant Parish attempted to deal with the situation that existed and for this reason its efforts and accomplishments are worthy of praise and acknowledgment. Its story began during the winter of 1948. Don Benedict and Bill Webber, both World War II veterans and seminary students at New York's Union Theological Seminary, convinced the Federal Council of Churches to experiment with an eighteen-month program. It allocated $10,200 to help with this experiment.[55] Bill Webber explains.

The East Harlem Protestant Parish started in 1948 and one of my colleagues, Don Benedict, insisted he wasn't going to work with a fancy church. We discovered East Harlem in the beginning of our fall senior year and Don dragged me over to the neighborhood. And both of us wrote a proposal for a storefront parish church in East Harlem. When I graduated from the seminary in June of 1948, four denominations raised enough money for the both of us to come to East Harlem.

Not long afterwards the New York City Mission Society allocated money for both men to survey East Harlem's churches. When they arrived in the neighborhood, they saw one of the most densely populated blocks in the city.[56]

Bill Webber: *Don Benedict, who lived in the union seminary, and I jumped in our truck and drove to First Avenue. When we arrived on 100th Street the place looked like a riot, for the block was packed with people. We got out and walked down the block from First to Second Avenue. And it was so crowded and that block was full of tenements and old coal bins. The residents were mostly African American and Puerto Rican and there was a synagogue there and a number of Italians, but soon they moved out. Some Italians were entrepreneurs and there were several businesses on 100th Street: the barber, the wine dealer, shoemaker and a pizza parlor. Don and I wanted to familiarize ourselves with the community. But the Mission Society said since you don't know the neighborhood, why don't you visit the churches, and we spent a couple of months visiting every church from 96th to 106th Streets. We saw the storefront churches, Catholic churches, and the Greek Orthodox Church next to the 103rd Street subway to get acquainted with the neighborhood.*

Shortly thereafter Benedict and Webber were ordained in a black church in nearby Harlem. Archie Hargraves, also an ordained minister and war veteran, became the third person to pilot this program. The three ministers did not open their churches right away as Webber split his time between East

6. 1950s — Three Strikes 137

Harlem and his position as Assistant Dean of Students at Union Theological Seminary until the early 1950s, when he moved into the George Washington Houses. But Benedict and Hargraves devoted their energies to the Protestant Parish.[57]

On a sweltering day in August, Hargraves, Benedict and Webber parked their truck in front of a one-story building that once served as a butcher shop on 102nd Street and Third Avenue. Their goal was to remodel the abandoned ground floor and turn it into a storefront church. But refuse from an adjacent tenement flooded the basement and damaged the building's structure. After prying the floorboards from the ground, they found that a foul stench of old sauerkraut enveloped the room. The putrid smell repelled the ministers back into the street. The trio tried to get the Sanitation Department to deal with the situation, but no help was forthcoming so they carted the odious waste and dumped it into the East River. After discarding the waste, the trio attracted the attention of the neighborhood's inquisitive youth. The youngsters responded by helping them with the excavation. And by nightfall the former butcher shop resembled a house of worship.[58] Bill Webber found another storefront church at 331 East 100th Street, but this acquisition was temporary, and by December, the East Harlem Protestant Parish moved into another storefront directly across the street at building number 322.[59] Finding the church was one thing, but finding acceptance was another problem as the trio discovered they were not well received by the community. They remained on the sidelines while the neighborhood waited for them to make their move. But if they were going work in East Harlem they had to make a real effort.

Bill Webber: *We came here and the children flocked to us out of curiosity, but we didn't have much of an impact. We asked "Why are we not communicating better?" We paid a research anthropologist to help us develop a better communication within the neighborhood. A month later the researcher said, "I know why this isn't working, you guys are a bunch of phonies. The great middle-class group of white saviors, out to help these poor broken-down people. And you three people are standing on the banks of East Harlem, safe and secure, throwing life jackets to these drowning people. Until you jump in and become the drowning person with the others and help find the meaning of life nothing will happen." And East Harlem became our home and we moved in.*

Moving into the neighborhood improved the relationship between the residents and the parish, but more effort was needed to win the neighborhood over. Many East Harlemites viewed anyone who helped them deal with their problems as their friend. At that time, this friend was Congressman Vito Marcantonio, who effectively dealt with his constituents' issues.[60] The parish ministers needed to emulate the services that Marcantonio's office provided if they were going to be successful, and this meant a victory was needed to build some trust between the parish ministers and the neighborhood. During the winter of 1949, an East Harlem landlord saved money on his fuel costs while his tenants were shivering from the brutal cold weather. When the tenants protested against this treatment, the landlord threatened them with eviction. The EHPP expressed its concern with the problem and Benedict encouraged the tenants to purchase a pocket thermostat in order to monitor the temperature throughout the building. For a whole day, the tenants kept an hour-by-hour report demonstrating that they were without heat. Afterwards the tenants turned in their findings to the city's housing official and their efforts paid off when the landlord was hauled into court, fined and threatened with jail if he continued to operate the building without heat. This episode proved that the ministers were able to back their words with action and gave the EHPP a reputation for social action.[61]

Another EHPP episode involved a fight against garbage. When the Rev. Norman C. Eddy, another World War II veteran, first arrived in the neighborhood in 1949, he jumped into the fray in East Harlem. Known for his work in the community, the Reverend Eddy, a retired minister, still continues to counsel many former acquaintances and associates who call him for guidance or prayer, a practice Norm established when he lived with his wife, the Rev. Peg Eddy, and their three children on 100th Street. Norm Eddy remembers when he arrived in East Harlem:

I heard of this experimental parish in East Harlem which, according to Benedict, Webber and Hargraves, the parish was a socially motivated and active church. I came over to East Harlem and volunteered once a week to see if I belonged here. And I was so moved by the people I met on 100th Street and by the work of the residents that I thought I should move to East Harlem. Back then I was at the Union Theological Seminary on 123rd Street and you were expected to do field work. I came to East Harlem spiritually searching for the right place to do God's will and be with the people. And try to make some changes in society. My wife Peg arrived in East Harlem earlier as an intern and she was already doing her own field work when I met her. Peg had been on her own spiritual search and we found we had a lot in common. She was then a fellow student and we hit it off and we got married here in East Harlem in 1950 and we lived on 100th Street for the next twenty years.

After he arrived, Eddy noticed how some tenants customarily dealt with their garbage by simply tossing it out of their apartment windows. This disposal method was convenient for the tenants who lived in the building, but was hazardous for everyone else in the neighborhood as a nearby lot became a garbage dump. Norm concentrated on cleaning both the block and lot with the aid of five church attendees, and everyone picked up a large broom and commenced to sweep up the block. The block's other residents joined the effort and the band of merry East Harlemites with broom in hand marched up to 100th Street to beat of their own anthem which was modeled after "Roll Out the Barrel." "Sweep, sweep East Harlem we've got dirt on the run Sweep, Sweep East Harlem Our job has just now begun Stop air mail garbage Because it fouls the air Now's time to use the ashcans Because that's why they're there."[62]

This time the sanitation department aided EHPP by providing large garbage cans, and also watered the street, which put the finishing touch on a successful day. After cleaning the block, several adolescents banded together and called themselves the Puritans. This new group continued the cleaning party by clearing a nearby lot. It was cleaned by the evening. And the EHPP held communion on the site, which later served as a community playground.[63] Norm and Peg both became pastors of the 100th Street church in June 1951 after Archie Hargraves left the church and moved to Chicago, Illinois, to head a similar program in the Windy City.[64] The EHPP opened its second church, called the church of the Son of Man, on 227 East 104th Street, and a third church, called the church of the Redeemer, located at 324 East 102nd Street between First and Second Avenues. The EHPP opened its final church, called the church of the Ascension, located on 340 East 106th Street. Originally it was the Old Italian Waldensian Church, once pastored by socialist Norman Thomas.[65]

The EHPP went beyond East Harlem when the organization procured parish Acres, a family retreat and vacation center located in Putnam Valley, New York. This retreat also served as a camp, conference place and retreat. This allowed the ministers, their families and members of the EHPP a place to relax and meditate.[66] The EHPP did more than establish churches. For example, it acquired a former synagogue on 100th Street and converted it into a multipurpose family center. In 1953, Dr. Beatrice Berlee, aided by several part-time doctors, nurses and two EHPP staff members, worked at the family health center at 311 East 100th Street.[67]

Another fundamental ingredient of the East Harlem Protestant Parish was the Group Ministry. Originally composed of the three ministers and their wives, at its zenith the Group Ministry grew to eighteen members and included different sects: Episcopalians, Methodists, Mennonites and Presbyterians. The Group Ministry was instrumental in mapping a strategy to deal with the problems in the East Harlem neighborhood. Each person derived strength from the Group Ministry. Aware of their gifts, talents and frailties, the members realized perfection wasn't obligatory, for in the EHPP they were free to learn and mature as God's servants. The group dealt with the neighborhood's problems through four disciplines. The first discipline was devotional, as each person prayed daily and read the Bible. The second discipline was economic, which allowed each minister's family to receive compensation based on financial need rather than their professional experience.

Also, all royalties generated from speeches went directly into a fund which paid for the parish's expenses. The third discipline was vocational, which mandated each member to spread the gospel in the neighborhood. Also, monthly constructive criticism was conferred upon by each member of the Group Ministry. The fourth discipline was political as the Group Ministry became involved in the social and political fabric of the East Harlem neighborhood. Don Benedict took this example and ran for the New York City Council. But more importantly, they committed themselves to stay in East Harlem for the foreseeable future. However, if the spirit took them in another direction, these ministers followed their heart. Benedict left East Harlem to pilot a similar program in Cleveland, Ohio.[68] Benedict's work was instrumental, but the EHPP was able to continue with the groundwork he contributed during the organization's early years. By now the EHPP had established a name for itself, but it refused to rest on its laurels. It looked for new challenges.

One night sixteen participants met at the parish church and the group engaged in a straightforward two-hour discussion. The first hour dealt with topics that ranged from sex to raising children to feelings about their parents. The second hour dealt with the group's monetary situation and it was this meeting that led to the formation of the Christian Economics Group. The following year the group expanded the idea to start a credit union.[69]

Ray Rodriguez: *We were trying to increase the economy of Puerto Ricans and Blacks and in the process better the neighborhood. Most residents were poor and we talked and we decided to start our own credit union and we met at Norm Eddy's house to discuss strategy. After two years of planning, the group felt it was ready to approach New York State and we contacted the New York State Credit League. This led to a meeting with Sidney Blitz and though we didn't get New York state certification we got the federal certification. The group became the first federal credit union in New York City and [New York] State. The name was the East Harlem Protestant Parish Federal Credit Union [EHPPFCU]. It was located between 105 and 106th Streets at 2050 Second Avenue. Johnny Sabatel was president and Norm was vice president. And after the group received its certification, we formulated questions [like] "what would you do with the money?" To receive a loan, each applicant filled out a form and the committee would meet and most of the time we approved the applicants. More people joined and by the first year we had twenty-three members. And the membership grew and 160–170 people took out loans the next year. We lasted twenty-eight years [1956–1984] until we merged with the Union Settlement Credit Union.*

One of the first loans the group approved was to an unemployed widow hampered by sickness and in debt with three children. A member of the Board of Directors' Credit Union sponsored her, as a friend rather than a loan collector. It was soon discovered that the interest on her debts prevented her from settling her accounts. With a sizable but manageable loan from the credit union, she was able to settle all her debts and pay back the money loaned to her from the union at a moderately reduced rate of interest. The credit union became an instrument to help other East Harlemites manage their finances as well.[70]

But more work was still in order and the EHPP met the challenge. Norm was appalled by the drug situation and its hold on the community. He, like other East Harlemites saw the damage that drug abuse did to these drug addicts. To confront this problem, EHPP would have to meet this situation head on. But the church, which had confronted garbage, housing and financial problems faced a situation without an easy solution. This problem required patience, resilience, prayers and hope. Something had to be done, and Louis "Pee-Wee" Leon was determined to do something.

Pee-Wee Leon lived on 100th Street and attended one of the EHPP churches. One day Leon walked down 100th Street where he met several addicts high on drugs. He became a confidant to many teenage drug addicts by conversing with them on the street. Though he couldn't offer much else

Former congressman Herman Badillo, seen here at the Three Kings Day parade (Los Tres Reyes de Magos). Mr. Badillo, a Puerto Rican, along with Jacqueline Foster, an African American, challenged the Democratic leadership in East Harlem during the early 1960s. This effort was successful and helped minorities win elected office in East Harlem.

to these addicts, they saw a friend who was sincerely interested in them. Pee-Wee Leon counseled the addicts who were willing to seek help.[71] Drug addicts under the age of twenty-one could only seek help at the Riverside Hospital on North Brother Island, but this facility only had one hundred and fifty beds and many addicts chose not to enroll here for enrollment meant jail. Even worse was the fact that New York State hospitals would only treat drug addicts over twenty-one.

Norman C. Eddy: *If you wanted to get clean, you went to court and pled guilty to a misdemeanor. The understanding judge could commit you to ... Rikers Island for a month to kick cold turkey because incarceration deprived you of the streets. The EHPP Narcotics Committee was started by Pee-Wee Leon, and when I was his minister one day he said, "Norm, we got to do something." ... East Harlem on 100th Street, like many other parts of East Harlem, had its share of heroin addicts. And we put together these meetings every Thursday for eight months and people were able obtain their vouchers to go to Kentucky and get clean. The Narcotics Ward at Metropolitan Hospital opened thanks to the work of the EHPP Narcotics Committee.*

Forty-five people attended the first meeting of the narcotics committee, and by year's end over 500 drug addicts were serviced there. Relatives of drug addicts, concerned citizens and a few ex-addicts attended as well. Norm dove head on into the struggle as he tutored himself by reading information on drugs and served as a liaison with the staff of the EHPP Parish Medical Center. Norm furthered his education by researching the effects of drugs on people. Finally, he forged alliances and conversed with doctors and patients in hospitals and officials in the legal and legislative communities.[72]

These meetings culminated in a medical group which provided drug-users with information on how they could obtain assistance at the city's limited, but accessible hospital centers. A neighborhood doctor was also on hand and demonstrated how drug addicts could obtain treatment while they lived in their own home. As Norm stated, Thursday night education seminars catered to drug addicts, ex-drug addicts and their associates. Professionals gave talks about drugs and how to combat the drug situation. Religious services were held at the center or at the church's upstate farmhouse, conducted by the clergy and several church members, some of whom were ex-drug users themselves. Some drug addicts sought treatment from these programs and successfully broke free of their addiction, while other drug addicts fell back into the cycle of dependency. But even with this effort, more work was needed to combat the problem, because in the three years since the East Harlem narcotics committee was founded only a few individuals out of the hundreds that passed through the doors of the EHPP medical clinic refrained from using drugs.[73]

But the narcotics committee kept up the battle and they concentrated on the next step with the medical community. Most doctors customarily refused to treat drug addicts and those doctors that offered treatment charged exorbitant fees. Also, the city wasted millions of dollars on incarceration. In short, though it was against the law to purchase drugs, there was no help for these addicts. The Narcotics Committee appealed to Mayor Robert F. Wagner to see if the city could do something. But all forms of communication — letters, telephone calls and telegrams to Mayor Wagner — were ignored.[74] Undaunted, the narcotics committee forged on. In early 1959, 200 marchers led protests in front of the city's hospitals and City Hall. The group kept up the pressure and soon they garnered support from forty of the city's prominent churches.

The narcotics Committee tried again to contact Mayor Wagner with respect to this issue, and this time the correspondence was buoyed by the support of the major national spokespersons in labor, politics, religion and medicine. The strategy paid off and soon the narcotics committee had an audience with Mayor Warner. The mayor responded by directing Metropolitan Hospital to set aside a fifty-five-bed research unit and a twenty-five-bed ward for drug-addicted men. This was certainly a start, but the narcotics committee knew that it was not enough, for there were 25,000 addicts statewide. More funding was needed to help these addicts receive treatment. Through the committee's efforts, a task force on drugs was created. It received further assistance from the state legislature, which appropriated $300,000 for the task force.[75] Two years later the EHPP Narcotics Committee received a grant from the Doris Duke Foundation and opened an office on 306 East 103rd Street. By the early 1960s the narcotics committee had procured an abandoned tenement that eventually became Exodus House.

Our last story associated with the East Harlem Protestant Parish is the East Harlem Tutorial Program (EHTP).[76]

The ETTP recently celebrated its golden anniversary and the organization can be proud of its achievements. Many alumni have gone on to become successful professionals, including United States Congressman Gregory Meeks. Dozens of artists from the literary, music and entertainment worlds and many corporations and benefactors from business and finance have donated their time to this worthwhile cause. It's a far cry from when the program first began in Bill and Helen Webber's living room apartment in 1958.[77] The Webbers explain the origin of the East Harlem Tutorial Program.

Bill Webber: *My wife had a little reading program in our living room for children after school on Saturdays which became the East Harlem Tutorial Program.*
Helen "Dibby" Webber: *It occurred to me there was a discrepancy that the students were receiving in education and this was ghastly. When I first moved*

to East Harlem and went into the children's homes there was hardly any books to read, maybe there were some newspapers. And I noticed that the neighbors' children in the Washington Houses liked to come and play at my apartment and once they saw our books they became curious about them. I think that's why I started the East Harlem Tutorial Program. Because I saw that the kids were really excited about books and having somebody read to them. But this was too small an operation, and we moved to the parish office on 2050 Second Avenue and they provided a place to store several bookshelves.

We were open two days a week and the children came and did their homework and borrowed a book. If they wanted help for their homework we provided that as well. The children began to receive tutoring and my idea was that it should be one-on-one to give undivided attention. We were able to recruit people from the churches and in the suburbs to provide one-on-one tutoring to the children. The East Harlem Protestant Parish was supported by many patrons in Westchester [County], and I guess they felt guilty that they had left the city. Nevertheless, their children enjoyed coming and tutoring our students. Some of the tutors studied at Dalton [a prestigious private school] and though some of the suburban parents were uncomfortable with sending their children to East Harlem, but their children continued to come to the neighborhood. At 2050 the Second Avenue parish ministers had their offices there and at one time they operated a narcotics [education] program and other social education programs. But the East Harlem Tutorial Program kept growing and finally took over the building.

Helen Webber had established a successful program, and she furthered her education, which served her and the program well.

I couldn't take on everything because it was impossible with the amount of people and I needed some extra staff. Also, I needed to some more training and since I was an English lit major, and I obtained my master's degree at Columbia and studied an urban education program at Yeshiva University, I took a lot of courses and got some advice about starting the tutorial program and what kind of materials and research I needed. There was so much to discover, for it was more than a program for children to borrow books and do homework. And the children needed to learn how to read, so they wouldn't fall behind in their school's reading level. The tutoring program taught basic math and how to write and we developed quite a few resources with the help of other educators. The mothers were also a big help, but the program that exists today took ten years to implement. It began when the tutorial program recruited an educator named Faye Edwards, who became a top-notch director, and she loved the children and was very outgoing. She remained with the program until the early 1970s. And other important assistance came from Mary Lindsey, who gave out scholarships to our children to advance their education, and many children [who] enrolled in the program went to college.

Today the East Harlem Tutorial Program operates sixteen successful programs such as the After-School Tutorial, Media/Technology Education, Social Work Services/Family Support and Parent Programs.

Helen Webber: *We now have a wide variety of programs for the children. Also, a social worker is on hand to work with the families and the organization is very successful at fund-raising for different programs. Carmen Vega [its former director] really developed a board that is very well motivated for fund-raising.*

By 1958, under the direction of the EHPP the office at 2050 Second Avenue operated many services: credit union, legal services, employment program and the tutorial program.[78] In 1963, for a lack of funds to pay his salary, the EHPP Group Ministry terminated the Reverend Eddy's services. However, during that decade Norman Eddy and the New York Mission Society helped Ramon Diaz start the Family Problem Clinic. Eddy also worked with several churches to start the Cooperating Christian Service, which became the church of the Resurrection and began holding its services inside the old Union Settlement auditorium on East 104th Street before moving to the church of the Ascension. Six years later, the church of the Resurrection welcomed its new home on 325 East 101st Street. The EHPP continued for nearly twenty years until 1982, when it ceased operation.

Bill Webber: *The churches were strong and each church was able to function independently. The churches would not be a missionary church and each one continued to run their own denomination. Now each church has its own board of directors and Norm remained in East Harlem and continued his ministry separately from the EHPP and I also continue to live here.*

The Rev. Norman C. Eddy still resides in East Harlem. The apartment in which Eddy and his family lived in East Harlem was demolished by the city in 1970. Bill and Helen Webber recently moved to New Jersey. Many of the offices and organizations have faded away with time, but the East Harlem Tutorial Program is still running strong as a lasting legacy to the East Harlem Protestant Parish. Sadly, the Rev. George Calvert, who arrived in East Harlem in 1953 and became a staff member of the EHPP, passed away in July 2005. Calvert established the church of the Living Hope and Hope Community during the 1960s. Since its founding in 1968, Hope Community has become one of the foremost housing organizations in East Harlem, renovating over 1300 apartments.[79]

7
1960s — Decade of Change

In this chapter, East Harlemites recall the events and people of the 1960s as John F. Kennedy, Martin Luther King, Jr., the Real Great Society and Vietnam became household names. And in East Harlem the 1960s practically began and ended on Lexington Avenue with Camelot on the Lucky Corner (116th Street) and ending with the Young Lords on 111th Street.

During the 1950s Italian East Harlem decreased significantly. The majority of East Harlem's electorate was now Puerto Ricans and African Americans. Both groups routinely voted for the Democrats; however, the Democratic Party moved slowly to embrace either group especially for elected office. The lone exception was Tony Mendez, who won a local race and became the first Puerto Rican district leader in New York City. Mendez' win was aided by the local Democratic Tammany boss Carmine DeSapio. Mendez' fealty was to the Democratic Party, so he supported the incumbent, City Councilman John Merli, an Italian East Harlemite, over the Puerto Rican candidate who vied for the same seat.[1]

The Democratic Party supported J. Lopez Ramos for the State Assembly in 1958; however, East Harlem's elected officials were still not Puerto Rican or African American. Today Herman Badillo, a Republican and a member of the Manhattan Institute think tank, has garnered nationwide attention for his book, *One Nation, One Standard*. But back in 1960 Badillo was a Democrat and with the help of Jacqueline Foster, an African American, both challenged the Democratic machine in East Harlem.

Herman Badillo was an orphan when he arrived from Puerto Rico in East Harlem with his aunt at age 11. He first settled on 104th Street between Lexington and Park Avenue. He briefly lived in Chicago and California before he returned to New York City to live with his uncle. Like many new Puerto Rican migrants Badillo couldn't speak English, but through hard work he mastered the language and graduated from City College and Brooklyn Law School and later became a certified public accountant. Badillo first learned politics from Tony Mendez, whose clubhouse was headquartered at 116th Street and Lexington Avenue: the Lucky Corner. It was here where Badillo met a future president.[2]

Herman Badillo: *In 1960, I was appointed by then Senator John F. Kennedy to run his presidential campaign [office] in East Harlem, at 2007 Third Avenue. Senator Kennedy came to East Harlem and spoke on the Lucky Corner, but the biggest hit was not for John Kennedy because it was for his wife, Jackie Kennedy, who spoke Spanish to the crowd. I registered many black and Latino voters and it was the largest increase in New York State which helped him win the presidency. During the Kennedy registration drive, no one ever heard my name and because I'm six foot one and slim, many people thought I was Italian. And I remember this Italian guy walks up to me and says, "you never seen all of the garbage that's coming to register." I said, "What do you mean, garbage?" The guy said, "... This fellow Badillo keeps bringing these blacks and Puerto Ricans to register and we gotta stop him." I said, "So what are we gonna do?" The guy says, "Well, the school is supposed to be open until 10:30 P.M., but I'm gonna close the school at 9:00 P.M., because that's when we get a big line and the blacks and Puerto Ricans wouldn't be able to register." And I replied, "Good idea." At 9:00 P.M. I stood outside with a pad and pencil, and sure enough they closed the school when there was a long line of blacks and Latinos waiting to register." I took down their names and I got the affidavits of fourteen Puerto Ricans and I brought a lawsuit and I established the fact that the voters had been on line and they were not allowed to register. Eventually they were registered by the board of elections and it was the first time that anyone established proof of voter discrimination against blacks and Puerto Ricans in New York City. And this is supposed to be a liberal city. But this action garnered me some notoriety in New York City, and even after Kennedy won the election, there was still more work to do.*

I ran for district leader against Alfred Santangelo, then the congressman who also served as a district leader. Back then, every politician in East Harlem was Italian. The congressman was Alfred Santangelo, the assemblyman was Frank Rossetti and the city councilman was John Merli. This was ironic because by then East Harlem was mostly black and Latino. I ran for district leader with a black woman, Jacqueline Foster, as my co-leader and it was a very tough battle because no one had run against Santangelo before and there were death threats. I lost by 110 votes, but I went to court and proved that 175 people were ineligible to vote because they moved out of the district a long time ago.

A new election was ordered, but since I was appointed housing commissioner by Mayor Robert F. Wagner, I couldn't accept the district leadership position because of the Hatch Act. This law prevented a commissioner who administered federal funds to simultaneously run for political office. Joe Arazo, another Puerto Rican, took my place. But this started the movement of blacks and Latinos in their bid to win control of the elected positions in East Harlem.

Afterwards, several Puerto Ricans won district leaderships and were elected to office in East Harlem. Carlos Rios became a district leader and later was elected to the state legislature. Councilman John Merli was defeated in 1961 and Santangelo's seat was redistricted out of the neighborhood the following year. Frank Rossetti served many nonconsecutive terms in the assembly until he retired in the early 1970s. Though Puerto Ricans won several local elective offices, but by the mid-1960s, the Commonwealth of Puerto Rico still remained the de facto spokesperson for many Puerto Ricans. Herman Badillo moved on to the Bronx and was elected to the Bronx borough presidency in 1965, but he voiced his disenchantment that Mayor John V. Lindsay still conferred with the Commonwealth Office rather than the city's Puerto Rican elected officials.[3] Still Badillo and Foster's efforts were successful in changing the political dynamics in East Harlem.

The next story is one of inspiration. Antonia Pantoja "Toni" was an advocate who was instrumental in helping Latino youth to develop their talents and abilities. Israeli prime minister Golda Meir once said, "If I am not for myself, who will be for me?" The same mantra could be said of Antonia Pantoja, whose mantra was "I am me and my circumstances." Manny Diaz, Jr., called her one of the ten most brilliant Puerto Ricans and a real motivator. Her memory lives on through the thousands of Puerto Ricans and Latinos who have benefited from Aspira. According to filmmaker Lillian Jimenez, who produced a documentary on Antonia Pantoja, East Harlem played a role in Pantoja's remarkable journey.[4]

Pantoja was born on September 13, 1921, in Puerta de Tierra, a poor section of old San Juan City. Shortly after Antonia's birth, her parents separated and the family moved to another neighborhood named Barrio Obrero, on Calle 14 [14th Street].[5] There she lived comfortably with her grandparents, but after her grandfather's death, the family's financial situation worsened. Plunged into poverty, Pantoja's family struggled to survive. To make matters worse, during her adolescence Pantoja was diagnosed with tuberculosis and spent three months convalescing in a sanitarium to regain her strength. She managed to graduate from high school and, following a reunification with her mother, Pantoja attended the University of Puerto Rico. However, she left school before a diploma was conferred upon her. She eventually earned her school certificate from Puerto Rico. Pantoja challenged herself by attending college during the day and worked part time to earn her bachelor's degree.[6] After her graduation, Pantoja moved to New York City with her childhood friend Carmen Laguna. In the city, she worked at several jobs before arriving in East Harlem to find employment with a local neighborhood community center on 110th Street while attending Hunter College to pursue her master's degree.

At Hunter College, she met Maggie Miranda, a fellow Puerto Rican, in her sociology class. Miranda introduced Pantoja to several other Puerto Rican students who banded together, and before long this group met in Pantoja's apartment. When her apartment became too small, the group convened at the Good Neighbor Community Center in East Harlem on 106th Street. Pantoja noticed how the city's Puerto Rican community received negative treatment in the press and wanted to so something about this. What a better place than to start with the group from Hunter College, but there were several differences[7] between Pantoja and the other group members. Whereas Pantoja was a seasoned student who was island born, in contrast the other group members were raised in the city. Yolanda Sanchez, the present director of the Puerto Rican Association for Community Affairs (PRACA), is a former associate of Pantoja and remembers the contrast between Pantoja and the group.

Toni was ten years older and there is a difference also, Toni was "the most Puerto Rican," because she had grown in up Puerto Rico to adulthood and the rest of us were either born here or came to New York from Puerto Rico as a child. And everyone in that group who was ten years older than me, I looked up to.

The staff from the Office of the Commonwealth of Puerto Rico and Puerto Ricans unaffiliated with any organization joined with Pantoja and increased the group's membership. This new membership made several important conclusions regarding the city's Puerto Ricans. One obstacle was that many Puerto Rican migrants had a problem communicating in English, which was a barrier because without this communication Puerto Ricans were unable to use the city's services. Their solution was to inform the city government that Puerto Ricans were lacking these services and ask how the city could address these issues. The Commonwealth of Puerto Rico had helped many Puerto Ricans acclimate themselves to the United States, but in the group's view, this organization could not solve these problems. Finally, the group decided it was not just a Puerto Rican problem but the city's problem.[8]

Manny Diaz, Jr.: *Every community goes through a process of developing institutions, and back then the only "institution" Puerto Ricans had was the Commonwealth of Puerto Rico. But this office was affiliated with the governor of Puerto Rico to direct the agency in New York to inform Puerto Ricans about their labor rights. Mayor Robert Wagner routinely asked Joe Monseratt [the director of the Commonwealth office] what Puerto Ricans were feeling in East Harlem. But Toni Pantoja realized the Commonwealth Office was a diplomatic office that didn't involve itself in politics or support any position.*

Pantoja and the members had a different vision to deal with many problems Puerto Ricans confronted in the city. This vision included developing and training new leaders and new community groups. They hoped that these leaders and community groups would work with the people. As for Pantoja's group, shortly thereafter it formally became the Hispanic Young Adult Association (HYAA).[9] HYAA's first project was to assist a neighborhood church organization called La Mission de Rescate [Rescue Mission] to procure donations from businesses, churches and community leaders. HYAA continued working in East Harlem and conducted a voter registration drive and a Puerto Rican youth conference. By the mid–1950s, HYAA decided that the word *Hispanic* was too broad and chose to celebrate its Puerto Rican heritage by adopting a new name: the Puerto Rican Association for Community Affairs.[10]

Yolanda Sanchez: *When I came out of college I was 22 years old and I wanted to join a Puerto Rican group. PRACA had a different name before, as we were known as the Hispanic Young Adult Association, but we ... changed it to what it is today.*

For many years, PRACA has played a key role in Puerto Rican and Latino issues in New York City and the organization continues this practice today.

Yolanda Sanchez: *Out of PRACA came a series of things. One of them was Aspira and other organizations. PRACA to me has been the most consistently alive and active since the 1950s. It has always been very progressive, and PRACA was there in the forefront for change and it had an office which was well funded. And if any Puerto Rican or Latino group was beginning to organize in those days and wanted a place to meet PRACA offered that. The Hispanic AIDS Forum was the first group to look at AIDS and its relationship to the Latino community. PRACA allowed the group to meet in its facility and organize itself on PRACA resources. Another organization was APRED, the Association of Puerto Rican Executive Directors, which was the forerunner to the Hispanic Federation. And this was funded by the united Way of New York and this came out of PRACA and became the prototype for which came the Hispanic Federation. This group also used PRACA's resources and this is lost to history.*

After Pantoja earned a master's degree, she won a scholarship to the New York School of Social Work, the forerunner to the Columbia University School of Social Work.[11] Professionally, Pantoja earned the right to call herself a social worker, but she really viewed herself as a builder of institutions. She wanted to work with the Puerto Rican community and find answers to the problems that confronted Puerto Ricans.

Pantoja got her chance when she became a member of the New York City Commission on Intergroup Relations, headed by Dr. Frank Horne. The commission was established to combat problems in housing, schools, and employment, and improve police relations. Pantoja used this model and founded the Puerto Rican Hispanic Leadership Forum. (Later, the word *Hispanic* was dropped.) The PRLF fought for equality for Puerto Ricans and patterned itself after other racial and religious organizations which also fought for human rights.[12] In 1961, the PRLF served as the first board of directors of Aspira. The etymology of the name Aspira derived from *aspire*. Aspira concentrated on building young leaders for the future. While in East Harlem, Pantoja's idea to form a youth club resulted from her association with a high school dropout. With her encouragement, he enrolled in night classes and earned his diploma. This success spurred her to form the youth club. Pantoja noticed how other ethnic groups developed their youth programs and with this in mind, she insisted that the youth club provide more than just social services.

However, she met resistance from several organizations that bypassed her project. However, Pantoja received backing from her old friend Dr. Horne, who agreed that Aspira would not be a referral center, but one that would uplift Puerto Rican youth through leadership training and help them select a profession that would enable them to provide for themselves and become community leaders. Also, within each club, young people would learn about their heritage and culture. The idea was that these adolescents would join a constructive organization as opposed to becoming involved in street gangs.[13] But who would head the organization?

At that time, Pantoja was ensconced in a comfortable position with the commission. But it was decided that there was only one person who could become Aspira's first chairperson: Antonia Pantoja. This decision was not easy, because she had never directed an organization. Undaunted, Pantoja ventured into schools, churches, the streets and anywhere adolescents could be found. But piloting Aspira became a challenge she never expected, and despite pouring her energies into Aspira there were problems. Infighting hampered the organization from the start and Aspira received torrents of abuse in the form of racist letters and audio recordings, and was threatened with violence whenever the organization applied for grant monies.

Aspira also faced opposition from the Board of Education which was against Aspira's attempt to organize Aspira clubs on school premises. Pantoja pressed on and eventually succeeded, and Aspira clubs existed in many New York City schools.[14] José Carrero was one of those adolescents who joined Aspira. Born in Brooklyn, New York, Carrero once worked with the New York City Economic Development Corporation as the market manager at La Marqueta in East Harlem. Carrero is also a community activist. He first arrived in the neighborhood during the late 1960s when he attended political education classes taught by the Young Lords, shortly after he had became an Apirante or member of Aspira. Here Carrero explains Aspira's mission and its impact on Latino students.

Aspira is a leadership program designed to develop leadership potential among Latinos and also promote educational tutoring and counseling. Aspira also assists

Hispanics and other minorities as they apply for college and focuses on adolescents that normally would have been pushed aside.

Carrero saw how important Aspira's was to his peers. He joined the organization, becoming part of a large family of Aspirantes.

José Carrero: *A friend of mine who attended Catholic school had joined Aspira's Brooklyn club and told me that Aspira was a great place. We were young teenagers and we were always looking to meet girls and this caught my attention. And I said, "I am going to check this out." At that time, Aviation High School, where I attended, did not have an Aspira club, but we joined the Brooklyn club which was established for students from different high schools who didn't have their own clubs. We met teenagers from many other Aspira clubs and we became part of the Aspira Federation.*

Early on Aspira thought of establishing a federation. These were Aspira clubs in the Bronx, Brooklyn and Manhattan, and if needed Aspira's central office was on hand to help prospective Aspirantes who did not attend school or whose school didn't have enough interest to form an Aspira club. Aspira clubs expanded to other large cities, such as Philadelphia and Chicago, and to other states with a Puerto Rican/Latino population.[15]

José Carrero: *Many Aspira clubs are located in the city's public schools, and to help the Aspirante a school counselor is assigned to the each Aspira club. An Aspirante will report their progress to the Aspira Club Federation, which is a citywide organization composed of the chairs and the executive committee of each club. That was the larger federation and those members held citywide meetings. At those meetings, members discussed citywide issues and for a teenager back then, this was pretty intense. But we also discussed educational issues such as studying in school and trying to enroll in college or look for scholarships to pay for college.*

By the end of the twentieth century, nearly forty years after it was created, Aspira clubs affected the lives of over 36,000 Puerto Rican and Latino youth.[16] Over the years Pantoja heard countless stories from former Aspirantes who entered the professional world and credited their success to Aspira. Antonia Pantoja's longtime collaborator and long-time partner, Dr. Wilhelmina Perry, recalls:

Antonia always kept in contact with Aspira and she would come in and do conferences and if one of the Aspira clubs were in a difficult situation they would call her. Time after time Aspirantes have talked about the opportunities that came through their association with Aspira. And many former Aspirantes have publicly acknowledged this. When we both traveled across the country, people would come up to us and say, "I am an Aspirante."

José Carrero concurs with Perry and credits his time with Aspira as very fruitful experience.

The leadership side of Aspira taught Aspirantes how to organize a group. And Aspira clubs also instructed us how to manage those organizations by building boards and corporations within the organizations. It also taught each Aspirante different skills such as organizing events, activities, parliamentary procedures, organizational structures and understanding the bylaws and regulations. It is not unusual to run into other Aspirantes today and many of them are in prominent positions like in the corporate sector, nonprofit institutions, or in the educational field and other institutions. Looking back on that period, Aspira was a fraternity that I had the privilege to belong to.

When Pantoja wasn't busy working to build institutions, she was still thinking of ways to improve the lives of Latinos. One day Pantoja was walking with her friend Alice Cardona when she noticed traffic signs were written only in English.

Pantoja envisioned a day when bilingual traffic signs would be a reality. Cardona retorted, "Yeah that will be the day."[17] Today, bilingual traffic signs are posted throughout many urban and suburban streets that contain a large Latino population.

After leading Aspira for five years Pantoja left the organization in the mid-1960s and was succeeded by Yolanda Sanchez. The fact Antonia Pantoja continued to work and challenge herself was not surprising. Many people who met her left with an indelible memory of a person who believed in people more than they believed in themselves.

José Carrero: *Antonia was an absolutely dynamic woman who was short, nonthreatening, but possessed a very strong presence. She was a woman who approached you and asked you to do things you have never dreamed of doing before. Just in her asking and in her mannerisms, this would make you feel totally empowered to do anything and wouldn't give a second thought about it. She was always positive with the people whom she dealt with, and this was manifested in everyone who was influenced by her. You couldn't refuse Antonia when she said you can do it, and you felt so good that you "could" do it. Antonia had the utmost confidence in all Aspirantes, which made you feel anything was possible.*

Dr. Wilhelmina Perry: *Antonia was a humble person who was also down to earth and she loved young people and that helped her to keep in touch with reality. She'd go to the White House, but she could talk to the farmer in the backyard and she identified with the oppressed and poor people. Though Antonia gotten her education and received awards and honorary degrees, she would say, "So what?" The awards never fazed her. One time in Albany, New York, Antonia was given an award, which was the Medal of Excellence by the New York State Board of Regents. And amidst the public accolades she gave the medal back and said, "Until every child has the opportunity to receive a quality education, I cannot accept this, it has no meaning."*

Pantoja agreed to serve on the Bundy Blue Ribbon Panel by invitation from New York City Mayor John V. Lindsay. The panel was headed by McGeorge Bundy, who served in the National Security Council during the Kennedy administration. The panel's objective was the decentralization of the New York City public school system. For thirty-five years decentralization paved the way for more minority participation in public schools. In 2002, the New York State Legislature abolished the board of education and its functions, replacing it with the department of education under the direction of the mayor of the city of New York. Nevertheless, minorities participated in the democratic process regarding their children's future. Pantoja's efforts also led to the establishment of bilingual education in New York City's public schools.[18] Pantoja returned to Puerto Rico in the late 1960s, and a decade later she moved to San Diego where she founded the Graduate School for Community Development. In 1996, Pantoja became the first Puerto Rican woman to receive the Congressional Medal of Freedom from President Bill Clinton. Pantoja returned to Puerto Rico and completed her memoir — aptly titled *Memoir of a Visionary* — written shortly before her death in June 2002.[19]

In the mid-1960s, the assassinations of President John F. Kennedy and Malcolm X were a prelude to the violence many Americans soon witnessed on television. Kennedy's successor, Lyndon B. Johnson, expanded America's involvement in Vietnam, and soon the war's daily casualties became part of the evening news. Several months before Kennedy's demise in Dallas, Texas, Americans applauded the eloquence of Dr. Martin Luther King, Jr.'s *I Have a Dream Speech*. Gus and Marty Trowbridge were caught up in this spirit. At that time, Gus Trowbridge taught at the prestigious Dalton School, but he and his wife Marty yearned for something more.

Gus Trowbridge: *Marty and I were living on the Upper East Side and like other New Yorkers we needed a larger apartment. We didn't have much money and if we did we were not anxious to stay in a white neighborhood like Yorkville. The both of us decided to start a school which was the embodiment of the Civil Rights movement. The school's mission back then remains the same today because there is no racial majority. And it's the fulfillment of Dr. King's dream which is consistent with our social philosophy. We figured that we should find a place in the neighborhood that was conducive to the dream. And this led us to move to 1270 Fifth Avenue—a private cooperative on 109th Street and Fifth Avenue. Harry Belafonte's wife lived there and they were selling the apartment for three thousand dollars.*

By 1965, in a small office on the Upper East Side, Gus and Marty Trowbridge laid the groundwork for the school. A year later they were ready for incorporation as a nonprofit: they had a board of trustees, certification and money to hire faculty and establish classrooms. The Trowbridges were also aided by the generosity of Gus' mother and her friends. These benefactors were not always keen on integration, but they believed everyone should have a fair chance in life to receive a quality education.[20] Throughout this journey, the Trowbridges met and allied themselves with people who shared their vision for equality for all Americans. These allies were clergy, social and community workers, civil-rights leaders and academicians. Also, professionals from the education, legal and political worlds sponsored the school. The Trowbridges looked to East Harlem to enroll black and Latino youth in their school.[21]

Gus Trowbridge: *When we started the school we concentrated on gathering support from the East Harlem community, for most of the students would be people of color. The two of us searched arduously to identify people and organizations and raise money. That's when we met Norm Eddy, and with his help, the both of us visited the social agencies in the neighborhood. First, we went to the East Harlem Protestant Parish and met Bill Webber. Then we met the black and Hispanic parents at the parish and they were dubious of us because we didn't look like we fit in. But our address at 1270 Fifth Avenue and 109th Street was a plus. And there was a term called "legitimate local" and we qualified technically because we lived in East Harlem. Still there was the issue that we were not Black or Hispanic. And Marty and I were tested by the parishioners at the East Harlem Protestant Parish. They wanted to know our sincerity, but I didn't feel any resistance. We also went to the parish's board members and the neighborhood people, which helped our cause.*

Despite their perception as outsiders, the Trowbridges pressed on and they secured over $200,000 in grants from foundations and corporations. The Kettering Foundation donated $60,000 and gave an additional $50,000 several months later. With this largesse, the Trowbridges acquired property on 7 East 96th Street. The building was a four-story mansion built by architect Ogden Codman in 1912. Codman, who once serviced the likes of John D. Rockefeller, Cornelius Vanderbilt and Edith Wharton, had decided to move to Paris. The property passed through several hands, but by the mid–1960s it was empty. Gus's timing was perfect because the building was scheduled to be sold, but the Trowbridges convinced the real estate agents to postpone the sell.[22] More importantly, the mansion served as an ideal location for the school, for 96th Street divided East Harlem from the Upper East Side, and the school's students bridged the racial and cultural divide. The next step was to choose the school's name.

Gus Trowbridge: *I remember how we selected the school's name. There was an institution called the Downtown School and we wanted to name the school the Uptown School. But a black friend of mine said 96th Street is not uptown, and it is not because 96th Street is the dividing line. However, the country was part of the* vision emanated through our upstate farm. And Marty went to a school called the city and Country School, which still exists. But we liked the name so we called the school the Manhattan Country School and we opened the school in 1966. We raised enough money and the faculty was mostly from private schools. Some of the teachers came from the Dalton School and I stole some of their teachers. And those teachers were as inspired by the movement and the times to want to be a part of an experiment as I was.

For most administrators and teachers, the first day of school is always filled with apprehension and excitement. For the Trowbridges, the first day of school in 1966 was no different. But the Trowbridges met their goal of a racially mixed school.

Marty Trowbridge: *It was the probably the heaviest rainfall of the century, but we had sixty-six children and only one child absent. The percentage of students was integrated and divided equally and we had open enrollment. The number was thirty per cent black and thirty percent Puerto Rican and the rest of the enrollment was made of white students. But today minority enrollment is over fifty percent and we met our goals.*

Gus Trowbridge: *We had problems, one, were we going to succeed financially, and two, to have a racially balanced school. And we committed ourselves to an enormous scholarship program. I can remember going to meet the mailman every day and depositing whatever checks were in the mail to the bank. And we struggled during the beginning and sometimes there were close calls.*

On January 1, 1966, East Harlem joined other New Yorkers when several labor unions went on strike. The most notable strike was that of the New York City Transit Authority. It crippled the city. Later that year the Black Panthers were founded and the new militant cry of black power made its way to the educational institutions as well.

Gus Trowbridge: *There were relatively few problems in terms of racial resistance to the school. We had one bomb threat, which didn't materialize. One problem we didn't foresee was the Civil Rights movement changed in the late 1960s. Black Power became such a strong force, for instance Stokeley Carmichael (who later became Kwame Ture) took over for John Lewis at SNCC and it was no longer nonviolent and espoused a more militant approach.*

Despite the cries of black power and separateness, the Trowbridges remained committed proponents of a racially balanced institution. *Life* magazine took notice of this commitment when it featured the school in an article titled "Making Prejudice Impossible." Manhattan Country School held seminars on racial awareness and imposed a sliding-scale tuition system that allowed parents to pay for their child's education according to their financial capabilities. And half of the students, teachers and administration were people of color, but still racial problems occurred.

Marty Trowbridge: *The school was right to take the audience and the black parents felt that it was safe to vent their frustration here in our school. Because where else were they going to go and vent?*

And parents did vent. A committee of black parents proclaimed "Pluralism at the Manhattan Country School is an incredible hypocrisy."²³ Despite all efforts, the Manhattan Country School still had to deal with race.

Gus Trowbridge: *We had a lot of fighting in the school and some militant black parents accused me of being a hypocrite and the same thing with the Hispanics.*

The Trowbridges hoped that racism would be less concentrated at the school, but Gus acknowledged that racism as well as classism affected the families at the Manhattan Country School.

Gus Trowbridge: *Preston Wilcox, one of our founding trustees [an African American former social worker with Union Settlement] later had a falling out with us. But he said one thing I'll never forget: "Be careful, for one of the most difficult things you will have is integrating the Negro with the Negro." By that he meant integrating middle-class blacks with lower-class blacks, and this was true during the first couple of years.*

The Manhattan Country School survived through the overriding spirit of providing good education and adhering to the spirit of the Civil Rights movement. This enabled to the school to withstand misunderstandings, and strained relationships, and minimized distrust amongst colleagues. Two years after founding, the Manhattan Country School purchased an upstate farm through the Trowbridges' friend from the Dalton School. The Trowbridges envisioned a place where children learned about food, farming and working with textiles. Also, the upstate farm has served as a tranquil setting miles away from the rigors of New York City.²⁴

Throughout the school's tenure, the students have been taught by the finest teachers and educators. Children who have graduated from the Manhattan Country School have moved on and attended outstanding public and private high schools and colleges. The Trowbridges maintained the vision of Dr. King for racial equality on an international level. The Manhattan Country School sponsored a seminar which urged private schools to divest their holdings from Apartheid South Africa. This legal practice separated people and imposed first and second class citizenship based on color. Those institutions and countries that divested from South Africa paved the way for apartheid's abolition in the early 1990s.²⁵ In 1998 the Trowbridges passed the directorship of the school to Michèle Solá. Michèle first worked with the school as its Spanish teacher and eighth-grade advisor. Today, Solá reaffirms the school's commitment to racial equality and good education. I posed to Solá the question regarding East Harlem's changing demographics and how they affect the Manhattan Country School.

Michèle Solá: *My experience with the school was there has always been change and that was a part of what Gus wanted. Which is to prepare people for the idea that society is always changing and therefore you don't just create a school that is defined and doesn't change. You create a place where you are always being changed by the student that comes in and their family's histories. Also, by the teachers who come to teach at the school with their passionate interests and talents. The philosophy then speaks to the children. I have certainly felt this as an educator. What it says to us is that you can be part of making change in the world. And the hope is that what you go about changing are those things that you think are unjust. So you are not just arguing one reading program over another program, or which program is better, or which lunch menu is important. And you say, "Wait a minute, there's racism in the world, there is sexism, gender problems out there. Major issues that I can have a role in making things better."*

By the time the students enter the 8th grade, they haven't seen much in life. We want them to have an experience where they are prepared to do things I don't even know yet, because you expect the world to change.

Manhattan Country School's setting allows children to discover the world and to develop their minds.

Michèle Solá: *The mission of this school from the beginning was to be a private school with a public mission. The "private school" part of the mission means providing a good education. And the public mission is to say, "Wait a minute, we're not just a great enclave with perfections." We're not perfect in the first place, we are a laboratory for trying to understand what could be in public schools, and to train teachers to go out and work in public schools. Let me tell you about the difference between the Manhattan Country School and the public school. Well, giving a simplistic answer, you walk into one of our classrooms and you see eight or nine children with a teacher. In public schools you will enter a classroom and you will see twenty-five to thirty-five children.*

First, we don't have classrooms big enough to hold thirty-five students. But we're staffed with two adults for eighteen children. This is one area where public and private schools differ and we are a private school. The other major difference is the funding of public schools and private schools. The way public schools are funded, the Parent Teacher Association has to raise money for the computers, raise money for the art teacher. PTAs are wonderful but PTAs change from one year to the next. The PTA might decide the school should teach music and the next year it might be art. In a private school, the curriculums that start with the children's questions are not restricted by school standards, the curriculum aims for higher goals, more in-depth thinking, and helping students realize there are meaningful connections between what they are learning and the world we live in. *Private schools are planned for the long term. We ask, "What is our arts curriculum?" "What is our music curriculum?" And this should be part of every child's life, and lastly, you create a group of good teachers.*

By the mid–1960s, cultural pride permeated throughout many urban cities. As Gus Trowbridge stated, the Civil Rights movement became more militant. This militancy veered away from integration and advocated for separation. East Harlemites Bill and Helen Webber, and their son Tom, lived in the Washington and the Wilson Houses. This family was one of the few non–Italian whites to live East Harlem during this period.

Today, Tom still lives in the neighborhood. He teaches at Hunter College. In some ways he is a minority living in a minority neighborhood. The dichotomy of Tom Webber's life is recounted in his book: *Flying over 96th Street: Memoir of an East Harlem White Boy*. He and activist Dylcie Pagan recall the changes during the this mid–1960s.

Tom Webber: *I went to college in 1965, and before 1965 a black guy wanted to be around a white guy. But when I returned to the neighborhood in the late 1960s it was totally different. There was a black consciousness and black power and you saw the black power salute on the streets and people sold [the Black Muslim newspaper] Muhammad Speaks and I felt the racism. In the late 1960s, I worked for New York City, and I remember going to a Black Power meeting on 116th Street. I went to the rally with a black friend, but I was still separated from him and because I am white, I sat in the press section with other whites.*[26]

Dylcia Pagan: *I went to Puerto Rico for the first time after my grandfather died. When I came back I had to go to public school, but we couldn't find one. I was born on October 15th and you had to be 5.9 years of age, meaning five years and nine months by September. I tried to enroll at Commander John J. Shea, but I was unsuccessful. Later, I went to Cathedral High School and at the time the main building was on Fifty-Second Street, but I guess because we were minorities we went to the school's annex on 127th Street and Madison Avenue. It was called All Saints–Sisters of Charities. And it was the first time I ever saw black nuns, which I'd never seen before ... they dressed differently from the other nuns. This was wonderful to have black nuns be your teachers because it was a whole different environment. I had a wonderful English teacher, Sister Concepta, who always stuttered. And many years later, when I got involved in the community and the Civil Rights movement, I heard, "Duh, duh, Dylcie." She was wearing a dashiki and an Afro. I said, "Sister Concepta!" She replied, "I am no longer a sister." I said, "What about all of the [other] nuns?" She replied, "We don't exist anymore." And she too became involved in the Civil Rights movement.*[27]

Two events in 1967 marked East Harlem's triumph and tragedy. The neighborhood's triumph was the publication of Piri Thomas' book *Down*

These Mean Streets. The book told the struggles of a half Puerto Rican and half Cuban of African descent growing up in El Barrio. What is remarkable about Piri's book is its brutal honesty about race, sex, and love. Piri Thomas also figures prominently on the subject of black consciousness as a Latino of African descent. Thomas, like other great black Latinos such as Roberto Clemente, Pedro Albizu Campos, Arturo Alfonso Schomburg, Sammy Davis, Jr., and countless others, proudly embraced both their African and Latino identity.

Thomas' life experience is similar to that of Malcolm X, who also developed his life's mission while he was in prison. Piri has said that he became free in prison. Though his body was incarcerated, his mind was alive, and it was in prison that his soul expanded. Thomas' life shows that one should not be ashamed of the past but should embrace it and learn from it. Piri explains the genesis of his classic book.

Piri Thomas: *When I was in prison I would dream I was back in East Harlem. I remember one time I got a big, black book with a red cover. I would sit by myself in cell C513 and I would look out at the valley and me in a 6 by 8 by 9 cellblock and I said this could be Grand Central Station. But I said to myself this was too fuckin' small. It [jail] had my body, but it didn't have my mind and my spirit. I looked at the pavement and I said, "Pavement, I am going to tell you a story." and I named the book right there "Home Sweet Harlem," which eventually became* Down These Mean Streets. *The book's title origin was because we, the people, were of these mean streets. There was a very famous writer and the publisher gave him my manuscript. His name was John, and I forgot his last name, but I was bursting to write the book and he wrote these words of encouragement. "A man who himself is not mean, can walk down these streets," and I called the book* Down These Mean Streets.

Ironically, East Harlem's tragedy also took place in the streets. The Civil Rights Act and Voting Rights Act passed during the mid–1960s mandated civil liberties and made explicit the voting rights of minorities. But legislation alone did not erase years of injustice overnight and, coupled with a lack of employment, set the stage for trouble. Many Americans at this time vented their frustrations through rioting. In 1964, riots took place in Harlem and in Bedford-Stuyvesant, Brooklyn. The following year in the Watts neighborhood of Los Angeles, rioting began. They continued into 1967, first in Newark, New Jersey, and Detroit, Michigan, and by July the riots reached East Harlem.

It all began when two police officers were heading home after the end of their midnight shifts. But this routine shift became hectic when patrolman Anthony Cinquemani saw José Rodriguez hovering over another man. When Officer Cinquemani went to investigate, Rodriguez took out a knife and gestured at him. The officer told Rodriguez to put his knife down, but Rodriguez ignored his commands and Cinquemani responded by discharging his weapon, killing Rodriguez. Later, a crowd of East Harlemites descended upon 110th Street between Lexington and Third Avenue, and the unrest and frustration which had been building for months finally erupted. East Harlem rioted for three days. Debris rained from rooftops, two East Harlemites were dead, and businesses along Lexington and Third Avenues were destroyed. Not even the heavy police presence, or the appearances of Herman Badillo and Jose "Chequi" Torres, former light heavyweight boxing champion, calmed the rioters. The rioting ended when New York City was hit by a heavy deluge of rain for two days.[28]

The year 1968 with its maelstrom of violence defined the dark side of the 1960s. The year began and ended with the capture and release of the crew from the USS *Pueblo* off the coast of North Korea. In the spring two men were cut down in their prime of their lives: Dr. Martin Luther King, Jr., and Senator Robert F. Kennedy. A week before he was assassinated, Dr. King had visited a youth center in East Harlem,[29] and Senator Robert F. Kennedy visited the neighborhood several times, first in the early '60s while campaigning for his older brother, John F. Kennedy, and later when he represented New York as a United States senator.[30]

In late August, protests and rioting took place at the Democratic National Convention in Chicago, Illinois. The protestors vented their anger at President Johnson's administration which by 1968 had committed half a million American troops to Vietnam. By this year the war had claimed the lives of over 25,000 American soldiers.

The Tet Offensive, launched in January 1968 by the Viet Cong, convinced many Americans that the United States was losing the war. American forces actually repelled the attack from the North Vietnamese, but the psychological damage had been done. Many Americans now believed the United States was mired in a stalemate over Vietnam. Many black, white and Latino soldiers who fought in the Vietnam War came from places like East Harlem. Next we will read a firsthand account from a former East Harlemite who fought in the Vietnam War.

Clarence Davis, originally born in Henderson, North Carolina, lived in East Harlem at 208 East 98th Street as a child. He vividly recalls the bathroom in the kitchen and the outside toilet that was shared by all the tenants on the same floor. Davis' family, like many other East Harlemites, were relocated to public housing, and his family next lived in the Melrose Houses in Central Harlem. But Davis returned to East Harlem as a student at Benjamin Franklin High School, located on 115th Street and Pleasant Avenue. After graduating he served in the Vietnam War. Here Davis recalls being inducted into the United States Army.[31]

I was drafted in May of 1967 and back then when you a received a letter from the selective service, you felt the envelope. And if you felt a token in the envelope it meant you were drafted. The armed services sent you a token because many draftees invented an excuse and stated they didn't have the carfare to get to the induction place. Because of this they mailed you the token with the notice so there were no more excuses. Afterwards I went to my induction place at Whitehall Street in lower Manhattan. I remember the armed services directed so many men to one large room and they said this half of the room to the marines and the other half went to the army. And I happened to be standing on the side that went to the army.

Clarence Davis recalls the racial breakdown of the inductees that went to Vietnam. He vividly recounts the waning months that culminated with his arrival in Vietnam.

The majority in the room were African American with a sprinkling of whites. After Whitehall Street the army put us on a bus which went directly to the airport. Next, we boarded a plane to Fort Jackson in Columbia, South Carolina, for basic training, then, Fort Gordon, Georgia, for advanced infantry training. Finally, I went to Fort Benning, Georgia, for paratrooper training, called jump school. And after that they gave me a month furlough and when the furlough was over I went to Vietnam. I went in the army on May 18th and by December I was in a Vietnamese town called Bien Hoa, South Vietnam. After I arrived there, I received my orders and they sent me to the 101st Air Force Division and a place called Phouc Vinh, Vietnam, where I was placed in the 101st Airborne Division, Delta Company 3/187.

In the previous American wars, including the Korean conflict, minorities served in a segregated unit. The Vietnam War became the first conflict in which units were integrated. Next, Davis recalls his tour of duty.

It [the unit] was mixed and the majority of the people in our unit did not come from upper-class families, and the whites that were in our unit came from a lower-class background or were poor whites. I was in a reactionary force and the duty of the reactionary force was, let's say if a soldier or soldiers went out in the battlefield and they were in trouble, the army sent our unit to retrieve them. We did that for a while or guarded the base camps or General (William) Westmorland. Our unit also went on patrol, which was called SND–Search and Destroy. I lost so many people that were close to me because when you're in a combat situation you develop a bond. And I even developed a close bond with the white fellows. We were like a family unit and the bond was so close that all the soldiers, blacks and whites, ate from the same plate, for we were all in the same situation.

Davis continues:

I don't know if I heard [about] the protests, or if it affected us because I was just thinking about how to keep myself from dying. But this is something that maybe a lot of people don't know or were not informed. There were a lot of soldiers that refused to fight in Vietnam for whatever reasons and these soldiers went to a place in Vietnam called LBJ. [The notorious U.S. Army Vietnam installation stockade was known to GIs as the Long Binh Jail, or simply Camp LBJ—as sarcastic reference to President Lyndon Baines Johnson]. This happened and when the soldiers filled the jails to full capacity, the army sent them to Okinawa, Japan, where they were locked up. I was on a mission one time and we got attacked and a white sergeant got hit in the back and became paralyzed. One of the black soldiers that witnessed it said if he ever got in that situation again, he would not go out in the field anymore. And we returned to the base camp and on the next mission the soldier refused to go. He was ordered and he said no. "I'm not going." And they said, "We're going to put you in jail." He said, "I'd rather go to jail than take a chance of being killed or injured." A lot of people took that stance or shot themselves in the foot to keep from going out there, but you had to follow orders in the military because if you came back with less than an honorable discharge you received nothing and you lost your benefits. Blacks represented nearly ninety percent of LBJ's inmate population.

Some combat soldiers, like Clarence Davis, lived through an arduous experience, and for America it was an expensive one.

I was in and out of the jungle for my entire tour. Swamp, rice paddies and there were central mountains everywhere and there was a lot of firing. One time we got into a battle which lasted all night and we spent 8,000 four-deuce mortars which cost thirty-eight dollars apiece back then, and we went through 8,000 of them. And not to mention the other armaments that was also used. But I had that feeling which went up my back, which was of dying all the time. Because every step you took could be your last step and I was wounded and received a Purple Heart. Have you ever heard of Agent Orange? That was true. It was an agent to defoliate and it was to kill the foliage so the Vietnamese could not hide in the bushes. And it was speculated that the bushes could take 100 years to grow back. But I was fortunate that I was not exposed to it and when I came back I took the tests and I have two children and there is nothing wrong with them.

Though Davis was not affected by Agent Orange, his memories of the war never left him.

I returned to the United States in December of 1968, and back then if you went into the army, and did your twelve months in Vietnam—in the marines it was thirteen months—the military would not send you back. It's different today, for you could remain in the service after your one-year duty. Because for one thing, there was the draft and the military constantly had people coming in.... For a while I was OK, but if I walked the streets and a car backfired I ducked for cover behind a car or another motor vehicle. I guess people looked at me and thought what was wrong with me. And I didn't keep in contact with some of my military buddies because these men spoke vengeful, crazy thoughts. Some of these men talked about becoming a MERC, or mercenaries. I didn't exchange any phone numbers with them because I just wanted to get away, for I didn't want to take part in any more killing. But posttraumatic stress is there and it could come down on you anytime—right now. You think you're cured and suddenly it could come back. I guess the World Trade Center attack [September 11, 2001] could bring flashbacks to some people or the nightly news about Iraq today. When you see soldiers getting killed, this can also bring back stress. And I know what those soldiers are going through today.

Though Davis experienced some flashbacks linked to the Vietnam War, he was able to secure employment and lead a successful life.

Juan Gonzalez, pioneering member of the Young Lords Party. Mr. Gonzalez first served the YLP as deputy minister of education. Later, he became chairman of the organization. The YLP brought attention to the issue of lead poisoning throughout East Harlem and need for free breakfast programs. Today, he is a newspaper columnist for the *New York Daily News*, where he still advocates for progressive issues.

When I got drafted I was already on the waiting list for the Transit Authority and the day I got back, the Transit Authority called me. But I couldn't take the job because I had another six months to do. I went to the Transit Authority and told them I was in the service and they said when you come out of the service, come back and see us. I got out of the army in May on a Friday and that Monday, I was pounding the pavement, looking for a job. I went to the Transit Authority and they told me they would call me for the next class. I found a job at the telephone company as an installer and I worked there until the Transit Authority called me forty-five days later. I got a job as a track repairman and I was employed with the Transit Authority for twenty-nine years until I retired in 1998. Throughout those years I received only one unemployment check and a lot of Vietnam veterans worked with me.

Other Vietnam veterans were not so lucky.

Josephine Carson: Black men were drafted into Vietnam and some of these men were my male friends.

7. 1960s — Decade of Change

If they didn't attend college they were drafted, and these soldiers were 18 or 19 years old when they went to Vietnam. And a couple of my friends were killed in Vietnam and those soldiers that saw action and returned, were different when they came back. Many of these returning soldiers were screwed up because the war really affected them. Most of the soldiers didn't want to talk about it and other returning soldiers coped with their experiences by using drugs, because the Vietnam War affected these soldiers for many years.

We end the decade in 1969 with two East Harlem organizations which sought to improve the neighborhood's conditions from the grassroots level. The first organization worked with the government to achieve their goals. The second organization, born of the first, adopted a socialist philosophy. When the year began, Johnson's presidency was near its end; the Vietnam War deprived the president of a second full term. Four years earlier Johnson had basked in the glow of his landslide election victory. In his 1965 inaugural address the president called his vision for the country the Great Society. In the early 1960s, several young Puerto Rican former gang members from the Lower East Side sought to implement Johnson's ideas at the local level. Calling themselves the "Real Great Society," these youths wanted to work for the public's good instead of fighting each other. The Real Great Society typified the early 1960s, which began with the hope and belief that anything was possible. In 1964, Chino García, Armando Pérez, Ángelo González and Ángelo Giordani all came together to change their direction from street gangs to something constructive.[32]

They sponsored dances at the church's community center, dubbed the "Fabulous Latin House," where the entrance was a dollar. This entrepreneural spirit translated into confidence that they could successfully

Felipe Luciano served as the first chairman of the New York Chapter of the Young Lords Party. A sought-after speaker and lecturer, Mr. Luciano has appeared on many television and radio programs throughout, such as WNBC, WCBS, and WNYC.

operate a business.³³ Ángelo Giordani first lived in East Harlem on 57 East 112th Street. His family, like many East Harlemites, was relocated to public housing.³⁴ As one of eight children, Ángelo honed his organizing skills.

Ángelo Giordani: *I met Chino García and Ángelo Gonzalez who lived on the Lower East Side. And I was asked to attend a meeting and there we discussed about doing something for the community. We started the Fabulous Latin House in the church basement on Grant Avenue. And from there we started thinking about the community along with organizing it, but to do that you needed an organization.*

The men brainstormed ideas with community leaders on transforming the harsh conditions many urbanites faced in poor neighborhoods. In 1965, at one of their gatherings, Chino García concluded that the power to improve conditions would come from the streets, because Garcia felt the Great Society did not exist in their neighborhood. Shortly thereafter, when Garcia and his friends were at a gathering, he said "Real Great Society" was needed, and the organization was born. The members floated ideas for their Real Great Society — jobs, entrepreneurship, safe streets and community control of schools. The following year, the Fabulous Latin House continued to make a profit, albeit modestly. And the members also worked odd jobs and managed a storefront operation that secured employment for neighborhood youth.³⁵

But the Real Great Society (RGS) aspired to do more; however, money was needed to make their aspirations a reality. Giordani and the RGS partnered with Fred Good, who was moved by these ambitious young men. Good assisted them and together they submitted their business proposal to the Office of Economic Opportunity. The group's proposal was denied, but they kept on and after several more submissions were denied, the RGS struck gold and received $ 15,000 from the Astor Foundation. The RGS established the University of the Streets, but this university differed from the traditional institution because this school literally came from the streets.

The idea was to take an individual and harness their talents to do something positive. This university taught whatever the participants wanted. No grades were awarded because the goal was to involve the community where it could benefit from something that it created.³⁶

With a supplemental grant of $25,000 from the Astor Foundation, the RGS operated in four floors of a neighborhood tenement and opened a satellite office in East Harlem at 1673 Madison Avenue, near 110th Street. The EHRGS received more good news when the Office of Economic Opportunity and the Ford Foundations, both awarded the RGS grants totaling over $50,000.

The RGS received $3.5 million total in grants from the aforementioned foundations and the government. In East Harlem, the RGS started a prep school for high school dropouts and reading classes for younger students. It also obtained a loan from Chemical Bank and opened a Blimpie's restaurant franchise in the neighborhood.[37]

Ángelo Giordani: *I wanted to take some of the ideas which emanated from the Real Great Society on the Lower East Side and transfer them to East Harlem. The East Harlem office opened right before the riots, but even before the riots took place there was a difference between both offices. The Lower East Side, which started the University of the Streets and had an art gallery, was more of a cultural group. But the East Harlem office was more involved with the issues that affected the community. We brought the Model Cities Program to the neighborhood and broached the idea of an economic development studio in East Harlem.*

The late 1960s changed the direction of the Real Great Society. The organization focused on militancy and radical and social conscience. And a split between the offices developed. Founding members believed that the Lower East Side Real Great Society should include everyone regardless of race, whereas the East Harlem office was imbued with Latino pride and believed that Puerto Ricans should control the direction of the organization.[38] But non–Puerto Ricans or Latinos were also welcomed into the RGS. Tom Webber was part of the Real Great Society of East Harlem.

In the late 1960s, I worked for the neighborhood youth corps and I met a bunch of ex-Viceroys and they were about to start an organization called the Real Great Society on the Lower East Side. And one of the guys, Ángelo Giordani, started an East Harlem branch of the Real Great Society and he stood up for me. I remember there was trouble and some guy complained about me being white. Angelo said "Tom's not white, he's from 102nd Street." It was a way of saying Tom is OK.

Another element helped the EHRGS assume its radical position. While foundation and government largesse went to the Lower East Side RGS, donations from the private sector allowed the East Harlem site to pursue its revolutionary stance.[39] This revolutionary ardor led the EHRGS to launch one of the first modern "garbage strikes" in East Harlem. They dumped garbage on the Triborough Bridge. The Young Lords replicated this move at their headquarters the following year.[40]

Ángelo Giordani: *In July of 1969 at our office at 1673 Madison Avenue, "La Sociedad de Abizu Campos" first met because we felt a more radical pro–Puerto Rican group was needed. We also believed there was a lack of the cultural influence, hence La Sociedad was created. And among those who attended the charter meeting was Felipe Luciano, Mickey Melendez and Harry Quintana. The Real Great Society organized and funded the organization, which changed its name to the Young Lords. [See pages 120–185.]*

The East Harlem RGS was on the move again. It brought two tenement buildings at 75 and 77 East 110th Street and converted them into the East

Harlem Educational Center. Afterwards, the East Harlem Prep School opened and both the center and prep school instructed children in reading, writing, science, math and history and helped adults gain their high school equivalency certificate.[41]

After the 1967 East Harlem riots, Giordani helped organize a youth conference. Some of the brightest youngsters in the neighborhood met with the East Harlem RGS. One of the themes discussed at the youth conference was a lack of community control. This idea led to the creation for the Urban Planning Studio, shepherded by William Vazquez, who received assistance from students at Columbia University. The Urban Planning Studio spent a year studying housing conditions in East Harlem. The plan was to take the abandoned buildings and empty lots and transform them into "uses that will improve community life." The study concluded that 39 empty lots and nearly 100 abandoned buildings existed from 100th Street to 121st Street from Park Avenue to the East River. But Vazquez and the Columbia students clashed over the Urban Planning Studio's mission. Vazquez felt that whites held progressive ideas but didn't want to hear his opinion and those of other EHRGS members. Harry Quintana, another member of the studio, dissolved the partnership between himself and the students and reconstituted the studio. The new planning studio still adhered to the urban planning theories of community redevelopment and welcomed a multiracial coalition of blacks, Latinos and whites. Quintana viewed the East Harlem RGS as an "oppositional movement." The main goal of the Urban Planning Studio was to simultaneously stop displacement and allow Puerto Ricans to maintain their roots in East Harlem. The Urban Planning Studio developed teams to carry out the latter mission on the East Harlem RGS. Each team included an architect, urban planner, lawyer, community organizer and project specialist.[42]

The Urban Studio Planning focused on various projects to include East Harlemites in the redevelopment of their community. Three of these projects were Barrio Nuevo, Taino Towers and Park East High School. Barrio Nuevo was designed to stem the encroachment of Yorkville developers and entrepreneurs into East Harlem. The target area for redevelopment was 98th to 106th Street from Lexington to Third Avenue. Studies were conducted and meetings were held in preparation for the Barrio Nuevo, but just prior to its implementation, Barrio Nuevo folded. The East Harlem Tenants Council, which began in the early 1960s under the leadership of (Isidro) Ted Velez, proposed building Taino Towers. These towers included four high-rise buildings located on 121st and 122nd Streets near Second and Third Avenue. The Urban Planning Studio had reservations with respect to high-rise developments, which in the past destroyed communities throughout East Harlem, but the Taino Towers would be built.

The planning studio was successful in convincing Taino Towers to construct a community-based center. Park East High School was originally scheduled to enroll 4,000 students and combine the Yorkville and East Harlem neighborhoods together at the former Rupert Brewery site on the Upper East Side. But New York City's fiscal crises of the 1970s halted construction of the school. Park East High eventually opened as an alternative school in the old Manhattan School of Music on 105th Street between Second and Third Avenue.[43]

By the late 1960s Real Great Society (RGS) was under attack by many Americans who felt that government money could not solve everyone's problems. The RGS East Harlem's branch with its ambitious projects sapped the organization's strength. And this led many to believe the organization may have overreached itself during this period. Tackling housing, education, drugs and crime was a tall order and there was only so much one organization could do. More problems arose as the EHRGS young progressive leadership alienated the old guard leadership in the neighborhood. Also, internal divisions, petty squabbling, political views, class differences, gender problems, anti-gay sentiments and administrative disorder also hurt the EHRGS. Finally, when Richard Nixon replaced Johnson as president he closed the Office of Economic Opportunity and a valuable funding source ended. The liberal era was replaced by the emerging conservative movement that vilified foundations that doled out money to antipoverty programs. The EHRGS's funding of the Young Lords exacerbated the issue and led to the group's appearance before the McClellan Committee.[44] (Led by U.S. Senator John McClellan.)

Tom Webber: *The Real Great Society was investigated to see if it was communist inspired or a branch of the Young Lords. I was in my father's car and I remember the police stopped me to see if any I had guns. Life magazine did an article on RGS and some of the people who worked for us were also investigated. Because of the investigation, the McClellan Committee wrote to the funding sources and the government said the Real Great Society is under investigation for its donations to radical groups.*

The investigation by the McClellan Committee hurt the East Harlem Real Great Society. Though the EHRGS lasted into the early 1970s, many foundations cut off its funding, which led to the organization's decline. Nevertheless, the East Harlem Real Great Society remains part of East Harlem's history. The organization was ahead of its time. It responded to what Aponte Pares called "community empowerment, advocacy planning and citizen participation." The ideas that the Real Great Society advocated for are still alive today. Presently, East Harlem is being redeveloped at an alarming rate. Later Ángelo Giordani attended Harvard University and graduated from the Harvard Business School. He and Tom Webber look back on the Real Great Society.

Ángelo Giordani: *Those were very exciting and formative years for me. A lot of strategy and development came from the Real Great Society.... We focused on housing, economic development, services for poor people, early voter participation, cultural enhancement, education and self-determination. We helped bring the Model Cities Program and Vista Volunteers to the neighborhood and funded the Taller Boricua.*

Tom Webber: *during those years, I got involved with the Rupert Educational Center, which founded the Park East High School. Then the school was in the basement of the St. Cecilia's Church until it moved to the old building of Manhattan School of Music after it abandoned the building in 1969. And the East Harlem Real Great Society secured six million dollars over two years and helped establish the Taller Boricua. Such artists as Carlos Osorio and Raphael Trufino had studios in our buildings.*

Fuerza Boricua

The Young Lords: They were young, dynamic and idealistic and their activism returned the neighborhood to the progressive ways of Vito Marcantonio. Their goal: change. The media, protests and demonstrations became their tool. Their story began when several Puerto Rican undergraduate students banded together to plot a course of action. These youngsters who attended high school or college also wanted to reaffirm their roots with the Puerto Rican community.[45] As winter became spring the group settled in East Harlem. By now they had found a venue to hold their events, but this membership was unstable. Those members who remained in the group concluded they had yet to accomplish anything. But one of the group's members remained committed to make a difference.

Pablo "Yoruba" Guzman joined the group in its second year. It was now called La Sociedad de Albizu Campos, or SAC (Society of Albizu Campos). Guzman, an undergraduate at the State University of New York in Old Westbury, had recently returned from Mexico. A Puerto Rican and Cuban of African descent, Guzman had identified with the plight of African people in the Americas. While in Mexico, Guzman reconnected with his Latino heritage and upon returning to New York, he sought to harness his energy into action. Guzman found his niche through a friend whose brother belonged to the SAC named David Perez, who was from Chicago by the way of Lares, Puerto Rico. He struck up an immediate friendship with Guzman. Denise Oliver, born in Brooklyn, New York, periodically visited her cousin in the George Washington Carver Housing Projects.

Later, Oliver lived in the neighborhood and worked at the East Harlem branch of the Real Great Society. And it was here where the first meeting of La Sociedad de Albizu Campos took place.[46]

Denise Oliver: *Some members of the Real Great Society also attended college and visited the campus at Old Westbury in Long Island to plan an experimental college. The people who were members of the experimental college were myself, Mickey Melendez, Bob Bunkley (who later went by the name Muntu) and Robert Ortiz. And the second year of this experiment we recruited a young man from the Bronx High School of Science named Paul Guzman [who later went by the name Pablo Yoruba] and more high school students followed.*

In early June, Guzman read an article in the Black Panther Party's newsletter. The piece mentioned the formation of the Rainbow Coalition, which was composed of several progressive organizations of different races and ethnicities. One of the groups that attracted Guzman's attention was the Young Lords Organization based in Chicago, Illinois.[47]

That same month the SAC met with another progressive Puerto Rican group from the Lower East Side which included Juan "Fi" Ortiz. Coincidentally this organization, too, planned to establish a chapter of the Young Lords. The groups merged, and established a New York chapter of the Young Lords.[48]

Another founding member was Juan Gonzalez, who was born in Ponce, Puerto Rico. Juan left the island shortly after his birth and arrived in New York City with his parents Juan and Florinda Gonzalez, a year later. They first lived on 112th Street near First Avenue until the family moved to the housing projects in East New York, Brooklyn. But Juan and his family often returned East Harlem to visit their relatives. Later, he joined the SAC and dropped out of Columbia University and worked for several antipoverty programs. Juan was living in East Harlem when he cofounded the New York chapter of the Young Lords.[49]

The Young Lords Organization was based in Chicago and several SAC members traveled there. The Chicago Young Lords had started a breakfast program and other programs in Chicago and some of us met with Cha Cha Jimenez and he authorized our group to start a New York branch. But after a year we had some differences with Cha Cha and we changed our name from the Young Lords Organization to the Young Lords Party. We opened our YLP office, which was the headquarters for the other YLP chapters on the East Coast. The cofounders of the Young Lords were myself, Pablo Guzman, Felipe Luciano, David Ortiz, and Juan "Fi" Ortiz who dropped out of high school.

It was a variety of reasons the Lords was founded—for one thing the Vietnam War was going on. We opened up our first YLP office in East Harlem on 111th Street and Madison Avenue. And we lived in apartments between Madison and Fifth Avenue or we had a bunch of apartments on 110th Street between Madison and Park Avenue. Our office was on the site of the current Arturo Schomburg housing complex.

Felipe Luciano, YLP's first New York chairman, explains how he joined the Young Lords.

Felipe Luciano: *I started with the group called the Last Poets on 125th Street and Madison Avenue. Also I was teaching at Queens College and developing a name for myself as a political educator. And the Puerto Ricans at the [Old Westbury] campus was Mickey Melendez, David Perez, Pablo Guzman and then came Juan Gonzalez. And all of them wondered, "Why isn't he with us?" But I thought to myself, did I want to join this organization? At Queens College, H. Rap Brown [now Jamil Abdullah Al-Amin] was coming to our lecture along with Stokely Carmichael, who later became Kwame Ture, and LeRoi Jones, who today is Amiri Baraka, also came there.*

But I was reluctant because I didn't think Puerto Ricans were ready. I had been organizing underground with some black souls. And I refused to join this Puerto Rican group for some time. Until Khanlen Kain of the Last Poets said, "You have helped blacks get our blackness and now you need to do the same and help Puerto Ricans. The Young Lords were beginning to form, to jell. After we got back from Chicago, I was elected chairman of the Young Lords in New York State. The Chicago Young Lords were more gangland oriented. Though they did the breakfast program and other things, but they had more of a street edge. Back in New York, the Young Lords included Hiram Maristany, who became the official photographer, and Betty Perez, who also was from East Harlem, joined.[50]

The Fearless Five — Pablo Guzman, David Perez, Juan Gonzalez, Felipe Luciano and Juan "Fi" Ortiz — each transferred their energy from classroom textbooks to the textbooks of the streets. They formed the General Committee of the Young Lords, and all five members received the title of deputy minister. Felipe Luciano was deputy chairman, David Perez was deputy minister of defense, Pablo Guzman was deputy minister of information, Juan Gonzalez was deputy minister of education and Juan "Fi" Ortiz was deputy minister of finance.[51] Other Young Lords who joined the group were members of the Dragons and Viceroys. They, too, were attracted to the Young Lords' approach to making a difference in the community. Mike Rivera recalls:

When Bobby Lemus and I first heard about the Young Lords, we were hesitant, for a lot of Viceroys were part of the YLP. One day Huskie Willie [William Jenkins] ... joined the Young Lords. And that day Bobby comes over and tells Georgie and me "Listen, I got a meeting with Huskie Willie in the YLP's office, and I will go alone." But we didn't trust them, and we took our guns and we stood outside the office, because if anything happened, we would come in. But nothing happened, instead we saw them hugging and crying and, you see, that is what the Young Lords did. Instead of killing each other it brought people together. Bobby Lemus spent many times in Huskie Willie's house. But Bobby Lemus died from cirrhosis of the liver several yeas ago in 2001.

The official introduction of the Young Lords Party took place at Tompkins Square Park on July 26, 1969.[52] The date was the 16th anniversary of the 26th of July movement, in which Cuban insurgents from the mountains led an unsuccessful attack on the Moncada army. (Fidel Castro, who was jailed over the revolt, later overthrew Fulgencio Batista's government and became the new ruler of Cuba.) With the organization and a steering committee in place, the Young Lords were ready to make a difference in East Harlem. Their first offensive was the garbage demonstration. Garbage cans were rarely seen in certain sections of East Harlem and the city's sanitation trucks traveled inconsistently to the neighborhood to collect the garbage. And if the garbage trucks arrived, only a half-hearted effort was made to clean the area. On a Sunday afternoon in early August, the Young Lords approached the sanitation depot to borrow some brooms to spruce up 110th Street between Second and Third Avenues, but they were rebuffed by the city's sanitation employees. The Young Lords forcefully took the brooms whereby they commenced to sweep the streets. Afterwards, they dutifully returned the brooms to the depot. They repeated this process a week later, but finally concluded the Sanitation Department was responsible for cleaning up the garbage. Instead, the Young Lords tried another strategy. Weeks later, they began dumping garbage on 110th Street near Park Avenue. Nearby residents joined the garbage demonstration and soon more garbage was dumped and burned. Though the demonstration was mild compared to the riots of two years ago, the group continued their offensive by overturning the abandoned cars and blocking traffic.[53] That day, one of the young protestors who spoke to the *New York Times* identified himself as "Yoruba."[54] Today, many New Yorkers know Pablo "Yoruba" Guzman who works as a correspondent for WCBS Channel Two News in New York City.

The Young Lords sent a message to New York Sanitation Department for its failure to clean up the streets of East Harlem. They succeeded as the city responded by providing more garbage cans throughout the neighborhood and implemented regular garbage pickups.

Felipe Luciano: *We had asked people what was the major contradiction in the community. And they said it was the garbage, which deflated our balloons a lot, since we wanted to go fighting. Needless to say we would have been killed because we had no idea of street fighting or what guerrilla warfare was all about, we learned that later.*

True to form, if you're a socialist and you're with the people, you do what they say. We went to the people and since that's what they wanted we took the garbage and put it in the bags and waited for the garbage trucks to come. And of course they didn't, so we waited and when the garbage trucks didn't come, we threw the garbage in the streets. And this stopped traffic, and once the garbage stopped the traffic, the police had the sanitation department remove the garbage. But we had a victory and we did this time and time again until people began to know us as the garbage people.

Denise Oliver: *The tenements had alleyways behind them and a lot of garbage was spread throughout the vacant lots as well. But the garbage was never picked up which rotted in the back and in the summertime the stench was unbelievable. It also attracted a huge number of rats and the unsanitary health conditions sent neighborhood children to the hospital. The sanitation department pretended as if East Harlem didn't exist, or garbage didn't need to be picked up above 96th Street.*

The Young Lords next concentrated on the health quality in East Harlem. In October 1969, as Mayor Lindsey vied for a second term, the city's Health Department issued a press release stating that 40,000 free test kits for lead paint poisoning would be available to the public. But the city never implemented a plan to disseminate the test kits, and after Lindsey was reelected, a city health official admitted that the free tests were just a press release, or put more bluntly, a publicity stunt. The Young Lords responded and circulated leaflets throughout East Harlem and began conducting their own lead poisoning test program with medical students. Another problem occurred when Metropolitan Hospital agreed to distribute 200 free kits to the Young Lords, but the hospital breached this agreement. The Young Lords responded by calling the health commissioner, Mary McLaughlin. However, Commissioner McLaughlin refused to acknowledge the Young Lords' entreaties.

On Monday, November 28, 1969, together with interns, nurses and health workers, the Young Lord's staged a protest at the city's Health Department offices. And again the city's health administration officials ignored them. Meanwhile, the test kits were left unused. By the end of the week, Jack Newfield, the *Village Voice* reporter who originally broke the story, also tried to contact Commissioner McLaughlin, but Newfield, like the Young Lords, was given the runaround by the Health Department. Eventually, the Young Lords received the kits and conducted the tests themselves. In short, the Young Lords were providing a free service while city officials were getting paid $35,000, then an appreciable sum of money, to remain idle.[55]

Denise Oliver: *We had been working with a group of leftist doctors and there was an issue where a number of children suffered from lead poisoning from the tenements. Paint chipped from the walls and fell on the floor and children ate the chipped paint. And nothing was being done about it and we developed a plan with these leftist doctors to collect urine samples from many East Harlem children. The children's urine sample came back and it tested positive for lead paint. We held con-*

ferences to address the issue, and again, as a result of our actions, new laws were placed on the books that mandated landlords remove lead paint.

The Young Lords opened another office in Newark, New Jersey, and developed a thirteen-point program. They kept growing and advocating like modern-day Robin Hoods. As autumn became winter, the Young Lords concentrated on their second offensive free breakfast program inside the First Spanish Methodist Church at 111th Street and Lexington Avenue.[56]

Denise Oliver: *The Black Panthers ran a free breakfast program in Harlem. The YLP tried to duplicate a similar program in East Harlem and one of the YLP members belonged to the first Spanish Methodist Church. And a relative of Pedro Pietri also belonged to the church as well. (Pedro Pietri wrote and performed [his poem] "Puerto Rican Obituary") the YLP approached the First Spanish Methodist Church's elders a couple of times. Some church members were not hostile, but the people were not receptive to the idea. Felipe was familiar with this church, for he was raised in the Pentecostal faith. He knew on Sundays that testimony was given in the church and at the church you could stand up and testify. We went there several Sundays, but what happened the third time we went to testify was horrendous.*

Rev. Norman C. Eddy: *The Young Lords kept going to the Methodist Church to give testimony, but the pastor was furious and the church's parishioners were upset too. This scene occurred for three or four Sundays and the pastor called the police to throw out the Young Lords. And the last time the Lords tried this Felipe got hit over the head.*

Felipe Luciano: *In October, during a church testimony, the cops were in the church and they beat me up and broke my arm in two places. And I needed seven stitches in my head and they arrested us.*[57]

Denise Oliver: *Felipe was beaten badly by this big policeman and one of the Young Lords' sisters actually jumped from a pew and landed on the policeman's back. The police was about to bash Felipe's head open. Actually, it was the women who fought the police and thirteen Young Lords were arrested and most of them were women.*

The men who accompanied and fought alongside the women were also arrested. The community responded the next day as the Reverend Eddy explains.

Rev. Norman C. Eddy: *The next morning the East Harlem Interfaith, a group composed of neighborhood and religious people, was studying the Bible. Then we received information from another Methodist minister about what had happened and what would be our next course of action. We thought we should visit the Young Lords, and when we did, one of the Catholic sisters who was also a nurse and dressed Felipe's wounds. We decided this little interfaith prayer and Bible study group would become [like] a UN peacekeeping force. And every Sunday we went to the* *church as a member of the congregation to try to keep the Young Lords quiet and keep the leadership of the church from doing anything negative.*

But the Young Lords refused to be silenced, and they continued their demand for a free breakfast program. The Young Lords met with the church's directors, but still their request was denied. On December 28, 1969, after the church services had concluded, Juan Gonzalez spoke to the congregation and reiterated the Young Lord's plea for a free breakfast program. Again they were denied, but this day it was different: the Young Lords announced that they were taking over the church.[58]

Juan Gonzalez: *We had started the breakfast program at the Theater Arts center at the [De Witt] Clinton Projects for quite a while before we took over the church. We also had a program at Emmaus House on 116th Street. After the church services closed, the Young Lords announced that we were going to take it over.*

Crosspieces were nailed outside the church's door. On the inside, the doors were chained. The minister, Humberto Carrazanno, who had defected from Cuba, viewed the Young Lords' action as a socialist reminder of Fidel Castro's regime back in his Caribbean homeland.

Rev. Norman C. Eddy: *It was only four or five of us and the East Harlem Interfaith went to the church every Sunday and on the third or fourth Sunday it happened. Suddenly, in the middle of the service a couple of young men walked down the aisle carrying chains that were clanging behind them. Next they went out in the back of the church and then we heard a pound, pound and pound. And a few minutes later one of the leaders moved to the vacant pulpit and proclaimed in a loud voice "This is the people's church." We were all locked in and the Young Lords talked for fifteen minutes. Afterwards, Felipe or one of the members said, "Will the Rev. Norman C. Eddy please come and meet with us." And I met with them and we worked out a negotiation that the East Harlem Interfaith would be allowed to leave if the Young Lords could take over the church. And our group left and indeed the YLP took over the church.*

Over 105 people participated in the church's takeover. On December 31, 1969, the 1960s ended. But the decade and its revolutionary spirit would never be forgotten and East Harlem and the rest of the world would never be the same again. The next day, January 1, 1970, began a new decade, but the spirit of the 1960s was still evident as the church's seizure entered its second week. Neighborhood children were treated to hot meals, and learned about Puerto Rican culture.

Felipe Luciano: *We went to the merchants in the community and we told them we wanted food and the merchants complied. And they gave us eggs, bacon, potatoes, milk, farina, and fruit, and they would bring the food to the church, or* *they would ask us to pick up the food. We also had supporters like Evelina Antonetti, Willie Soto, José "Chequi" Torres, Bette Midler, Jack Newfield, Jane Fonda, and the 1199 Union, support us. And Mayor Lindsay told the cops to stay away.*

Denise Oliver: *Doctors came in and gave us assistance if we had any medical problems. Also the YLP established a free health clinic, clothing drive and breakfast and lunch programs, in addition, political education classes, poetry readings and a music festival. We also received a check from Sammy Davis Jr., in the name of his mother [Elvira "Baby" Sanchez]. And most people didn't know that his mother was a Latina. The responses and the thousands of people that came through the church was amazing.*

But one individual who supported the Young Lords paid the consequences for his action.

Arnie Segarra: *I lost my job as Mayor Lindsay's assistant because I supported the Young Lords.*

On January 7, 1970, the eleven-day church seizure ended when the Young Lords' lawyers and a representative from the sheriff's office reached an agreement. The Young Lords complied with the order and vacated the church. The church seizure was over. The Young Lords' next battle was the contempt of court charges. The Young Lords again received the community's support.

In late February the contempt of court charges were dismissed, and more good news arrived when the church and the city came together and created a day care center on the church premises. The city appropriated $200,000 for the day care center, but the city stipulated that the Young Lords would not reoccupy the church.[59]

In the spring of 1970, the Young Lords opened an office in the South Bronx and began to spread their wings in the media. They published their newspaper, *Palante*, and delivered weekly broadcasts on 99.5 WBAI-FM, and they opened more offices on the Lower East Side and in Philadelphia.[60] Olguie Robles, who was born in East Harlem and moved to the Bronx with her parents at age two came of age during the Civil Rights movement and was eventually recruited into the Young Lords.

Olguie Robles: *I was about sixteen when my friend Selena brought me one of the first issues of the Lords' paper,* Palante, *and she said, "Ougie, you should look at this paper. They are talking about the Puerto Ricans." I looked at* Palante *and, except for the curse words, I liked what I read. However, I thought it might be a problem for many elderly people who might support the Young Lords, they wouldn't like the curse words that appeared in the paper. I went to the Young Lords' branch office in the Bronx and I told them how I liked the article's content. Richie Perez said, "You seem pretty bright, why don't you join our organization?" And that's how the Young Lords recruited me.*

But one was not admitted into the Young Lords overnight. And before one became a full-fledged member all potential recruits had to convince the organization they were serious about joining the Young Lords.

Olguie Robles: *First, you became a friend of the Lords because you had to prove yourself. And as a friend of the Young Lords I helped out the organization and I did whatever was requested. For example I did odd jobs, sold newspapers and then I made the commitment. Later, I was in charge of political education classes two or three times a day and this improved my reading ability. When I first entered the Young Lords I had a sixth-grade reading level, and through leading these political education classes my reading level advanced to the twelfth-grade level. I would meet up with six people and asked each group member to teach to six other people. I taught cultural history, for instance Puerto Rican and African American history, sociology and economics because the Young Lords tried to be broad as possible.*

THE LORDS OF THE DAY

As Olguie mentioned, all Young Lords were required to perform certain responsibilities. After each member entered the Young Lords' storefront office they would sign in and receive their daily orders from the officer of the day, a Young Lord official positioned at the front desk. Work was divided equally amongst the women and men and some of the work was on the breakfast program, lead poisoning and tuberculosis testing, or tending the church's day care center. If a Young Lord was not working, each member received stipend money for breakfast, lunch or dinner. And the Young Lords also collected and gave away clothes in the community.[61]

Olgui Robles joined the Young Lords Party at age sixteen. Robles, along with the other female members, led an effort to address the importance of women's role within the organization. This effort was successful as several women gained prominent positions within the Young Lords Party. Today, Robles still advocates as an unpaid substance abuse counselor and tenant organizer.

Felipe Luciano: *We would come to the office and we were given our orders. To sell papers, clean up the office, go to the Bronx, put out the paper or speaking engagements. And everybody was given a role to play, for example the political education lessons, or the YLP went around the neighborhood to talk about our organization, to advocate. And we had a group that simply advocated for people who need help to pay a Con Ed Bill, or if they needed translation with the Welfare Department or if you needed help with the homework.*

Mike Rivera: *Bobby Lemus told me about an educational program and after work I went to the Lords' office. I participated in tuberculosis testing and still visited the stores and collected food to maintain the free breakfast program. The Lords advocated or passed out leaflets, and held demonstrations that we called "hit and run." And we also advocated for students' or squatters' rights.*

Denise Oliver: *The Lords were a full-time occupation organized on paramilitary lines and it was difficult for some people to give 100 percent to the Lords. Suppose you had a significant other who was not political or interested, you had to make a choice.*

There were problems within the group, and the organization needed to clean its own house. Women in the Young Lords were not treated as equals. When the organization was founded, only a few women belonged to the Young Lords. Back then women worked as secretaries or held lower-level positions within the organization, but this would soon change.[62]

Marcos Dimas, is pictured here with Gloria Calero (center) and an unidentified woman. Mr. Dimas became part of an emerging group of artists that arrived in East Harlem during the early 1970s. Today, he works at the Taller Boricua (Puerto Rican Workshop). Taller Boricua displays art from many minority artists.

Olguie Robles: *In the beginning, it was not easy and there were a lot of issues. And people practice what they learn and if you learn machismo, you practice machismo and if you learn a double standard, you practice a double standard. Until the issue is addressed and that transformation occurs, then no changes will happen.*

Denise Oliver: *How could machismo not exist? It was prevalent in the community.*

And the issue was addressed.

Olguie Robles: *The Lords were not practicing what they were preaching and we started to talk about the manifestations of passivity and machismo in the movement and how this needed to be changed. The Young Lords held general meetings which opened up a dialogue amongst the group and through this dialogue the Young Lords were able to discuss and settle our differences. And this allowed the group to move forward and we developed a woman's group and a men's group. Within each group you had leadership roles and for the women you had Denise Oliver and Iris Morales.*

Denise Oliver became minister of finance; Iris Morales was education captain and Gloria Cruz became field marshal of the Young Lords. Now the six-member governing central committee included women.[63] According to Felipe Luciano, membership was estimated at 350 and women comprised forty percent of the group. Many members were of mixed ethnicity. Puerto Ricans, African Americans, a Panamanian, and both Richie Perez and Geraldo Rivera, the Young Lords' lawyer, both share Puerto Rican–Jewish heritage.

After dealing with the issue of machismo, the Young Lords returned to advocating on behalf of the community. Following the death of Carmen Rodriguez from a botched medical procedure at Lincoln Hospital, the Young Lords geared up for their third offensive. They believed the hospital ignored the atrocious conditions that existed there. The Young Lords briefly took over the hospital and held a press conference and discussed the serious conditions with Health Department officials. They also managed to get their point across before the police executed their arrest warrants.[64] The Young Lords then executed their fourth offensive and commandeered the tuberculosis van on 111th Street. Even after many years of study, East Harlem still accounted for the highest number of tuberculosis in cases the city. The Health Department had made available a mobile testing truck to conduct tuberculosis tests; however, it never stopped in East Harlem. The Young Lords repeatedly demanded the Health Department provide a truck to conduct tuberculosis tests in East Harlem. But they were ignored and as before, the Young Lords took matters into their own hands and seized the mobile truck. Soon a volunteer medical team was conducting tests in East Harlem.[65]

The cohesion the Young Lords enjoyed would not last. In early September, Felipe Luciano, New York chairman of the Young Lords Party, was suspended from his position and decided not to return. Before Luciano left the group, the central committee convened and reevaluated the Young Lords Party. This meeting resulted in clear definitions, duties and responsibilities of the Young Lords, which became known as democratic centralism. Henceforth, every level of the Young Lords Party was subject to review.[66] Finally, the Central Committee reshuffled the office of deputy ministers.

The press reported on the high number of suicides among African American and Puerto Rican inmates. A large number of these incidents were suspicious. In mid–October, Julio Roldan, a member of the Young Lords, became the latest casualty.[67] However, the Young Lords speculated that while he was in jail, the security guards beat Roldan to death.

Denise Oliver: *The correctional department said he hung himself in jail and we didn't believe that. Because the Lords were arrested many times, for example for selling newspapers and we constantly had to bail our members out of jail, which depleted our funds. Despite this situation the Lords believed anyone who was arrested would soon be released. It was illogical that anybody arrested by the police would be killed. But that was the correctional department's history, because people supposedly hung themselves after they were beaten up in jail.*

Olguie Robles has a blunt answer to this mystery.

Olguie Robles: *He was murdered and the police said he hung himself, but we say he was murdered. When you go to jail, the police took away your shoestrings and your belt, so how can you hang yourself because you have nothing to hang yourself with.*

Roldan's passing led to another seizure of the first Spanish Methodist Church on October 18. Unlike last year's seizure, this time the Young Lords were armed and Julio Roldan's coffin was displayed inside the church. He was dressed in a black leather jacket with a rifle inside his casket. After the public paid their last respects, Roldan's funeral services were held. This followed a procession by the Young Lords who carried Roldan's body through the streets of East Harlem. The Rev. Juan Antonio Velazquez, the newly appointed minister, backed the Young Lords takeover of the church. They tried to buy the First Spanish Methodist Church but the church administration denied the Young Lords' offer.[68] Twelve days later, the Young Lords commemorated the 20th anniversary of Puerto Rico's Nationalist Party's by marching with 10,000 people on the united Nations.[69]

Denise Oliver: *That was an incredible moment because we were able to turn out huge numbers of people. We organized with the Puerto Rican students union and other youth conferences. We also worked with a lot of progressive organizations. There were white groups like Youth Against War and Fascism, and the Black Panthers.*

The United Nations march was one of the high points for the Young Lords because that year the group made a fateful decision to open a branch in Ponce, Puerto Rico. Denise Oliver, Pablo Guzman and Gloria Gonzalez traveled to Puerto Rico to explore the possibility of branching out on the island. The trio met with a group of leftist Puerto Ricans composed mostly of lawyers who were unprepared for the exploration of African–Puerto Rican roots which the trio presented to them. But Ruben Berrios, one of the progressives, was receptive to the exploration of an African culture amongst the island's Puerto Ricans. But Gloria Gonzalez, who grew up in Puerto Rico, was comfortable with the realization that the island did not concentrate on African culture.

According to Denise Oliver, she and Pablo Guzman felt the decision to establish a base in Puerto Rico was unwise. Both of them believed the reception they received from the island's leftist lawyers didn't look promising. Another problem manifested itself with some YLP members who weren't fluent in Spanish, and communicating with mainland Puerto Ricans proved difficult. Finally, many Young Lords were Nuyoricans—born in New York City or came there when they were young. All this indicated that the YLP had little if no attachment to the island. Still, Gloria Gonzalez and David Perez wanted to establish a foothold on the island. When they returned to New York City the Young Lords decided to vote on the issue, but the decision became a very heated one and one member of the Central Committee suggested that Denise shouldn't vote on the issue because she wasn't Puerto Rican. Denise was allowed to vote and voted no, and by a close margin the Young Lords decided to open up an office in Puerto Rico. As a founding member, Denise felt appalled that her ethnicity became a wedge issue that could have prevented her from voting. She ultimately resigned from the Young Lords.[70] Denise later joined the Black Panther Party.[71] The Young Lords moved on and established a branch in Puerto Rico.

Olguie Robles: *That happened during the later years of the Young Lords because one of the members believed that we had to make changes. But Puerto Rico was different and we Puerto Ricans born in New York were more urbanized. In contrast, Puerto Rico was more rural, with a different setting, and if you are not from that setting you are not familiar with that lifestyle. And the quality of life in Puerto Rico then was much harder. Because the amenities were not available as opposed to New York and I stayed in little houses and shacks.*

The Young Lords continued and operated in both East Harlem and the Bronx, but the organization underwent several changes in leadership, name and mission.

Juan Gonzalez: *After Felipe left, the leadership chose me as the leader (chairperson) and I led the organization from October 1970 to May 1972, until we changed the name.*

In 1972, the Young Lords became the Puerto Rican New Revolutionary Workers Organization.

Juan Gonzalez: *We became more of a Marxist kind of group and we decided the name "the Young Lords" had derived from the gang period. And we wanted to have more of a political name and also we concentrated on less community organizing and more organizing of Puerto Rican workers in factories. This is why we changed the name and I left the organization in 1974, and a form of the group lasted until 1975. COINTELPRO [investigation] and infighting amongst themselves and little by little we dissipated until we broke apart. In addition to COINTELPRO [the FBI's program to wipe out radical movement organizations], the chapter office in Puerto Rico was another reason that led to the demise of the organization.*

Olguie Robles: *I think it the experience in Puerto Rico weakened us because we had to split our forces and we became disengaged to what was taking place in New York. Also, that weakness was played on by COINTELPRO and the undercover forces. The other factor was our own weakness. If you had a weakness like sex or drugs, or whatever, COINTELPRO took advantage of it.*

After the dissolution of the Young Lords/Puerto Rican New Revolutionary Workers Organization many former members have led successful lives. Felipe Luciano, Juan Gonzalez, and Pablo Guzman have succeeded in the media. Felipe Luciano has appeared on numerous television shows. Pablo Guzman still works at WCBS Channel 2 News. Other Young Lords have branched out into other successful careers. Juan Gonzalez was a columnist for the *Daily News* and was recently recognized by the Latino community for his contribution as a journalist. Other ex-members became educators, social workers and public administrators. Iris Morales became an attorney; Denise Oliver became an anthropologist; Mickey Melendez teaches at Hunter College and works for the Department of Education in New York City.[72] His book *We Took the Streets* gives more a detailed account on the Young Lords Party. But after the Young Lords ended some former members were not so successful, and it took some time before they were able to put their experiences behind them.

Mike Rivera: *The Young Lords got infiltrated by COINTELPRO and it became "if I didn't know you?" who are you and we couldn't trust who was who. After the Young Lords broke up, some of us got into to drugs and it was a real depression. It took a while, then people started to come back.*

Olguie Robles: *I was very depressed and I became very distrustful of people. I was in the Young Lords until 1975 and then the Young Lords went back underground. And when it was over, I was isolated for nearly seven years and I worked real hard to keep myself from feeling and thinking about what happened, and this lasted nearly eight years.*

But Robles forged on and after years of isolation, she reemerged and continued her activism.

Olguie Robles: *I got into tenant organizing in Queens to help people keep their homes. And I returned to school and earned my high school diploma and college degree. Later I also returned into organizing because that's were my heart is and today I am an unpaid substance abuse counselor. I became a Young Lord because I wanted to make qualitative changes in the world. And if I could save one person from being addicted, from the madness of substance abuse addiction, then I have made qualitative changes.*

The Young Lords reflect on their impact in East Harlem and the rest of America.

Felipe Luciano: *The most electrifying moment in the United States' Puerto Rican history; the most profoundly revolutionary moment in the United States" Puerto Rican history. One that coalesced and put Puerto Ricans on the map in the United States ... dispelled the myth that we were brown teddy bears ... that we Puerto Ricans couldn't defend ourselves and confront the system. And it brought together three classes of people, blacks, the educated youth, and drug and gang members. The first integrated people of color and not just black and white people for our group were proud of being Puerto Rican. We were the finest group and as a result of that we are still alive today.*

Juan Gonzalez: *The Young Lords raised the issue of lead poisoning in the city and forced the city to pass all kinds of legislation to eliminate lead poisoning. Our organization battle on health care literally forced the city to build a new Lincoln Hospital. The city had promised they were gong to build the hospital for twenty-five years and never did. All of the Latino–Puerto Rican studies at the colleges were established because the Young Lords advocated for the need to study Puerto Rican history. And the Young Lords organized students to demand that these programs be implemented. The free lunch programs that are available in public schools today happened because of the Young Lords and the Black Panthers. Both groups raised the issue that children were going to school without eating. This expanded nationally and there are free lunch programs for poor children coast to coast. But the most important thing, it elevated and put the Puerto Rican community in the United States on the map as a group that needed to be respected. And it established for whole generations of young Latinos that we had a right to be treated equally with all Americans.*

Olguie Robles: *I believe it was the first modern Puerto Rican revolutionary movement. There were antipoverty movements and many Puerto Ricans tried to change the system. But I don't think there was a movement that addressed the essence of what many Puerto Ricans felt with respect to injustice, discovering their culture and their history until the Young Lords. It also helped me become a better person,* *where I can address political, economic or social issues and not become narrow minded. The Young Lords also helped me understand on a human level the importance to take care of ourselves holistically and set priorities because not everything is about money.*

Denise Oliver: *I think it had an incredible impact and some of the things that are available now like the free breakfast program wouldn't be there if we hadn't fought for those changes. We addressed the housing conditions such as lead poisoning, and changes in the consciousness of the people in East Harlem. And East Harlem became part of the political landscape of New York and in the United States. In many ways the Young Lords put El Barrio on the map.*

Some of the Young Lords have died since the group disbanded, among them Richie Perez. After the Young Lords folded, Perez went on to found the National Congress for Puerto Rican Rights, which was at the forefront of fighting injustice for all oppressed peoples. Perez died in 2004.

Mike Rivera: *I'll tell you what type of guy Richie was. One day Richie called me and said, "Hey, Mickey Melendez wrote a book,* We Took the Streets. *Next day I got an email. "Be on the lookout for it," Richie said. I got the book the following day. He air-mailed it and I didn't ask him for it, I just said to get me the information about the book. And I emailed him to say thanks and that's the type of guy Richie was.*

Sadly, Mike Rivera also passed away in 2004.

In 1990, I was a junior at John Jay College, part of the city University of New York (CUNY). The CUNY Board of Trustees wanted to raise CUNY's tuition from $625 to $725. To the mostly working-class students, African Americans, Latinos and whites the tuition increase was an extra burden. Students from all of the CUNY campuses responded to the proposed increases and seized their respective colleges to protest the tuition increase. As the Young Lords had long ago, the students locked and chained the doors and Hunter College, City College and John Jay College all shut down. At John Jay, the occupying students began chanting "By Any Means Necessary" and "Palante" attributed to both Malcolm X and the Young Lords. Viva Palante. The protests worked, briefly, for CUNY's Board of Trustees decided not to raise CUNY's tuition in 1990. They did in 1991, however.

8
1970s — Fruits of Labor

In this chapter we revisit the struggles and gains made in the 1960s that paved the way for individual and cultural achievements in East Harlem during the 1970s. On January 20, 1969, Richard M. Nixon replaced Lyndon B. Johnson as president. American combat troops remained in Vietnam. Also that year, a half million Americans descended on the Mall in Washington, D.C., to protest the war, which continued into the early 1970s. On May 4, 1970, the National Guard killed four Kent State University students who were protesting the Vietnam War. The event shocked the nation, and outrage over their deaths made its way to New York City. In East Harlem, neighborhood artists demonstrated their outrage and protested the Kent State killings.

The organization called Taller Boricua is located at the Julia De Burgos Latino Cultural Center between 105th and 106th Streets and Lexington Avenue. Marcos Dimas, one of the directors, was born in Cabo Rojo, Puerto Rico, and came to the United States and settled in the South Bronx where he was schooled and raised. After a stint in the army, Dimas used the G.I. Bill and attended the School of Visual Arts. There he befriended other Puerto Rican artists and together they formed Art Workers Coalition, a multiracial artists' organization. The Art Workers Coalition led a series of demonstrations protesting issues from the Vietnam War to the decentralization of the arts. These demonstrations eventually led Dimas to East Harlem and the founding of Taller Boricua.

Marcos Dimas: *After the deaths of four students at Kent State University in May 1970, the Art Workers Coalition helped close the Museum of the city of New York in East Harlem. And this action was in solidarity with the Kent State massacre. Another reason for the protest was that our organization demanded the museum, located in East Harlem, become more available to the community and promote exhibitions that related to the Latino and African American population in the neighborhood. This was successful and the museum responded to our demands by hiring Betty Mangot, a woman, and the Art Workers Coalition shifted our priority from protests to concentrate on East Harlem. After we did a street exhibition the group created a liaison with the Real Great Society. And they were instrumental in grand-*

fathering us into the community by way of donating space in their building on 110th and 111th Streets and Madison Avenue. Also with the Young Lords across the street, the block itself was fervent with activity and we created silk screen workshops and took those exhibitions and workshops to different parts of the city. We did portraits on Puerto Rican historical figures like Pedro Albizu Campos, Lolita Lebron and Julia De Burgos and gave them away. The art became a tool for social change, for identity and for self-worth and political empowerment. The founders of Taller Boricua were myself, Armando Soto, Adrian Garcia and Martin Rubio.

Marcos Dimas recalls how the organization chose the name Taller Boricua.

Marcos Dimas: *Manuel Otero and Tom Webber met with a lawyer to obtain the incorporation papers. But the name was never discussed because we never held a meeting and the organization immediately needed a title and our lawyer arbitrarily called it the Puerto Rican Workshop. The name was in English because you couldn't use the Spanish translation which at the time it wasn't popular. But today, you could have a Spanish name for an organization. Originally, the place was called Taller Alma Boricua, which means Puerto Rican Soul Workshop. Until our members dropped Alma and we became Taller Boricua (Puerto Rican workshop) because it was easy. Carlos Osorio and Raphael Tufinó were our link to Puerto Rico and the development of Puerto Rican art. And they were also our artistic mentors, because many of our members were Nuyo-ricans, which means born or raised in New York.*

Taller Boricua was about to begin a journey that would usher all of its members into a new realm of Puerto Rican art in the United States. But their stay at their original headquarters ended when the Real Great Society closed.

Marcos Dimas: *After the Real Great Society closed, Taller Boricua had some stipends to pay the rent, but after those stipends ended, and after the winter arrived we moved out because Con Edison cut off the electricity and it was cold.*

Taller Boricua moved to several locations throughout East Harlem during the mid 1970s and 1980s. This move also coincided with staff changes. Adrián García, Armando Soto, Martín Rubio, Rafael Tufinó and Carlos Osorio left. They were replaced by Jorge Soto, Raphael Colon Morales and Fernando Sallicrup. In 1997, Taller Boricua moved to its present home. Marcos Dimas discusses Taller Boricua today.

Marcos Dimas: *Taller Boricua maintains its mission and its basic philosophy is in the arts and cultural organizations. We debut anywhere from twelve to thirty-five artists a year and these artists are from a cross-section of the city: Puerto Ricans, Latin Americans, African Americans and Asian Americans and Caucasians. We also host music and poetry events. We donated space to Julia Jam, a place where musicians come and play. Groups like Yerba Buena, Son Del Barrio and other professional bands have played here. Besides those artists Taller Boricua sponsors* *swing nights on Mondays and has an instructor who gives swing and salsa dance lessons.*[1]

Another arts institution founded by Puerto Ricans was El Museo del Barrio. Like Taller Boricua its origins date back to the late 1960s. A coalition of Puerto Rican parents, educators, artists and community activists founded El Museo del Barrio. The genesis of El Museo began with School District Four Superintendent Martin J. Frey, whose school district lines covered both East and West Harlem. He was cognizant of the numerous African American cultural amenities in the area. But no comparable cultural organization existed for the Puerto Rican community.

An opportunity to create a Puerto Rican cultural center was available and Frey leapt into action. Through the Community Education Center, state monies were available to establish a cultural center for the Puerto Rican community. Frey collaborated with Rafael Ortiz, a teacher from the High School of Music and Art, to work on this project and became its first director. Both men traveled to Puerto Rico and visited the museums on the island to broaden their scope, which helped them to establish the cultural center. A year later the cultural center became El Museo del Barrio, and in 1970, School District Four was redrawn to cover the entire East Harlem neighborhood.

At that time El Museo del Barrio was still headquartered at P.S. 125, located at 425 West 125th Street. In its infancy El Museo del Barrio was primarily a children's museum, staffed by ten people. One of its first two exhibitions included a needlework display by Puerto Rican women, and paintings and graphic work. But El Museo del Barrio was devoid of any security personnel or permanent collection and its possessions were placed in cardboard boxes. This organization taught through an accumulation of cultural objects that instilled cultural pride for many Puerto Ricans in El Barrio and beyond.[2]

Its first location was 116th Street near Third Avenue, but this was temporary. Marta Moreno Vega was chosen as its second director. From 1970 to 1977 El Museo was headquartered in several neighborhood storefronts until it finally secured a home of its own at its present location on Fifth Avenue between 103rd and 104th Streets. The move provided the organization with a modicum of prestige. For example, El Museo became a member of the Cultural Institutions Group as it helped found the Museum Mile. Hiram Maristany succeeded Marta Vega and became interim director, until he was replaced by Jack Agueros, who became its permanent director during this transition period. He changed El Museo del Barrio's direction from a children's museum to one that welcomed artwork from Latino artists throughout the Latin diaspora. More important, El Museo obtained grants from the National Endowment of the Arts, and the New York State Council of the Arts, and gained prestige alongside the other prestigious museums located on Fifth Avenue, such as the Guggenheim Museum. And soon its exhibitions were covered by the *New York Times*. Jack Agueros' tenure at El Museo lasted for ten years. He left his mark on El Museo del Barrio through the Three Kings Day (Los Tres Reyes de Magos) parade which takes place in the neighborhood on or about January 6. Originally, the parade began on the Lower East Side where Jack worked at the Mobilization for Youth. When he became director of the museum, Jack transferred the parade to East Harlem. Today the parade starts on 106th Street; and Fifth Avenue and proceeds to Third Avenue until it reaches 116th Street; then it returns to El Museo del Barrio.[3] It brings a host of politicians who eagerly participate in the parade.

The women's rights movement of the late 1960s and early 1970s, followed in the spirit of the suffrage and Civil Rights movements. This modern protest for equality can be said to have culminated in the Equal Rights Amendment. Though the Amendment was never ratified, women throughout America made their voices heard.

This man championed women's rights and backed his stance with not only words but action. Leo Bailey, who grew up in East Harlem, had a lasting impact on New York State when he worked for the Department of Civil Service. In March 1971, this department asked its staff members to submit their ideas to improve the organization. In recognition of the female workforce throughout the state, Bailey suggested the Workman's Compensation Board be renamed the Workers Compensation Board (WCB).[4]

Bailey was informed his suggestion could only be implemented by the state legislature. Undaunted, Bailey pressed on. He hoped to avoid the state legislature by approaching the Civil Commission to rename the organization. He was again informed that his suggestion was ineligible because it was not conducive to improving the economy and efficiency of the Civil Service Commission. The Civil Service Commission urged Bailey to again approach the state legislature to rename the office to the Workers Compensation Board.[5] Meanwhile, Bailey had gotten press coverage from mainstream magazines, including *Ms.* magazine.[6] Bailey again approached the State Legislature. From 1975 to 1977 several measures were put forth before the state assembly, but each year the bill failed to garner enough votes to pass the first hurdle, and it died in committee. Finally, in 1978, Leo Bailey found an ally, Assemblyman Seymour Posner. (He later worked for the WCB.) Posner reintroduced the bill in the assembly. Assemblyman Posner was joined by State Senators Roy Goodman and John Flynn, who introduced an identical version in the State Senate.

This time the bill passed both houses in the State Legislature and the Worker's Compensation Board became a reality on April 18, 1978. Leo Bailey was hailed in the press for his seven-year odyssey that ended in triumph and he was honored by many organizations and received many awards. State Senator Olga Mendez, who represented east Harlem, presented Leo Bailey with Senate resolution in recognition of his effort.

Piri Thomas' book *Down These Mean Streets*, written in the late 1960s, unofficially began East Harlem's literary flowering. In the next decade other East Harlem writers published books, including Judge Edwin Torres' books *After Hours, Carlito's Way* and *Q and A*. One Puerto Rican woman, Nicholasa Mohr, also first published in the 1970s. Mohr, like Thomas, spent her early childhood in East Harlem and is an artist of many talents. In addition to being a writer, she had an early successful career as a visual artist.

When she submitted her manuscript to her art agent, he assumed that everyone who was raised in East Harlem must have lived the same experience as Thomas. Mohr's book *Nilda* totally rejects this notion. She too writes about several themes also mentioned in Thomas' book, such as playing the numbers, Mohr gives a touching, and often poignant and moving account partially reminiscent of her early East Harlem years. Here Mohr describes how she went from artist to prolific writer. And like Langston Hughes, she confronted and overcame stereotypes attributed to many minorities and women.[7]

Nicholasa Mohr: *The way I started in writing came about from an art agent who handled my graphic art. And, this collector who was the head of a publishing house bought some of my artwork from my art agent. It was he who suggested that I write a book about my experiences. "The artist's work has so much graffiti in it that she seems to be a frustrated writer," said the collector. "Why doesn't she write something about her experiences? "Piri's wonderful book had just come out a few years earlier and the agent brought him up. I replied that I was not a writer, but I also told him that since I was a child I've always been able to write. I am a self-taught writer. Before I went to school, I could read, count, write, similar to someone who can play the piano by ear. The art agent was very persistent, asking, "Why don't you give us fifty pages?" I'd written some art reviews, but that was very simple writing. I replied, "I am an artist, and I'm not a writer. And why would I write?" Then he asked, "How many books do you know are about or written by Puerto Ricans: "And except for Piri's book, there were none. After thinking it over carefully, I decided to give it a try. The art agent didn't tell me who the collector was. The reason is that art agents fear the collectors will go directly to the artist studio to buy work and thereby cancel their commission. I was never told who it was that wanted me to write a book about my experiences. Later, I found out that it was the head of a publishing house.*

I began to write, with difficulty, and cried a lot because it brought up painful memories, but my brother Vincent, and my husband were both helpful by giving me moral support. Somehow, I managed fifty pages, but after reading my work, the agent responded by saying, "Look, we were very disappointed. We wanted something real but this does not sound authentic and this is not what we really want. You need to write about the real guts of your life, you know about gang life in the streets and sexual experiences." I felt not only disrespected but also devastated and I told my agent that I could not write such a book. Instead I suggested that he and the collector go visit a women's prison and find a talented woman who could write the book about her experiences for them. In addition, I also proposed that he would find my present life boring because I was married, had two sons and was living in a lovely home in the suburbs with my husband. "And I was never in a gang, nor have I ever stolen anything or been a prostitute." He apologized and replied that I should not be offended and assured me that the publishing house would find someone to help me write my story. I wanted to send him to hell and leave, but at the same time, he was my art agent and he was allowing me to sell my work and make a good income. I decided not to become confrontational or argue, and with great self-control I simply told him that I was not going to do the book. Because it was a daunting experience, I felt battered and very bad. I had poured out my heart and this racist tells me that my story is not authentic. It's so shocking, even to this day, because he didn't have a clue that his racism was so insulting.

However, Mohr knew she had a wonderful story to tell and she gives an account how her art work led to a fortuitous moment and helped her publish *Nilda*.

I had an exhibit at the 1199 gallery near Lincoln Center and received a great review in the New York Times. *Subsequently, I was recommended by someone who needed an artist to illustrate a book of poetry to be published by Harper & Row. It was 1972 and multiculturalism was just rearing its head and this book of poems contained work by Native American, Black, Asian and Latino writers. I was not a commercial artist and had never illustrated a book. Nevertheless, I took my portfolio to Harper and the editor-in-chief loved my work but responded by saying that my work was not quite what they wanted. However, I took the opportunity to tell her about the fifty pages I'd written. And since I was nice enough to bring in my artwork, she reluctantly agreed to read my short manuscript, also adding that they usually did not accept or read unsolicited work. I sent her my written work and within three weeks the editor in chief at Harper & Row sent me a letter offering me a contract and an advance if I agreed to write a novel based on my short submission.*

It taught me an important lesson, that one opinion is just one opinion. That very summer I got accepted at the MacDowell Colony, a wonderful colony in Peterborough, New Hampshire, for creative artists. Instead of doing artwork, I took this time to write the first eighty pages of Nilda. *Harper & Row sent a letter offering me a contract. A few months later I finished my first novel,* Nilda, *published in*

1974. *I thought this writing career was not going to last and that I was only doing this one book because my intention was to return to my artwork. And now some forty years later, I am still writing. You never know where life takes you.*

In 1974 Nilda was dubbed one of the ten best books of the year by the *New York Times*. And she also won Jane Addams Peace Award and several other awards and rave reviews.

Nicholasa Mohr: *I was both shocked and pleased by the* New York Times Book Review *and their placement of my novel. Harper & Row then wanted a sequel to* Nilda. *But, I was really adamant in my desire to write a collection of short stories and even agreed to take a lower advance. And that book is* El Bronx Remembered *and today both these titles are still in print and selling very well indeed.*

Though Latinos broke through in the literary world, they had yet to conquer the media. For the media hadn't featured any program from a Latino perspective. East Harlem Puerto Ricans sought to ameliorate the situation by joining with other Puerto Ricans and Latino communities to push for Latino-themed television. And this effort resulted in Realidades.

Philanthropist Eugene M. Lang lived in East Harlem during his youth and attended Public School 121 in the neighborhood. Fifty years after he graduated from grammar school, Lang returned to his alma mater. As he went to the podium to address the audience, he thought of Dr. King's famous speech at the Lincoln Memorial. He spontaneously promised to provide college scholarships to the sixth-grade graduating class. Several years later, he founded the I Have a Dream Program. Lang is shown meeting with several students from that sixth grade class (photograph courtesy Eugene M. Lang).

Humberto Cintron: *At that time, I got together with Jack Agueros, Manny Diaz, Jr. [and others]. And we organized the Wednesday night group which featured Puerto Rican guys in leadership. And we decided to make an issue of the media's consciousness regarding Latinos. A friend of mine named José Garcia said WNET has not done any Latino programming in their eleven years of existence. Except for ... "The World of Piri Thomas," about his book* Down These Mean Streets. *But this episode appeared on a black themed program. Channel Thirteen listened and responded to Mr. Garcia's claim.*

And they did a pilot called La Carretta, *"The Ox Cart." But they didn't want to air it, or fund it. Instead we protested and took to the streets. Folks from East Harlem, the West Side, El Comite, the Young Lords and people from the Lower East Side all got together. We had a way where we could call the Lower East Side, Brooklyn and others from the Puerto Rican community do a demonstration.*

Marcos Dimas: *José Garcia used a Puerto Rican play called* La Carretta, *"The Ox Cart," as a pilot project. And basically slanted it toward a social consciousness vehicle and he took it to WNET 13. But they wouldn't accept it, for it was politically charged; however, by today's standards it would be considered mild. Because they didn't want to fund it, José got on the phone and put people together and we demonstrated.*[8]

Humberto Cintron: *We picketed but Channel Thirteen ignored us and finally we got really pissed off. And we took them off the air, by going in and [sitting] in the studio. We closed the door and said, "That's it, nothing will be aired on Channel Thirteen." Then, Channel Thirteen decided they would talk to us. In the meantime, they were recruiting, trying to figure out if we can get a budget, how we want money and a series. We wanted Channel Thirteen to hire José Garcia, but they refused. Then they said, "We have some money, and we will find someone else to do the program." But we said, "You don't have to search anywhere, we got a candidate, and that's part of the deal. We have a person that we think you are gonna like because we heard a lot about him. His name is Humberto Cintron and he worked for the Community News Service." We also said they [Channel Thirteen] interviewed him, but that was bullshit, because I was standing right there and I was on the picket line.*

And Channel Thirteen said "OK," but they didn't know it was me. And the next day, I walked in and the guy from Channel Thirteen almost died. [laughs] I was the first guy climbing up on the desk and now I was working for them. And that's how I got hired.

Channel Thirteen gave us money for fifteen shows, but we did nineteen and we finally aired La Carretta. *And many people learned about producing, for example Marcos Dimas did a show for us.*

Marcos Dimas: *Out of that demonstration many people from the community became producers. I was able to attend WNET film and television school and came out and found work right away. With* Realidades *I produced a couple of pieces with* my co-producer Larry Varas. *The first piece I produced was called* Your Collective Expression, *which was a piece on Puerto Rican art. The second piece was called* Mestizajes, *the Spanish word for "mixture." It featured three Latinos pieces dealing with the question of identity and it focused on the Puerto Rican, Cuban and Mexican experience which was the three main Latinos back then.*

Humberto Cintron: *We also did an advocacy program and taught people all over the country to do license challenges. And we filed license challenges in every station in the city and the news organizations had to listen. Now, they were competing and needed to support their license. That's how we opened the doors for all these other people, David Diaz, J. J. Gonzalez and Raquel Ortiz, who later became television correspondents.*

Many in the Hispanic community in the media learned from their association with *Realidades*. *Realidades* not only catered to Latinos, it helped all people of color. Orlando Blackwell, who is black, became a cameraman, and David Chang, who is Asian and works as an NBC cameraman, also came from *Realidades*. The program also laid the groundwork for *Tony Brown's Journal*. Originally it was called *Tony Brown's Third World Minority Workshop*. In short, *Realidades* was a groundbreaking experience for many people.

Humberto Cintron: *Realidades aired for five years from 1972 to 1977. And many people had the opportunity to broadcast their own films and also work in the industry.*

We conclude our look at East Harlem's renaissance period with Johnny Colon, who returned to East Harlem and lived in the East River Houses. After performing all over the world and making several recordings, Colon used his musical training and instructed the next generation of musicians. And eventually, he opened a music school that was headquartered for many years on 104th Street between Lexington and Third Avenue.

Johnny Colon: *I started the music school in 1962 out of my mother's apartment. And one time I wrote a proposal for the music school, but I was told to disregard it and I kept teaching music out of my mother's apartment.*[9]

Many children I taught at my school went right into any available band because that's how you did it. You expose the musician to the bands and if someone wanted the musician that person went directly into a band. And then other musical students came and they were exposed until that musician was integrated into a band as well. I was fortunate I had my own band and I recorded an album and it became a monster hit, "Bugaloo Blues," which sold three million copies. This was during the era of the Latin bugaloo, but I got ripped off on royalties, still I was working seven days a week. I played many instruments such as trombone, piano, and I also sang and wrote all of my arrangements.

One day I see José Arguayo, then the deputy commissioner for the New York

City Youth Board. And he approaches me and says "Do I know you? You wouldn't happen to be Johnny Colon?" I replied "Yes, I am." He says "I love you, and my kids have all of your records." Then he says, "What are you doing here?" I told him my plans and he replied "Here's my card, why don't you come up and see me." Through his assistance I received funding for a pilot project for nineteen children for the summer, but I ended up with forty-five children.

The next year I was funded only for forty-five children but it was increased to 150 children. Back then I operated out of the Hunter School on 94th Street and Park Avenue. The pilot was so successful that I moved to Public School 171 [19 East 103rd Street] next to Boys Harbor, but unfortunately it didn't work out. I rebounded through the help of my friends and my wife Stephanie and through their help I started up the music school.

Johnny's wife, Stephanie, was an indispensable entity to Johnny Colon's music school. She served as grant writer and administrator, but she also counseled many students, dispensing advice, and cared about each student as if they were her own children. Not surprisingly, these students called her Mom. Besides managing a $2 million operation at the Union Settlement House, Stephanie always felt that the mission of Johnny Colon's music school was important to the East Harlem neighborhood. But after performing at several political functions, Johnny felt uneasy with this association and he parted ways with his politically connected associate.

Colon moved again and opened up his school at 104th Street between Lexington and Third Avenue. There Johnny Colon taught and mentored some of the biggest names in Latin music, including Marc Antonio Muniz, now known as Marc Anthony, who also grew up in East Harlem.

Johnny Colon: *The school did very well and we developed a lot of talented musicians. Every major salsa orchestra which made it big came out of the music school. Tito Puente had many band members who studied at the school. For example, Joe Dejesus who played trombone and Jaime Delgado who played guitar in Tito Puente's band studied here. And Machito and Ray Barretto also used musicians from our school. Plus, Eddie Palmieri and his brother, Charlie Palmieri, who was an instructor at the school, stopped by as well. Finally, Marc Anthony was a student here and I first met Marc when he was eight years old. Both Marc and his sister studied with me when they were children. And he was a very energetic and bright student with exceptional leadership qualities. For example Marc distributed the instruments to the students and in class he studied music and piano theory and he loved to sing. And Marc was always singing songs, but back then Marc sang rhythm and blues. Marc studied at the school for several years until he was about twelve or fourteen. After he left the school, I heard he went to Puerto Rico and years later and he's singing salsa and made his own album. It was* salsa romantica *style and Marc became very successful and he signed with Sony.*

Colon remained at this location until Hope Community Incorporated, a housing organization that owned the place where Colon operated his music school, decided to replace that business. Afterward, Colon moved his music school to 106th street. Sadly, it was also during this period that his beloved Stephanie died. His music school closed in 1993. This setback did not deter Johnny Colon from continuing his love of playing and teaching music; he still teaches music to a new generation of students. Presently, he is a school teacher.

East Harlem's cultural renaissance showed the world the beauty and artistry of the neighborhood, but these achievements were overshadowed as East Harlem faced mounting problems over health conditions, drugs, infanticide and mental illnesses. After the neighborhood's support systems—neighbors living in small buildings and businesses—disappeared during the 1950s, this left many East Harlemites depending more on the city's social services, and these problems were magnified by the 1970s. East Harlem's health centers were overwhelmed and inadequate to deal with these problems. Before long, East Harlem fell on hard times. As before, the New York City Department of City Planning deemed East Harlem a major area for redevelopment. East Harlem was joined by Harlem in the Model Cities Program, a federal initiative created in the late 1960s to help poor neighborhoods enhance their community through a network of social services. Some of these initiatives were education and job training.

On paper the Model Cities Program (MCP) looked promising, but as with the plans of 1937 and 1945, the goal to uplift East Harlem failed.

In retrospect, the MCP needed a strong administrator to serve as a conduit between the MCP and the city. To make matters worse ethnic tensions rose with the merging of East and Central Harlem into one MCP unit. Finally, labor unions were reluctant to assist the MCP. The unions feared that training MCP members would siphon off jobs from union members.[10] Despite these problems, funds were still available when the MCP ended in 1972. But the failure of the MCP reflected the failure of the anti-poverty programs across the country. The MCP was a hold over from the Johnson administration's anti-poverty programs of the 1960s. The Office of Economic Opportunity, once instrumental to the East Harlem Real Great Society, was replaced by President Nixon's Community Services Administration (CSA) in 1969, and the CSA was ended by President Ronald Regan in 1981.[11]

Some antipoverty programs survived during the 1970s. Federal monies were still available to economically distressed communities in East Harlem. These antipoverty agencies provided jobs as the old-style patronage system once did.

Arnie Segarra: *In the late 1960s or early 1970s the reform movement phased out the patronage system. The Anti Poverty Programs became the new Patronage System.*

The demise of the political bosses ended the patronage system, but it opened the plantation system in the guise of antipoverty "pimps." Puerto Ricans and to a lesser extent African Americans utilized these antipoverty programs during this period to attain political power. However, Harlem and East Harlem operated under different circumstances. Harlem, with its entrenched politicians such as Adam Clayton Powell, Jr., and power broker Raymond Jones, the "Harlem Fox," knew how to control the community through the antipoverty money. In contrast East Harlem's Puerto Rican community still lacked a powerful politician.[12]

Felipe Luciano: *The Civil Rights movement fell into East Harlem at the end of the movement's last years. And so many antipoverty programs came to the neighborhood and affected East Harlem economically. The poverty pimp regime was born and we ended up having more antipoverty programs in this particular community than any other community. And corruption became a way of life.*

The Massive Economic Neighborhood Development Program (MEND) became the most successful antipoverty program in East Harlem. MEND began in the 1960s, after Preston Wilcox, a social worker who once worked at Union Settlement, wrote the proposal for the program.[13] MEND was established to combat the neighborhood's problems: joblessness, drugs, and crime. These antipoverty programs had one thing in common: brevity. Government-funded programs had to produce results within a specific time or the funding would end. Even if these organizations succeeded, their funding could still end. Many observers surmised that anti-poverty programs like MEND would inevitably end due to the changing markets in production, technology and employment skills. And some directors within MEND aimed to uplift themselves rather than their constituents.

Ultimately MEND had other ideas, and the social service agency reconstituted itself from a service center to an organization that wielded political power. MEND consolidated its empire by gaining control of the community's health and advisory boards. Through MEND, the Puerto Rican leadership rose and reached its zenith in East Harlem during the early 1970s. The agency helped elect an Assemblyman to the State Legislature and won several districts.[14] However, despite the human rights, literary and cultural achievements of Marcos Dimas, Leo Bailey, Nicholasa Mohr and Johnny Colon, many East Harlemites lived with the criminal element that existed in the neighborhood. Loan sharking, drug dealing and the numbers racket thrived in East and West Harlem, Bedford Stuyvesant and the South Bronx. This profit making scheme sapped hundreds of millions of dollars from these urban neighborhoods.[15] Also during the 1970s, East Harlem lost several of its treasures. The Washburn Wire Factory which provided employment for thousands of East Harlemites closed. The original La Marqueta, which first operated outdoors and served many generations, was damaged by a fire and never returned to its original form. It faded into history.[16] A new version of La Marqueta opened in the late 1990s; however, it pales in comparison to the original La Marqueta.

Henry Calderon: *It was competition now. People could buy their certain foods in the neighborhood stores. And La Marqueta no longer exclusively sold those products. Plus, the population had changed.*

The neighborhood's movie theaters also closed during this period. The Azteca and the Eagle closed in the 1970s. The Cosmo, the last local East Harlem movie theater, closed in 1987. The 1970s saw many tenements destroyed by arson or abandoned by their landlords. It was not as prevalent as in the South Bronx, still East Harlem had its fare share of abandoned buildings and became a blighted neighborhood.[17]

David Givens: *The community just deteriorated and it was very depressing. I remember the 1977 blackout. And many people robbed the Bargain World store on 125th Street and Fifth Avenue and took many transistor radios. Besides the blackout, I remember walking from an office on 115th Street and Madison Avenue and you saw abandoned buildings from 117th to 123rd Streets. It was a ghost town. And any unoccupied and abandoned building was seized by drug addicts who went in there, did drugs. North General and Joint Diseases hospitals on 122nd and 123rd Streets during one weekend just abandoned those buildings. They packed up their expensive equipment and went downtown and the neighborhood was left with an aging building built in 1919. And many methadone clinics moved to the neighborhood and East Harlem became oversaturated with them.*

Other neighborhoods throughout the city successfully fought and prevented methadone clinics or more social service agencies from opening in their community. But these centers opened in East Harlem because of its lower-class status. As for the neighborhood itself, the population declined from 154,000 to 114,000 by the decade's end.[18]

9

1980s — Dr. King's Dream Lives On

The next story represents the very essence of this book. Here we will read how one man's vision helped dozens of East Harlem students attend college and touched the lives of thousands of Americans. The problems that plagued the neighborhood in the 1970s, poverty, drugs and crime, continued in the 1980s. Crack, a cheap, derivative form of cocaine, became the neighborhood's latest problem. The drug, very addictive, accounted for many of the neighborhood's violent deaths. Many East Harlemites again felt under siege.

Despite these difficult times, it was during the 1980s, when Eugene Lang conceived the renowned I Have a Dream Foundation in East Harlem. Today Lang, a successful philanthropist, has inspired many corporate executives throughout America to "adopt" thousands of children in low-class communities to help them earn a college education. Lang, born in 1919, is the son of immigrant parents. His father hailed from Hungary and his mother hailed from France. He spent his early years growing up in an East Harlem railroad flat. Lang attended P.S. 121, located on East 103rd Street between Lexington and Third Avenue, from the first to the sixth grades. It was his machinist father who insisted he should learn to use tools because in his view these instruments or a skill meant his son would never starve.

Later, Lang's family moved several blocks south to 87th Street, and eventually to Westchester County. He applied for and gained admission to the distinguished Townsend Harris High School (THH). And upon completion of the intensive three year high school curriculum he graduated in 1929. He was assured admission without cost to City College. However, his high school years were during the Great Depression. The Lang family suffered periods of unemployment. Eugene frequently saved subway or trolley fare by walking from his home on 87th Street to the high school, located 23rd Street. He worked as a busboy in a small restaurant located between his home and school while simultaneously serving as an advertising manager of the THH annual book, *The Crimson and Gold* — an experience which proved valuable in his later years.

As he approached his THH graduation in January 1934 fate intervened in his favor as Lang replaced a co-worker who was ill that day. Lang was summoned to serve a regular customer at the restaurant, but this person was not just anyone: He happened to be a trustee at Swarthmore College who liked what he saw in Lang and set up an interview for him. Lang passed the interview and won a scholarship to Swarthmore in Pennsylvania. He was an economics major and graduated in 1938. He then furthered his education at Columbia Business School. In the early 1950s, Lang founded Refac, a company that organized cooperative manufacturing enterprises with many corporations in over forty countries around the globe. Lang's life is an American success story,[1] but for many East Harlemites during the early 1980s, the chance of pursuing a successful career like Eugene Lang's was improbable. But as before, fate played a role in Eugene Lang's life.

Eugene Lang: *Back in 1981, the school's new principal was about to preside over his first sixth-grade commencement class and he wanted to have a guest speaker that would attract publicity. Actor Burt Lancaster, who also was from East Harlem and a P.S. 121 graduate, was an ideal guest speaker. The principal tried repeatedly to contact Burt Lancaster, but he received no response. And he was prepared to give up on the idea of attracting a newsworthy person, but he read a coincidental New York Times article about me. The article mentioned that I had attended P.S. 121, which apparently qualified me as a noteworthy person for the invitation to address his school's 1981 commencement. And I accepted his invitation. I had given commencement speeches before, usually to college graduates. But when I got to P.S. 121, I realized this was a different audience and they were from the sixth grade, about twelve years old and mostly with Hispanic parents who did not speak English. I had expected to give a conventional commencement speech. But I realized to talk to these young kids and their parents the same way I talked to college students didn't make any sense. In fact, I was not sure what I was going to say as I sat there on the dais, agonizing, waiting for my time to speak.*

Just before he was about to speak, the memory of King's "I Have a Dream" speech planted the seed for Mr. Lang's stunning surprise.

Eugene Lang: *As I walked to the rostrum to give my commencement address, I kept thinking to myself, "What am I gonna say?" Suddenly, I felt a flash of inspiration. I thought back to the day in Washington, D.C. when I heard Martin Luther King, Jr., give his tremendous "I Have a Dream" speech at the Lincoln Memorial, and that became my theme. I began talking to these children and I told them how I'd grown up in the neighborhood and I was [brought up] to realize that you had to stay in school. In the past you needed only muscles to find a job, but now you also needed education. I said this is your first graduation, some will go to junior high school, and then on to high school and then to college. But as I talked I thought to* *myself, Am I being realistic? Most of these kids had never thought about college. In fact, many of them would not even finish high school, and drop out. So I urged them to stay in school and I impulsively told them if you stay in school, graduate from high school, and when you do I'll give you the tuition scholarship so you can go to college' And this promise was completely impulsive. The audience was enthusiastic even though I didn't think they understood what college meant, but when you're a kid, you take what you can get.*

Lang could have stopped with his promise, but a conversation with the school's principal spurred him to take further action.

Eugene Lang: *Actually, that was far as I thought it would go and after the ceremony the principal told me, "That was a great thing you did." I replied I was glad that I did it. Now, as I calmly began calculating how much it might cost to send sixty-one students to college, the principal said, "Don't worry about it because most of these children will drop out. Because only a few students will graduate high school, truthfully maybe one or two might make it to college." I thought to myself, that's a hell of a note. I'm promising these children that I will help pay for their college education and he was telling me that my promise didn't mean anything. And this bothered me. I thought to myself maybe I shouldn't have made that promise, but having made it, I would keep my word. I would figure out some way to encourage them to stay in school. The principal said, "I'll figure out a way and we'll develop a budget and then you can take care of it. Then I replied. I was surprised that if he thought it so important, why as a principal he wouldn't do something about it.*

He answered, "I'm used to spending my school's budgeted money, but I can recommend some people to work a budget for you." I replied, "You can send me their resumes, but I hire my own people." He said, "We'll get a press release on what you said." I replied, "Please don't do that. I'm not doing this for publicity, only for the children." And he was no longer interested in the promise I made and washed his hands of the affair. I asked him for the list of the graduates and their addresses and he refused, but I obtained them and invited them to a graduation party on a Saturday afternoon at the neighborhood Y. They came and I enthusiastically decided to "Have a Dream for the First I have a Dream Project." I domiciled them in the Youth Action Program, then on 109th Street and Fifth Avenue, and Dorothy Stoneman was a big help with the program because she gave a home to the I Have a Dream Project [IHAD], and my children became the first Dreamers.

Lang was committed to his IHAD project, and was cognizant that these children faced many problems growing up in East Harlem. Since their 1981 graduation, Lang has maintained contact with his "Dreamers." And he has taken a genuine interest in many of the students. These relationships encompass group discussions on school related and personal issues.[2] And their parents or guardians are often involved. Also, Mr. Lang has embellished their lives in other ways by arranging camping trips, career advice and introductions, educational and job opportunities and personal advice.

For example, in late 1985, Lang and twenty Dreamers attended a Broadway production of *The Marriage of Figaro* starring the late Christopher Reeve. After the performance ended, the Dreamers met the actor, who stressed the importance of his college education, which prepared him for adulthood and his subsequent acting career.[3] In September 1986 Lang established the I Have a Dream Foundation and traveled across the country telling local audiences how average citizens could help children from economically challenged backgrounds attend college. Lang traveled around spreading a message that the best investment the nation can make is in its youth. Many cities from coast to coast were receptive to his idea of encouraging and sponsoring children to college. Today, hundreds of individuals have sponsored IHAD projects.

Eugene Lang: *For several years, I made sure I Have a Dream was private affair for I did not intend to spread the program's message. But the word gets around that this successful guy is doing this program in East Harlem, with these children. And when people asked me questions, I turned a deaf ear and I kept it private for four years until June of 1986. Then Dorothy Stoneman said, "You don't realize it, but all of your children are still in school." That's when I realized this was succeeding and ... perhaps a miracle had happened considering the odds against possible failure. And the Dreamers were halfway through their high school years. I asked myself, "What, really, did I do?" Well, I developed personal relationships with the students and focused on encouragement with their education and their future. And I provided things like a show here or there. But IHAD didn't seem to me like any big deal. And I was getting as much pleasure and reward as the children and their parents, perhaps even more.*

I thought to myself, if it's so easy to generate these happy relationships and if anybody could offer children scholarships to attend college then why not? That was when, for the first time, I decided to inform the public of the I Have a Dream Program. Clearly many children needed the personal support that IHAD provides. In September 1985 a New York Times reporter interviewing me on another personal subject asked me what else I was doing. And [then] the clouds opened up with questions and interest stemming from television with respect to the I Have a Dream Program. They wanted to know how IHAD could be replicated. And that's when I formally organized the I Have a Dream Project. Within a year we started twenty projects in New York City and the message spread across the country.

In 1987, forty-eight out of the sixty-one original dreamers graduated from high school and ten students had moved away from East Harlem. However, many of the original class pursued "the dream" and attended college. And five Dreamers, like Mr. Lang, went to Swarthmore College.[4]

IHAD has grown exponentially since Mr. Lang's visited P.S. 121 in June

1981. The program does more than just provide scholarships for disadvantaged youth. IHAD's mission is that it directly assists children from kindergarten to the 12th grade with year-long instructional programs that encompass education, cultural awareness, and social and recreational outings. After a few years Dreamers will earn a high school diploma and acquire the skills to obtain employment.

IHAD sponsors are subjected to a rigorous process. Each is directly and personally involved with the Dreamer, focusing on developing the young person to earn an education and learn skills to compete in society. The cost of sponsoring a project varies depending on the program. Each sponsor selects a complete elementary class from public school, starting no later than in the third grade, or a public housing authority, which constitutes a formal IHAD project. The average project may include 30 to 100 children.

Sponsors must reside in the community with the project. This arrangement will develop a personal bond between the long-term sponsor(s) and the Dreamers. The arrangement enriches the lives of both the provider (sponsor) and the Dreamer (recipient). To facilitate these relationships each sponsor (or group) employs a project coordinator who maintains contact with the Dreamers. In addition, the sponsor also addresses the educational issues that are important to the project, which includes input from the teachers and their families. The community is also important in helping develop and sustain the Dreamers and their sponsor. The "community" could be a religious leader, local elected official, or community based organizations, churches, synagogues or other houses of worship. These organizations can help by donating space, time and energy to their local IHAD project.[5]

In 1993, IHAD branched out and sponsors were invited to select public housing residents as Dreamers. Five years later, Congress passed the GEAR UP legislation, patterned after IHAD. IHAD continues to inspire many Americans from government and the corporations to help, sponsor, and support the programs. Secretary of Education Arne Duncan, who once headed Chicago's public school system, was a dedicated sponsor for ten years. In addition, IHAD sponsors have provided Dreamers with access to part-time jobs, internships, and career counseling. Presently over two hundred colleges and Universities support IHAD. Some have assured that Dreamers who are admitted to college receive needed scholarships and financial aid.[6]

Thirty years after I Have a Dream was founded, over 200 projects have been undertaken in twenty-seven states. Some 16,000 lives have been touched during this period. For his efforts, Eugene Lang's I Have a Dream Foundation has been recognized by Presidents Ronald Reagan, Bill Clinton and George W. Bush. And Alvarado Aristedes, an original Dreamer, received an audience with First Lady Barbara Bush, who spoke at an IHAD Convention.[7]

Eugene Lang is still in touch with the first class of the I Have a Dream Project.

Eugene Lang: *I still see the students and their families and they individually call or drop by my midtown office to see how I'm doing. And the students each year have arranged a Father's Day party for me.*

Like Lang, another East Harlemite, James De La Vega, envisioned a dream, and though his dream is different, this artist/philosopher has moved thousands of New Yorkers with his simple message "Become Your Dream." Unlike the El Museo del Barrio or Taller Boricua, this dreamer works alone. And De La Vega's work can still be seen on many East Harlem buildings throughout the neighborhood. Tito Puente stated he was a street musician, and likewise James De La Vega is a street artist. He was raised and learned his craft during East Harlem's lean years of the 1970s and 1980s.[8]

James De La Vega: *I was born in Spanish [East] Harlem between Park and Lexington Avenues, where I still live, and both of my parents are Puerto Rican. My father is from Caguas, Puerto Rico, and my mother was born in East Harlem and moved to the West Side before she came back to the neighborhood. I was the only child from that union, although I have another brother from my father, but my mother raised me. My stepfather was there, but my mother was the key figure and she always kept me pretty isolated from the neighborhood. And I witnessed the streets from my father's eyes by watching him because he was very popular in the area. And these guys would drink in the corner together in the social club and this was my experience growing up in the neighborhood as a kid. But I was pretty lucky that my mother, who is a strong lady, guided and took care of me and I think that influence came from my father's effect on her. I know my father was involved in the day-to-day hustle from the streets, but she wasn't and she protected me from all that.*

Though he was raised by his mother, De La Vega's artistry came from his father's side. Like Lang, Vega branched out of East Harlem and returned to help the neighborhood.

James De La Vega: *When I was a child my father loved to draw, and though I didn't live with him, I spent many times with him. And when we were together he drew these little pictures for me and it was those pictures which made me appreciate art and enjoy the magic of it. Also, to watch somebody's hand to create Superman or another character was great. And my mother always encouraged me to draw and she brought me boxes of crayons or coloring books. Eventually, she sent me to the Whitney Museum for their after-school art programs. Later, I attended York Preparatory high school, but I didn't think I wanted to be an artist. Even though I liked doing art, it wasn't until my senior year when my guidance counselor suggested that I attend college and study something I enjoyed, which was art. This led me to study art at Cornell University. But I hadn't decided if I wanted to live as an artist, or* do art as a profession until I was a freshman in college. At Cornell, as a freshman art student, I took art classes, did paintings and drawings, all with mixed paints. And I studied with many professors who were really serious about doing art.

De La Vega's works are reminiscent of those of another artist whose style is similar, Keith Haring, who died in 1990, De La Vega's first year in college.

James De La Vega: *I remember when I was a junior or a senior when one of my fraternity brothers drew some of Keith Haring's materials, but I didn't pay it any mind. However, I heard about Keith Haring after I graduated from college and he was an influence on me through his works and he inspired one of my works.*

After De La Vega graduated from college, the urban blight that plagued the neighborhood had not dissipated. Though crack cocaine was on the wane, it was still in the neighborhood. Despite these surroundings, De La Vega did not let the situation deter him from making art.

James De La Vega: *After I graduated from college I wanted to do something in East Harlem to make the neighborhood a better place. I remembered there were two vacant lots on 102nd Street between Lexington and Park Avenue. And this was the first time I really got involved in politics or any neighborhood activism. Once we cleaned out the lot, we held many poetry readings there. And before you know it, people did poetry and talked politics. And some of the poets were Sandra Maria Estevez, Panama Alba, Richie Perez, Papoleto (Melendez) and Pedro Pietri or any poet you could name came there.*

The poetry readings were successful, but De La Vega wanted to move in a different direction. He turned to his art to beautify the neighborhood by painting murals on many buildings throughout East Harlem.

James De La Vega: *I was tired of being part of the political scene, for I felt it was going nowhere. I graduated from a good university and I couldn't accomplish something meaningful to help people realize their dreams. I figured, let me apply my own ability as an artist, and little by little I began painting on the neighborhood's abandoned buildings or empty walls. And my artwork made people think. One of my earliest paintings was for this child named Sammy who was seventeen years old when he died. And when I was painting I noticed there was a power to working on the streets. Not only was it a nice way to beautify the abandoned buildings, but it brought a lot of excitement and enthusiasm to the streets. I have painted [Puerto Rican independence leaders] Don Pedro Albizu Campos and Lolita Lebron, Mexican leader Emilio Zapata, Malcolm X, the late Tejano singer Selena, and many religious themes.*

De La Vega went further as an artist and has written in chalk the words that have become his mantra, "Become your Dream." This slogan has appeared on many East Harlem streets as well as elsewhere in New York City.

James De La Vega: *People have always asked where "Become Your Dream" originated from. I don't remember, but I know what the idea means to me. It is the artwork I have done on the streets and it is about getting people to rethink themselves and to rethink the world around them. Also, "Become Your Dream" brings inspiration and brings people together. Why feel lonely, isolated or depressed, and this whole idea of "Becoming Your Dream" is a concept about inspiring people to really dig deep into themselves and think about what they want to do. And go out and do it, because in the dangerous times we live in, the events might crush people's dreams.*

De La Vega's artwork transcends East Harlem. His former neighborhood storefront art studio on 104th Street and Lexington Avenue became a tourist attraction for many New Yorkers and many community residents. Many art world figures like LeRoy Neiman visited his storefront to see De La Vega's work. In 2005, he relocated to St. Mark's Place in downtown Manhattan, but recently De La Vega returned to East Harlem.

James De La Vega: *One of the messages I've learned along the way is to teach other people to break beyond [their] limitations. Just the same way the world is right now as people outside 96th Street have entered East Harlem, and I think we should enter their world. Rather than East Harlem residents seeing ourselves as victims, we need to take charge of our situation and let the world see we have no limits. I like the idea of going into St. Mark's or Union Square and people say who in the hell is De La Vega. It didn't matter who I was, or that people didn't know what I looked like. And that is one of the reasons the work has become interesting because people have seen "Become Your Dream." We have been able to communicate with simple mediums. Like chalk on the sidewalk, or putting little thoughts on T-shirts, and finally painting on abandoned buildings. And we've used art not only to renovate buildings, but renovate people's lives.*

10
1990s — Rebirth of East Harlem

The first story of the neighborhood's rebirth focuses on the music of the Boys Choir of Harlem. Traveling around the globe, the young singers have entertained thousands of fans for several decades. They were the Boys Choir of Harlem.

They were first led by Dr. Walter Turnbull, originally from Greenville, Mississippi. He received a scholarship to and graduated from Tupelo College, outside Jackson, Mississippi. After receiving his college degree, Turnbull arrived in East Harlem and attended the Manhattan School of Music. Turnbull also taught in the neighborhood at Junior High School 99. Later he received his Master's degree from the Manhattan School of Music.

The choir was founded in 1968, but was officially incorporated in 1975. The choir was headquartered at the Ephesus Church on Lenox Avenue until it burned down, and then the choir moved to the Marcus Garvey Center. At the center, the choir met Ambassador Franklin Williams of Ghana, who liked the choir and connected it to the Phelps Stokes Fund and the choir took off.

Dr. Turnbull ventured into the public schools to find his future choir members. After passing a rigorous audition they were admitted into the choir. Members of the Boys Choir of Harlem wear burgundy blazers and dark slacks.

The Boys Choir of Harlem has an excellent reputation which garnered invitations to perform all over the world, including Israel, Japan, Singapore and the Netherlands. In addition to their international performances, the Boys Choir of Harlem has performed for several presidents at the White House, at the united Nations, and before Pope John Paul II with an estimated audience of over 125,000 in Central Park. They can be heard on such movie soundtracks as *Glory* and *Malcolm X*, both of which starred Denzel Washington; on former Beatle Paul McCartney's *Liverpool Oratorio*; with the Ballet Hispanico; on Broadway and at the Apollo.[1]

In 1993, the Boys Choir of Harlem moved to the Choir Academy of Harlem, located on East 127th and Madison Avenue, where the school catered to over 550 students from the fourth to twelfth grade. In 2000, one of the choir members stated he was sexually abused by a staff person. Afterwards, funding to the Boys Choir of Harlem declined. Six year later, the Boys Choir of Harlem was evicted by the Department of Education from the Choir Academy of Harlem building. After the eviction, the Boys Choir of Harlem operated in East Harlem at 127th Street and Fifth Avenue. But, the guiding force behind the choir, Dr. Walter Turnbull, died in April 2007. Since then, the Boys Choir of Harlem has remained silent.

Next this story delves into how East Harlem's Pathmark supermarket came to the neighborhood. Many small businesses and franchises opened in East Harlem during the late 1990s and afterward, but the neighborhood's biggest and addition was the pathmark supermarket that opened in 1999. Its origin dates back to late September 1994, when the Community Development Local Initiatives Support Corporation (LISC), a nonprofit organization, composed of ten corporations amassed $24 million to pursue a business venture. LISC soon focused on bringing a Pathmark supermarket to East 125th Street between Lexington Avenue and Third Avenue, a space which once operated as a community garden. Proponents of this proposal claimed Pathmark would be an upgrade in contrast to the expensive but poor quality foods sold in the neighborhood. Another incentive for bringing Pathmark to East Harlem was the prospect of securing over 250 jobs for the neighborhood.[2]

Monies earned from this development would be returned to the community to build housing and health care facilities. One of Pathmark's biggest supporters was the East Harlem Triangle, an area from 125th Street to the Harlem River near 132nd Street. The triangle began in 1961, when the Community Association of the East Harlem Triangle was formed. Its founders were Alice Kornegay, Virginia Watson, Vivian Taylor, Gilberta Peterson, Flossie Pope and the Rev. Melvin Schoonover, a white minister. Residents in this community not only advocated for civil rights, they also believed in economic and community improvement. The organization name was later shortened to the East Harlem Triangle.

Today, Hannah Brockington is the president of the East Harlem Triangle. Brockington was a member of Chambers Memorial Baptist Church when Schoonover arrived. As in most black inspired movements, the church played a vital role in its creation. She recalls with Schoonover's participation and much needed community services that led to the Triangle's formation.[3]

Hannah Brockington: *I became involved with the East Harlem Triangle through the Chambers Memorial Church, and the church did many things for the community. For example, through the church our members became aware of their civil rights and health benefits. Before, many residents who went to the nearby hospital and had their temperature taken, but many times these patients were uninformed about their results and other city agencies did this.*

Whether it was the social services agency or the housing authority, a majority of our residents believed their status as low-income New Yorkers was the reason they were not informed. Basically, the Triangle was established because many residents needed to know their rights and obtain neighborhood services like after-school programs and day care. The church was headed by Melvin Schoonover, who introduced the Triangle. When the Triangle was built it was then located on 129th Street and Lexington Avenue. And the Triangle also operated as a referral service or the organization advocated for the community. It advocated the need for good schools and there were also housing issues, but the city just built housing projects. And many residents needed to live in affordable housing, but didn't want to live in more housing projects.

Several studies were commissioned regarding the Triangle's economic and housing status. And one report cited a need to improve the housing and economic conditions within the Triangle. By the late 1960s, the Triangle joined the Architects Renewal Committee in Harlem to implement the aforementioned changes. And out of this study grew the Neighborhood Economic Development Board (NEDB).

The Triangle operated and controlled the NEDB and they met with private companies to create businesses. Some of the businesses that were created were in the areas of catering, laundry and maintenance. The NEDB gave financial and consulting advice to retail new businesses. Hannah Brockington describes the success of this program.

Hannah Brockington: *One young man opened two laundry stores and men and women gained valuable experience in the business sector and it made a difference. And there was the Beatrice Lewis Senior Center which has a day care center which still operates today. A job readiness program and Each One, Teach One founded by Bob McCullough.*

The organization did more than just create businesses and senior and day care centers. It also instructed the Triangle's residents on the fundamentals of employment etiquette, and in the legal and social services.

Hannah Brockington: *Employment counselors did role playing and they stressed punctuality and people were taught to dress properly. And they also learned how to professionally answer phones and this instruction is needed today. Also legal aid counseling and Peace Corps volunteers helped the Triangle. We also had at the Chambers Houses a social worker who provided assistance and if the residents had problems with alcoholism, an alcoholic treatment or referral service was there as well. The Triangle also gave advice to young parents on how to take care of their children, develop a budget to pay their rent and buy food. And out of that success came the opportunity to build housing from 126th Street to 130th Street.*

Within this same period, the organization changed its mission from a social services provider to housing developer. The Triangle helped rehabilitate

Triangle Apartments/Chambers Houses and this effort yielded 179 refurbished apartments. Finally in, 1968, P.S. 30/31, the Raphael Hernandez and Langston Hughes School, opened. But many of the Triangle's successful programs and services that the organization began in the late 1960s were phased out or were taken over by the city. The Triangle suffered through a dry period from the mid- to late 1980s as no housing was constructed or rehabilitated. But by the early 1990s, the organization rebounded. The Tweemill Houses opened, and a year later, with assistance from the Triangle, the Addicts Rehabilitation Center welcomed its new facility on 128th Street and Madison Avenue.

In 1997, the Triangle continued this resurgence when it partnered with Mt. Sinai Hospital, Union Settlement and Chambers Memorial Baptist Church and created 77 units of housing for senior citizens.[4] The next project involved the Pathmark supermarket. But first Pathmark's officials needed convincing before they agreed to a supermarket in East Harlem.

David Givens: *Pathmark didn't want to come to East Harlem, but Alice Kornegay, myself and Bob McCullough went to the company's headquarters in Cataract, New Jersey. And Alice explained to them with the new developments there would be a substantial population to support a Pathmark which is why it should be open in East Harlem. But Pathmark didn't think East Harlem residents had the money to shop at one of their stores. Then Bob, Alice and I again went to their headquarters to convince them there was a market in East Harlem. Because when you drove around the block, they didn't see anyone living on 125th Street, but they didn't realize that people who traveled on the Triborough Bridge and people from other neighborhoods would drive over to shop if the Pathmark was built.*

Meanwhile the mainstream press wrote that the Pathmark of East Harlem was turning into a racial issue, even as Harlem's Abyssinian Baptist Church, located on West 137th Street and Frederick Douglass Boulevard, partnered with the East Harlem Triangle. Some Latinos in East Harlem viewed Pathmark's sponsors, the Abyssinian Baptist Church and the Triangle, whose population was dominated by African Americans, as a black venture.

Compounding the arguments was the proposed Pathmark would be built in East 125th Street (El Barrio) and not in West Harlem. Some Latino bodega and supermarket owners feared Pathmark threatened their businesses and distributors. They also objected to the federal and state subsidies awarded. The National Supermarket Association (NSA) headed by Eligio Peña, Mariano Diaz and Al Rodriguez, was part of this group and objected to the project. Ironically, the major players in this drama didn't even live in East Harlem. Some small bodega owners lived in East Harlem, but the majority of them and supermarket owners were Dominican entrepreneurs who resided in Washington Heights or other parts of the city. Conversely, the Abyssinian

Baptist Church, which backed the Pathmark Supermarket, was located in Harlem.[5]

Nelson Antonio Denis, a lawyer and activist, arrived in East Harlem in the early 1990s. Immediately, Denis became involved in the neighborhood and joined Community Board 11. He ran against the political leadership, which by early 1990s was dominated by Angelo Del Toro. After several elections, Denis won the State Assembly seat once held by Del Toro, who died in 1994. Denis served two terms in the State Assembly. After leaving office, Denis wrote and directed the film *Vote for Me*. A year before Denis was elected to the assembly he too joined the fight for the Pathmark supermarket. Though he backed the NSA, Denis asserts the Pathmark was not a racial issue as the press reported.

Nelson Denis: *Al Rodriguez never saw this as a racial issue because his own supermarket serviced everybody, but he saw this as an economic issue. Al had people to feed, his own family, and his workers to pay and their produce was set at good prices. I strenuously avoided and repudiated any effort to make this a racial issue, because the only color that mattered was green. Abyssinian Baptist Church did not involve themselves to make Pathmark a racial statement and neither was Alfredo. When one individual or group asserts their economic interest it becomes community oriented and when someone else of color does it, it's become racial and this is a double standard.*

The groups fiercely fought for and against this project. Thousands of petition signatures were gathered from East Harlem residents.

Nelson Denis: *Aurora Flores, a writer and performer, held a press conference at the Tweemill Houses in East Harlem. And together we brought shopping carts and did a shopping cart demonstration, while the Pathmark was being discussed. Our side obtained between five and ten thousand signatures and I presented my viewpoint on a televised discussion between the Rev. Calvin Butts and myself on [the television channel] New York One.*

The National Supermarkets Association came up with a solution which the organization thought would be acceptable to both sides, but the idea went nowhere.

Nelson Denis: *The NSA proposed an alternative supermarket for the same site. And the architectural group was Gotham Grid Properties who made a presentation to Community Board number 11. Bottom line, Pathmark supermarket presented their side and the Community Board agreed that it was deemed necessary for this supermarket to go forward.*

With that hurdle passed, the next step was City Hall. Rudolph W. Giuliani, the pro-business mayor elected in 1993, was expected to support the

Pathmark. But Giuliani, who defeated David Dinkins, the city's first black mayor, was at a disadvantage in forging a strong relationship with a majority of black New Yorkers. But Giuliani also did not want to strain relations with the Latino community. Surprisingly, Giuliani remained silent on the issue. While the mayor remained mute, the Pathmark's fate hinged on the Manhattan Borough Board: ten of City Council members from Manhattan, the chairperson of Community Board 11, and the Manhattan borough president, Ruth Messinger. But the Manhattan borough president would only vote if there were a tie. In late April 1995, it appeared that the opponents of the Pathmark had enough votes to kill the project. The day before the scheduled vote, City Councilman Guillermo Linares, the first person from the Dominican Republic elected to office in New York State, told fellow Dominican Al Rodriguez of his assured no vote, which would effectively kill the Pathmark supermarket.[6]

Nelson Denis: *Then it came down to a borough board vote and Councilman Linares was viewed as a solid anti-Pathmark supermarket vote. And he agreed that the pathmark supermarket was a bad idea. Even as Linares rode up the elevator with Al Rodriguez to cast his vote, he stated he would vote against the Pathmark.*

But, when the roll call was made, Linares literally switched sides at the last minute and voted to approve the project. The final vote was 7–5 and the contentious issue even solicited a vote from Messinger, who supposedly could not vote. But she claimed she voted to avoid any doubt on the final outcome. And Linares stated he voted yes because if the proposal was defeated the racial polarization between blacks and Latinos would worsen.

With the borough board vote decided, there was still the delicate issue between the Latino and black communities over the Pathmark supermarket. To appease the Latino community, the city under Mayor Giuliani would retain 49 percent interest in the project until a Latino-owned corporation could be found. On August 23, 1997, ground was broken for the supermarket at East 125th Street and Lexington Avenue.

On April 15, 1999, Pathmark officially opened[7] and the fears of the bodegas and supermarket owners that Pathmark would siphon away their customers never materialized. Pathmark has been open for over a decade and many of the neighborhood's bodegas and smaller supermarkets today remain open.

David Givens: *Not one bodega has closed, because the average person who shops at the bodegas mostly purchases very small items which are cookies, a container of milk, or maybe cold cuts and canned foods. Otherwise nobody does large shopping at the bodegas.*

But according to Nelson Denis at least one supermarket closed.

Nelson Denis: *For a while the supermarket on 122nd Street and Third Avenue, not far from the Pathmark, closed, because the supermarket couldn't maintain their finances and it had to refinance and build back up again.*

Nevertheless, the Pathmark supermarket became a successful venture and paved the way for future businesses and building construction in East Harlem.

David Givens: *East Harlem is the last frontier and it has its advantages and disadvantages. The potential of East Harlem is finally realized, but at the same time it's grown to the point that the average person can't live here. They [the realtors] have driven the up the renting price and apartments once rented for $450 a month and now someone is willing to pay up to $1000 a month. And this will push the current resident out of that market because they can no longer afford to live in an apartment that once rented for $450 two years ago. And then there is the growing trend of people. You look at the history of East Harlem and it has always been a transitional community, as opposed to Central Harlem, which went from white to black and for the time being it remains black. East Harlem has always been a transitional community because if you always look at the housing stock and the facilities you realize it was never intended for people to stay there. It was done to develop yourself and move on to somewhere else. Even the NYCHA buildings, they were supposed to be transitional. The churches, they were built by the Irish and today some of them are ninety percent black. Holy Rosary Church, years ago some Italians were there, but the church was mostly Puerto Rican. I went back there two years ago to Our Lady of Guadalupe and that church is mostly Mexican.*

Since 1980 Mexican immigrants have comprised the majority of immigrants to the U.S. By 2006, over eleven and a half million Mexican immigrants lived in the United States. Eighty-three percent of Mexican immigrants live in Illinois, Colorado, Georgia, Nevada, Florida, Arizona, North Carolina, South Dakota and New York.[8] It is estimated that 200,000 Mexican immigrants live in New York City, making them the third largest Latino group in the city. Puerto Ricans and Dominicans are the first and second largest Latino groups respectively. More Mexican men than women have immigrated to the city, but the high birth rate means more women have recently arrived to the city as well. From 2001 to 2005, the number of babies born to Mexican women have increased by 28 percent.[9] As for East Harlem, in the last fifteen years the neighborhood's Mexican population has grown exponentially. The 2000 census revealed that 10,000 Mexicans reside in East Harlem, but the number could be high as 15,000. Now El Barrio has two meanings: the traditional Puerto Rican community and the emerging Mexican one.[10]

Following the pattern of other immigrant groups, Mexican East Harlemites founded several organizations to assist other Mexican immigrants in East Harlem. Mexican Unidos en Nueva York (UNIMEX); an East Harlem branch of Tepayac, an organization that represents Mexican rights throughout the city; Mexican Community Center (CECOMEX); Mexican American Workers Association (AMAT) and Esperanza del Barrio. Another group founded by Latinos which has helped Mexican immigrants is the Moviemento para Justicia del Barrio.[11]

Esperanza del Barrio was established by five Latinas to bring about change in Latino neighborhoods throughout the city. Satellite groups can be found in East Harlem, Brooklyn, Queens and the Bronx, totaling over 500 members. This organization provides youth programs, legal support and counseling service, job training, leadership mentoring, nutrition, mental health and parenting skills. Esperanza del Barrio seeks to foster friendships and understanding between immigrant and non-immigrant communities. Like Italian East Harlem whose immigrants hailed from southern Italy, the majority of Mexican immigrants hail from the southern part of Mexico. In keeping with the theme of diversity within East Harlem, this story will profile two Mexican East Harlemites. Francisco Xavier Guzman first witnessed the Mexican East Harlem community in its infancy when he arrived here two decades ago.

Francisco Guzman: *I was born in Guerrero in the 1960s, which is located in the southern part of Mexico. I grew up in that village and when I turned seventeen I left that area to look for work to improve myself. First, I went to Mexico City to enroll in college, but I was unsuccessful as my grades were low and there was a tremendous amount of competition. Not long afterward I got married in Mexico and through my wife's relatives. I was invited and accepted an opportunity to live in New York.*

I arrived in the city on October 12, 1988, and by October 13th my relative found a job for me. I first lived in Brooklyn, until I moved to the West Side of Manhattan. And my brother-in-law lived in the neighborhood and we connected with him. He helped my wife and I locate an apartment in East Harlem. I worked twelve hours a day at Minerva's Grocery Store which was located on 8th Street and First Avenue. Here in East Harlem I looked for familiar people and that's where I met Walter Torres [a Puerto Rican East Harlemite]. And he introduced me to different neighborhood organizations in East Harlem, his friends and the places where he attended. And this is how I met many East Harlemites in the neighborhood.

The Growth of the Mexican Community

I believe there were a few Mexicans when I arrived, but not too many. Mexico Lindo was a first modern Mexican store that opened East Harlem in 1992. And the

Mexican population grew tremendously in the 1990s, especially the Mexican youth. The vast majority of Mexicans that immigrated to East Harlem and New York City as a whole averaged twenty years of age. And from this group many Mexicans hailed from three main towns in southern Mexico. They are Guerrero, my home town, Guayarcha and Pueblo Alto. And like many immigrants before, I think Mexicans have started working in the service industry such as restaurants, as office cleaners and in construction.

LEADERSHIP

I believe the Mexicans who have moved to East Harlem find it difficult to develop a leadership position. The Cinco de Mayo festival might [make it] seem that the Mexican community has established roots in East Harlem. But it's very difficult and Mexicans don't see themselves truly represented. I don't think the people who organize these celebrations or festivals are guiding or representing the Mexicans' interests. Even though we might see these parades or festivals in the media, I feel that these are sponsors. However, many Mexicans are not organized to run a political race.

STRUGGLES IN EAST HARLEM

Like the padrone system in Italian East Harlem a century ago,

Many Mexicans have been exploited by contractors who promised them work, but fail to deliver. I am a member and one of the founders of the best Mexican organization in the city, La Association de Tepeyac. And we know many cases of Mexican laborers who have been taken advantage of. The language barrier is a problem and Mexican immigrants are oblivious of the laws to protect them. Mexicans also feel they don't have any rights in this country and there are many cases right here in East Harlem where Mexicans feel they are under attack. Then there was a case in Long Island, where some Mexican laborers were almost killed and our organization traveled there to protest the mistreatment of those Mexican laborers. And the bosses and even the police in that town tried to cover it up that incident. Still today a lot of work needs to be done on human rights issues for Mexicans and for other immigrants.

FUTURE

I think the Mexican community will continue to grow. Recently I saw on television where Mexicans were leaving the northern part Mexico and immigrating to the United States or to another country. And I believe there are a million and a half Mexicans in the tri-state area according to the Associación de Tepeyac, but the city's *census as accounted for only 200,000. As Mexicans continue to grow in this country hopefully we will soon have meaningful representation.*

We will now hear from a recent transplant from the West Coast. Aurora Anaya-Cerda was born in Los Angeles, California, in Boyle Heights, a neighborhood between downtown and East Los Angeles. Though many Mexican East Harlemites migrated from the southern part of Mexico, Aurora's family hailed from Jalisco, the central part of Mexico.

Aurora Anaya-Cerda: *My parents are both Mexican and my entire family is from Jalisco, which is a central state in Mexico. I have been living in El Barrio for about six years now and when I first arrived and walked around the Mexican part of East Harlem, I knew that Mexicans had lived in this area. But these Mexicans originated from the southern part of Mexico. And because of this these Mexicans look different from those who live in the central or northern part. I even struggled to convince Mexican people that I'm Mexican because I don't "look Mexican," at least not from 116th Street. Because the Mexicans from the northern part like Chihuahua or central Mexico are light-skinned.*

Two decades after Francisco Guzman arrived in the neighborhood, Aurora describes how this community changed from a Puerto Rican to a Mexican one.

Aurora Anaya-Cerda: *In May 2004, right after the Cinco De Mayo festival, I saw the Mexican flags flew over the tenements on 116th Street. And for one week I lived with friends on 118th Street and Pleasant Avenue. As we walked through 116th Street to get the subway I became acquainted with the community. Ten years earlier my friend lived here when this area was a Puerto Rican community. And she told me how surprised she was to see the change from a Puerto Rican community to a Mexican community. I was also drawn to the Mexican culture here in East Harlem which is similar to my hometown. And moving to El Barrio was not difficult because I could travel to 116th Street and buy the same ingredients for whatever food as if I were back home in California. This made living here a smooth transition and I was able to find my niche. It has also led to a positive experience living in El Barrio. And the similarities that I found here are that every Mexican has immigrated to New York to find work. Some Mexican immigrants believed they didn't make enough money or hardly earned any income when they lived in Mexico, while other Mexican farmers either lost their land or couldn't provide for their families. They also came here to find work and send money home or try to provide a better life for their children.*

I haven't met anyone from Jalisco or any part of central Mexico, but I have met people from Guerrero, Puebla, Morelos, Chiapas, which are the southern part of Mexico. And all of these places are states in Mexico and different people from different regions in Mexico will migrate to different parts of the United States. Jalisco is one of the largest states in Mexico and many people from Jalisco migrate to California or Chicago. For example half of my family lives in Chicago and the other half lives in California.

Though jobs are plentiful in New York City, why would Mexicans travel so far north east to find employment and housing?

Aurora Anaya-Cerda: *I asked several Mexican East Harlemites why they would immigrate from southern part of Mexico to New York City and not Texas or to the Midwestern States. The reason is simple: because there are no Immigration and Naturalization Service Patrols or raids like the ones which happen in Texas or California. If one person travels to a certain place and they find employment they will tell their cousins, uncles, neighbors and friends. Other Mexicans will then migrate there and the same situation exists in East Harlem.*

New York State law prohibits law enforcement officials from questioning any immigrant's naturalization status. As a former community outreach worker with the East Harlem Tutorial Program, Aurora is able to communicate with the Mexican immigrant community and its organizations in East Harlem.

Aurora Anaya-Cerda: *Gentrification has pushed many Mexican immigrants out of East Harlem and this is a problem. If one Mexican family is forced out of their apartment they will live with another family and you have two families living in an apartment. Then, it will become three families in one apartment. And another problem arises when the rent becomes too expensive, or they have been threatened by the landlord or it's just fear. To avoid this, the Mexican family will relocate to the South Bronx or Queens.*

There are other forms of harassment as Mexican immigrants are the latest group to have met resistance in East Harlem from Puerto Ricans and blacks. Ironically, black and Puerto Rican East Harlemites once fought the Italians who once fought with the Jews as Jews once fought the Irish and Germans.

Aurora Anaya-Cerda: *I have heard about Mexican youths beaten up by gangs and these attacks took place in school or just as they were hanging out with friends. And they were attacked just because they were Mexican.*

Though Mexican youth were attacked by black and Puerto Rican youth, Puerto Rican entrepreneurs and local elected officials were helpful to several members in the aforementioned Mexican organizations in East Harlem. Similar to the ethnic groups profiled earlier, Mexican East Harlemites work as low-skilled and semi-skilled laborers in the service sector.

Aurora Anaya-Cerda: *Mexicans are the cooks in restaurants, custodians, delivery boys or maintenance. Basically all service jobs. And when you visit any Upper East Side restaurant and look in the kitchen, you'll see a Mexican.*

What is the future of Little Mexico in El Barrio? When I first interviewed Francisco Javier Guzman, he was hopeful that the Mexican community would expand in East Harlem like other ethnic communities have done in the past. But a new housing movement has taken place in East Harlem. The construction of luxury housing coupled with gentrification has changed the dynamics of East Harlem.

Aurora Anaya-Cerda: *An uncertain future exists for Mexican immigrants. Just in the past two years, I've seen new buildings rise and these rents are outrageous. And many people have been very quickly displaced and people and businesses are pushed out because they cannot afford the rent. I would like to open a bookstore, but I can't find any affordable space. If we fast forward five years from now we will have to look at who will be living here and what types of businesses will exist. Of course you will have catered to whoever is living here. Historically, this has happened to many neighborhoods. It happened to the Lower East Side and in my hometown in East Los Angeles. But it's unfortunate that so much culture is lost when gentrification happens. The question is what will happen to the Mexican community in East Harlem. Truthfully, I think the large Mexican wave has already happened. And if there is an annual growth, it might have stopped. I mean the offspring will be born, but the new immigrants might not come to East Harlem. And where are they going to live, because again the lack of affordable housing?*

In June 2012, Aurora Anaya-Cerda found a location in East Harlem and opened her bookstore: La Casa de Azul Bookstore (The Blue House Bookstore).

Epilogue

We have come to the end of this book, but the story of East Harlem continues. Whether it becomes Spa Ha (Spanish Harlem) Upper East Side, Carnegie Hill or Upper Yorkville, these stories proved that East Harlem was a special neighborhood in the past and is still a special neighborhood today. Could East Harlem's name change? It was unimaginable years ago that the Hell's Kitchen neighborhood could today be called Clinton. There is some good news, because after declining population throughout the twentieth century, East Harlem began the Twenty-First with an increase. The 2000 census reported that 117,000 residents live in East Harlem.[1] As of 2011 more housing units have been constructed throughout the neighborhood and this will result in an even larger population increase when the 2010 census is recorded. Presently, Latinos comprise the ethnic majority of East Harlem at 52.1 percent. Puerto Ricans are the largest Latino group in East Harlem at 30.1 percent. But since the last census was taken in 1990 more than 8,000 Puerto Ricans, or 18.8 percent left the neighborhood.

Mexican immigrants represent the next largest group of Latino East Harlemites. Since 1990, the Mexican population has grown from slightly over 760 to over 10,000. Now Mexicans represent nearly 9 percent of East Harlem. Dominicans, Cubans, and Latinos from Central and South America and other parts of the world account for the rest of the Latino population in East Harlem. African Americans at 35.1 percent make up the second largest ethnic group in East Harlem, but some African Americans have left the neighborhood in the last twenty-years as Puerto Ricans have. Whites have made a significant move into East Harlem in the last decade. The 2000 census puts the white population at 7.3 percent, a noticeable increase from .02 percent since 1990. Asians and other nationalities account for the other 4.9 percent. East Harlem is once again a diverse and cultural community. Many whites and minorities who once shunned East Harlem now look upon the neighborhood as a convenient and affordable place. James De La Vega shares with us how some East Harlemites feel about the neighborhood's new arrivals.

James De La Vega: *I don't mind when new people move into the neighborhood. But what concerns me is when these new residents move here and become indifferent to those current residents or those longtime residents of East Harlem. For example, if people only move to East Harlem just for the cheap rent, this bothers me. I understand everybody wants a good deal, which I think is fair, but I think it's important that those who move into East Harlem try to contribute and make this neighborhood a better place to live.*

Longtime East Harlemites are trying to avoid displacement to other boroughs and neighborhoods. East Harlemites face several challenges: Any vacant lot will likely see housing construction as soon as possible — but will this new housing be affordable? And gentrification: the dichotomy of East Harlem will remain as long as low-income housing projects are surrounded by market rate and luxury housing. Presently East Harlemites reside in 14,000 units of public housing, but public housing federal subsidies have declined during the past several years. For the first time many housing residents have seen rent increases and parking space on public housing lots was raised from five to seventy-five dollars.[2]

What will become of these residents? Can East Harlem survive when its public housing residents are surrounded by market rate and luxury buildings? East Harlem's twenty-first-century housing boom is the latest plan to redevelop the neighborhood. The first redevelopment stages took place in 1937 and 1945 when both the city and business community urged construction of public housing. But, as we noted, this period saw loss of businesses and residents. The second wave to redevelop the neighborhood occurred during the mid–1960s and 1970s when the federal government instituted Model Cities and other antipoverty programs. The federal and city governments poured monies into poor neighborhoods like East Harlem. Both believed the infusion of money would empower people through job training and education. But private developers passed on the idea of redevelopment and the antipoverty programs ended by the mid 1970s. And the neighborhood's housing and economic problems continued.

During the early and mid–1980s the familiar refrain echoed that East Harlem was ready for redevelopment. In 1982, the New York City Department of City Planning issued the report "A Neighborhood Strategy for East Harlem." But by this period the federal monies were gone and many landlords abandoned their property throughout East Harlem. And by default New York City became their landlord. Again, plans were drawn to develop housing for low and moderate families, revamp the neighborhood's main commercial corridors, and encourage entrepreneurship to combat the negative effects of vacant properties in East Harlem. The city believed that East Harlem needed more moderate and middle income families to bring some stability to the neighborhood and sold several buildings in East Harlem for only one dollar to encourage homeownership.

In 1985 New York City's Office of Business Development announced "El Nuevo Barrio," a plan to develop a "Latin Quarter" in East Harlem which would highlight and celebrate the neighborhood's Latino character. But this plan was consistent of the previous plans to redevelop the neighborhood.[3] And East Harlem's aforementioned problems continued.

New York City has adopted a new plan to redevelop poor neighborhoods like East Harlem. The City Council passed 421-A and this legislation is designed to insure affordable housing in low-income neighborhoods.[4] Unlike the past, new housing has risen, but the luxury buildings that have been built are unaffordable for most East Harlem residents. The city has partnered with some agencies to build moderate and low income housing. Lastly, the East River Plaza stands on the former site of the Washburn Wire Factory. It opened in 2009 and many businesses including Costco, Target and Best Buy have opened at the plaza.

Crime and poor health continue to be problems in East Harlem. These problems pose serious challenges, but as we have seen East Harlemites will not shy away from them. And despite these problems I still fondly recall those stories of my godmother and mother years ago. And I am heartened by the recollections of many who contributed to this book. They have lived, loved and enjoyed being a part of a neighborhood and they have touched my life. God Bless you all for your help in bringing this story to life.

Chapter Notes

Introduction

1. Donald Stewart, *A Short History of East Harlem* (New York: The Museum of the City of New York, 1972), 8.
2. James P. Riker, *History of Harlem* (New York: New Harlem Publishing Company, 1904), 109.
3. *Ibid.*, 118; Stewart, 13–15.
4. Riker, 169–171.
5. *Ibid.*, 230; Stewart, 24.
6. Stewart, 22–23.
7. Riker, 211.
8. Gilbert Osofsky, *Harlem Making of a Ghetto* (New York: Harper and Row, 1971), 72.
9. *Ibid.*, 9; Stewart, 31–32.
10. *New York Times*, March 22, 2011.
11. Richard Peck, *New York Times*, "Harlem: Valley of Myths," April 11, 1976.
12. Stewart, 33–34.
13. *Ibid.*, 36.
14. Jeffrey Gurock, *When Harlem Was Jewish* (New York: Columbia University Press, 1979), 6.
15. D. T. Valentine, *Manual of the Corporation of the city of New York* (New York: Edmond Jones, 1861).
16. Gurock, 7, 15.
17. Lawrence Stelter and Lothar Stelter, *By the El: Third Avenue and Its El at Mid-Century* (Flushing, NY: H&M Productions, 1995), 8–9, 107.
18. "Robinson's Atlas of the city of New York 1885," by E. Robinson and R. H. Pidgeon.
19. Gurock, 32.
20. *Ibid.*, 45.

Chapter 1

1. Eric Homberger, *The Historical Atlas of New York City* (New York: Henry Holt and Co, 1994), 42.
2. Gurock, 7.
3. *Ibid.*, 9–12.
4. *Ibid.*, 14–15, 18, 24.
5. *Ibid.*, 15, 20.
6. *Ibid.*, 21–22, 28.
7. *Ibid.*, 36.
8. *Ibid.*, 27–28, 30, 34, 42.
9. *Ibid.*, 36, 38–40, 52, 55.
10. *Ibid.*, 50.
11. *Ibid.*, 58.
12. *Ibid.*, 59–60.
13. *Ibid.*, 66–73.
14. *Ibid.*, 74–85.
15. *Ibid.*
16. *Ibid.*, 94–98, 100–102.
17. *Ibid.*, 98, 114–115.
18. *Ibid.*, 114–117.
19. *Ibid.*, 118–122.
20. *Ibid.*, 126–127, 134, 154, 156.
21. Robert Orsi, *Madonna of 115th Street: Faith and Community in Italian Harlem, 1880–1950* (New Haven: Yale University Press, 1985), 14.
22. Robert Charles Freeman, *Exploring the Path of Community Change in East Harlem, 1870–1970: A Multi-Factor Approach* (Thesis, Ph.D.)— Fordham University, 1994, 17–18.
23. Orsi, 14.
24. *Ibid.*, 14–16, 18.
25. *Ibid.*, 51–53; Gerald Meyer, *Vito Marcantonio: Radical Politician, 1902–1954* (Albany, N.Y.: State University of New York Press, 1989), 113–114.
26. Orsi, 54, 59.
27. Freeman, 23–24; Orsi, 25.
28. Orsi, 25–27.
29. *Ibid.*, 22–24.
30. *Ibid.*, 28–29.
31. *Ibid.*, 17; Meyer, 114.
32. Meyer, 113.
33. Orsi, 16.
34. Freeman, 35.
35. *Ibid.*, 45.

36. Orsi, 34.
37. Ibid., 28, 35.
38. Ibid., 45–46.
39. Ibid., 34; Meyer, 123.
40. Orsi, 21, 34.
41. Ibid., 35, 46.
42. Ibid., 35; Meyer, 7, 114; Freeman, 128–130.
43. Meyer, 114; Freeman, 128.
44. Meyer, 7.
45. Orsi, 41.
46. Orsi, 35, 46.
47. Meyer, 10–11.
48. Orsi, 35; Freeman, 101.
49. Nathan Glazer and Daniel Patrick Moynihan, *Beyond the Melting Pot: The Negroes, Puerto Ricans, Jews, Italians, and Irish of New York City* (Cambridge, Mass: M.I.T. Press, 1963), 219.
50. Virginia Sánchez Korrol, *From Colonia to Community: The History of Puerto Ricans in New York City, 1917–1948* (Westport, Conn: Greenwood Press, 1983), 11–12.
51. Bernardo Vega and César Andreu Iglesias, *Memoirs of Bernardo Vega: A Contribution to the History of the Puerto Rican Community in New York* (New York: Monthly Review Press, 1984), 45.
52. James Jennings and Monte Rivera, *Puerto Rican Politics in Urban America* (Westport, Conn: Greenwood Press, 1984), 17–19; Sánchez Korrol, 13.
53. Vega, 53, 77.
54. Jesse Hoffnung-Garskof, *The Migrations of Arturo Schomburg: On Being Antillano, Negro and Puerto Rican in New York, 1891–1938* ([New Brunswick: N.J.] Transaction Periodicals Consortium, Rutgers University, 2001), 18–24.
55. Sánchez Korrol, 17–18.
56. Ibid., 29, 31.
57. Ibid., 41, 45.
58. Lawrence Royce Chenault, *The Puerto Rican Migrant in New York City* (New York: Columbia University Press, 1938), 55–56.
59. Sánchez Korrol, 39–52.
60. Ibid., 58–62.
61. Vega, 9.
62. Sánchez Korrol, 71–76.
63. Ibid., 92.
64. Ortiz, *Altagracia Cimarron* Vol. 1 #3, Spring 1988, p. 40.
65. Sánchez Korrol, 96.
66. Ibid., 135–137, 162.
67. Ibid., 142.
68. Ibid., 144, 147.
69. Ibid., 150–153.
70. Ibid., 153–155.
71. Jennings and Rivera, 23; Sánchez Korrol, 183.
72. Sánchez Korrol, 184.
73. Arthur Mann, *La Guardia, a Fighter against His Times* (Philadelphia: Lippincott, 1959), 319–320.
74. Sánchez Korrol, 190–191.
75. Eric Homberger, *The Historical Atlas of New York City* (New York: Henry Holt and Co., 1994); James Weldon Johnson, *Black Manhattan* (New York: A.A. Knopf, 1930), 4–5.
76. Riker, 134.
77. Stewart, 36.
78. Riker, 238, 260.
79. Stewart, 36.
80. Osofsky, 4, 5, 21–23.
81. Ibid., 84–85.
82. Ibid., 131–135.
83. Ibid.
84. Ibid.

Chapter 2

1. New York (N.Y.) *East Harlem Community Study. Mayor's Committee on City Planning in Cooperation with the Works Progress Administration*, 1937, 11.
2. Ibid., 13–14.
3. Ibid.
4. Ibid., 16.
5. Ibid., 17–18.
6. Ibid., 24.
7. Ibid., 33, 38–39.
8. Ibid., 44.
9. Gurock, 145.
10. Ibid., 140–144.
11. Ibid., 144–146.
12. Ibid., 149–150.
13. Ibid., 155–6.
14. Freeman, 168–200.
15. *New York Times*, March 4, 1940.
16. "East River Report," New York City Housing Authority, 1941, 3, 15; Freeman, 168–200; *New York Times*, April 2, 1941.
17. "East River Report," New York City Housing Authority, 1941, 10, 14–16.

Chapter 3

1. Meyer, 7–8.
2. Ibid., 8; Salvatore John LaGumina, *Vito Marcantonio, The People's Politician* (Dubuque, Iowa: Kendall/Hunt, 1969), 2.
3. LaGumina, 2.
4. Meyer, 9.

5. *Ibid.*
6. LaGumina, 3; Meyer 10.
7. Meyer, 9–10.
8. Alan Schaffer, *Vito Marcantonio, Radical in Congress* (Syracuse, N.Y.: Syracuse University Press, 1966), 10.
9. Meyer, 10–13.
10. *Ibid.*, 12, 15; Schaffer, 12–13; LaGumina, 4.
11. Meyer, 11; LaGumina, 4.
12. Meyer, 12, 15; LaGumina, 5–6.
13. Meyer, 17.
14. *Ibid.*, 16–17.
15. Meyer, 17–18.
16. LaGumina, 6.
17. Schaffer, 10; Meyer, 21–26; LaGumina, 8–9.
18. LaGumina, 8–9; Schaffer, 28; Meyer, 18.
19. Schaffer, 37–38.
20. LaGumina, 42–43.
21. Schaffer, 65.
22. Annette Rubenstein, ed., *I Vote My Conscience: Debates, Speeches and Writings of Vito Marcantonio* (New York: The Vito Marcantonio Memorial, 1956), 16.
23. Schaffer, 19, 23.
24. Meyer, 134, 136–137.
25. Orsi, 44.
26. Meyer, 152, 159.
27. *Ibid.*, 144, 156, 165.
28. *Ibid.*, 128.
29. LaGumina, 71.
30. Meyer, 59–60; LaGumina, 76–79.
31. LaGumina, 71–75.
32. Meyer, 54, 56–57, 65.
33. LaGumina, 37.
34. Meyer, 40; LaGumina, 56–57.
35. LaGumina, 62–63.
36. Meyer, 92–93.
37. *Ibid.*, 31.
38. Meyer, 35–56; LaGumina, 84.
39. LaGumina, 92–93, 95.
40. Schaffer, 166.
41. LaGumina, 92–95.
42. Meyer, 35–36; LaGumina, 113.
43. Meyer, 63–64; LaGumina, 118.
44. Schaffer, 171, 174.
45. David G. McCullough, *Truman* (New York: Simon & Schuster, 1992), 566, 707–711.
46. Schaffer, 188–190.
47. Meyer, 46, 99.
48. LaGumina, 107, 112.
49. *Ibid.*, 109; Meyer, 62, 63.
50. LaGumina, 133, 135.
51. *Ibid.*; Rubenstein, 352–355.
52. LaGumina, 135, 136.
53. *Ibid.*, 138–139; Meyer, 182.
54. Meyer, 183.

Chapter 4

1. *New York Daily News*, December 29, 2004.
2. Clarence O. Senior, *Strangers Then Neighbors: From Pilgrims to Puerto Ricans* (New York: Freedom Books, 1961), 39–40.
3. Jennings and Rivera, and Sherrie P. Braver, 93.
4. *Ibid.*, Jennings and Rivera.
5. Sánchez Korrol, 212–3.
6. *Ibid.*, 77, 81; Jennings and Rivera, 42.
7. *Centro Journal* Volume 16, No. 1, Spring 2004, 161–162.
8. Patricia Cayo Sexton, *Spanish Harlem* (New York: Harper & Row, 1965), 9.
9. *Ibid.*, 36, 40.
10. *Ibid.*
11. Arnold Rampersad, *The Life of Langston Hughes, Volume I: 1901–1941: I, Too, Sing America* (New York: Oxford University Press, 1986), 11, 19–20, 23–26, 33, 44–45, 52.
12. *Ibid.*, 116, 171, 252–254.
13. Arnold Rampersad, *The Life of Langston Hughes, Volume 2: 1942–1967* (New York: Oxford University Press, 1988), 3–10, 45.
14. *Ibid.*, 145, 146–150.
15. *Ibid.*, 278–279.
16. *Ibid.*, 148.
17. *Ibid.*
18. *Ibid.*, 64–65.
19. *Ibid.*, 148.
20. *Ibid.*, 278–279.
21. *Ibid.*, 190–191, 197.
22. *Ibid.*, 213–218.
23. *Ibid.*, 115, 309, 412.
24. *Ibid.*, 298.
25. *Ibid.*, 232, 238, 297.

Chapter 5

1. Leonard Covello, *The Heart Is a Teacher* (New York: McGraw-Hill, 1958), 185.

Chapter 6

1. Jane Jacobs, *The Death and Life of Great American Cities* (New York: Random House, 1961), 353–379.
2. *Ibid.*, 390–405.
3. Jacobs, 29–34, 277, 445.
4. *New York Times*, July 30, 1981; Ric Burns, *New York a Documentary Film*. [United States]: PBS Home Video, Part 7, 2000.

5. *Ibid.*; Samuel Zipp, *Manhattan Projects: The Rise and Fall of Urban Renewal in Cold War New York* (Oxford: Oxford University Press, 2010), 284–287.
6. Freeman, 418–419.
7. *New York Times*, Nov. 26, 1951, Feb. 28, 1953.
8. Richard Plunz, *A History of Housing in New York City: Dwelling Type and Social Change in the American Metropolis* (New York: Columbia University Press, 1990), 245–246; Manhattan Development Committee, and Harold Reeve Sleeper. *A Realistic Approach to Private Investment in Urban Redevelopment Applied to East Harlem As a Blighted Area* New York City: Architectural Forum, Time Inc, 1945).
9. *New York Times*, December 24, 1947.
10. *New York Times*, January 7, 1951.
11. *New York Times*, January 26, 1955.
12. *New York Times*, October 4, 1955.
13. Jacobs, 306; Freeman, 432.
14. *New York Times*, June 23, 1957.
15. *Ibid.*
16. Public Hearing before John J. Merli, January 16, 1956; "East Harlem Small Business Survey & Planning Committee"; *New York Times*, March 5, 1962.
17. "East Harlem Merchants Association: Progress Report," July 18, 1956.
18. "East Harlem Merchants Association: Progress Report," February 28, 1957.
19. Ric Burns, *New York a documentary film*.
20. Sexton, 9, 36.
21. *Fact Sheet on Public Housing in East Harlem*.
22. Sexton, 37.
23. Ric Burns, *New York a documentary film*.
24. *New York Times*, October 16, November 12, 1961.
25. Freeman, 420, 424; Sexton, 13–14., 36.
26. *New York Times*: May 30, 1966, October 15, 1968.
27. Hulan E. Jack, *Fifty Years a Democrat: The Autobiography of Hulan E. Jack* (New York: New Benjamin Franklin House, 1982), 66–67; *New York Times* October 24, 1951; February 16, 1952; September 21–22, 1952; November 18, 1952.
28. Eric C. Schneider, *Vampires, Dragons, and Egyptian Kings* (Princeton (N.J.): Princeton University Press, 1999), 28–30.
29. *Ibid.*, 31–33.
30. *Ibid.*, 55.
31. *Ibid.*, 41, 78–79.
32. *Ibid.*, 41, 94–105.
33. *Ibid.*, 91–93.
34. *Ibid.*, 76–77.
35. *Ibid.*, 71–72.
36. Carlos de Jesus, *That Old Gang of Mine*, New York, NY: Filmakers Library, 1998.
37. Eric C. Schneider, 160–161.
38. *Ibid.*, 124–125.
39. *Ibid.*
40. *Ibid.*, 137–143.
41. *Ibid.*, 137, 143–148.
42. *Ibid.*, 148–151, 159–163.
43. *New York Times*. June 2, 1958, June 10, 1958.
44. Good Neighbor Week Committee Bulletin, April–May 1962.
45. *New York Journal-American*, January 3, 1960.
46. Schneider, 165–166.
47. Bruce Kenrick, *Come Out the Wilderness: The Story of East Harlem Protestant Parish* (New York: Harper, 1962), 216–219.
48. Schneider, 168–170.
49. *Ibid.*, 171.
50. *Ibid.*, 174–177, 183–187.
51. *Ibid.*, 183–185.
52. *Ibid.*, 217–218, 236, 241, 245.
53. Freeman, 414–415.
54. *Ibid.*; Sexton, 95–105.
55. Kenrick, 30.
56. *Ibid.*, 4–8, 23–27.
57. *Ibid.*, 8, 31.
58. *Ibid.*, 31, 32.
59. East Harlem Protestant Parish and its Offshoots, pamphlet, 1.
60. Kenrick, 36.
61. *Ibid.*, 38–39.
62. *Ibid.*, 39–41.
63. *NY Daily News*, August 5, 1951.
64. Kenrick, 66.
65. *Ibid.*; East Harlem Protestant Parish and its Offshoots, pamphlet, 1–2.
66. Kenrick, 70–71.
67. *Ibid.*, 43, East Harlem Protestant Parish and its Offshoots, pamphlet, 1–2.
68. Kenrick, 32–33, 73–80, 126–127.
69. *Ibid.*, 43–45.
70. *Ibid.*
71. *Ibid.*, 184–185.
72. *Ibid.*, 186–187.
73. *Ibid.*, 188–189; East Harlem Protestant Parish and its Offshoots, pamphlet, 1–2.
74. *Ibid.*, 191–192.
75. *Ibid.*, 193–195.
76. East Harlem Protestant Parish and its Offshoots, 1–2.

77. Interview with Helen "Dibby" and Bill Webber. East Harlem Tutorial Program 40th Anniversary Celebration, program, 3.
78. East Harlem Protestant Parish and its Offshoots, pamphlet, 1–2.
79. *New York Times*, 2005.

Chapter 7

1. Jennings and Rivera, 44.
2. Interview with Herman Badillo.
3. Jennings and Rivera, 45–46.
4. Antonia Pantoja, *Memoir of a Visionary: Antonia Pantoja* (Houston, Tex: Arte Publico Press, 2002), 75.
5. *Ibid.*, 2–7, 32–33, 40, 51–53, 70–71.
6. *Ibid.*, 71–73.
7. *Ibid.*, 73, 77.
8. *Ibid.*, 74.
9. *Ibid.*
10. *Ibid.*, 75–76.
11. *Ibid.*, 79, 83–89, 90–93.
12. *Ibid.*, 90–93, 98–99.
13. *Ibid.*, 100–103.
14. *Ibid.*, 99, 106–107.
15. *Ibid.*, 106–107; Lillian Jiménez and Edward James Olmos, *Antonia Pantoja ¡Presente!* (New York, NY: Distributed by Women Make Movies, 2009).
16. Pantoja, 106.
17. Lillian Jiménez and Edward James Olmos. *Antonia Pantoja lPresente!*
18. Pantoja, 132–133.
19. *Ibid.*, 13.
20. Celebrating Manhattan Country School's 35th Anniversary, 19.
21. Manhattan Country School Newsletter, Winter 2001, 6–7.
22. *Ibid.*, 9.
23. Celebrating Manhattan Country School's 35th Anniversary, 40.
24. *Ibid.*, 33.
25. *Ibid.*, 41.
26. Interview with Thomas Webber.
27. Interview with Dylcia Pagan.
28. *New York Times*, July 25 — 27, 1967.
29. *New York Times*, March 27, 1968.
30. *New York Times*, August 24, 1960, October 18, 1964, September 29, 1967, June 8, 1968.
31. Interview with Clarence Davis.
32. *LIFE*, September, 1967.
33. Joseph P. Blank, *Reader's Digest*, January, 1969, 135–140.
34. Interview with Angelo Giordani.
35. Blank, 135–140.
36. *Ibid.*
37. *Ibid.*; Mary Kelly, *The Christian Science Monitor*, February 7, 1969; Interview with Angelo Giordani.
38. Luis Aponte-Pares, "Lessons from el Barrio— Caucus for a New Political Science" in *Latino Social Movements: Historical and Theoretical Perspectives: A New Political Science Reader*, Rodolfo D. Torres and George N. Katsiaficas, eds. (New York: Routledge, 1999), 51–52.
39. Interview with Angelo Giordani.
40. *Ibid.*; Planners Network Publications— The East Harlem Real Great Society. Luis Aponte Pares. March/April 1999.
41. *New York Times*, March 19, 1968; Lessons from el Barrio— Caucus for a New Political Science © 1998, 52, by Luis Aponte Pares.
42. *New York Times*, April 29, 1969, 54–64.
43. *Ibid.*
44. *Ibid.*, 64–69.
45. Young Lords Party and Michael Abramson, *Palante: Young Lords Party* (New York: McGraw-Hill, 1971.
46. *Ibid.*
47. *Ibid.*
48. *Ibid.*
49. Juan González, *Harvest of Empire: A History of Latinos in America* (New York: Viking, 2000); Interview with Juan González.
50. Interview with Felipe Luciano.
51. *Caribe*, vol. 7, issue 4, "The Young Lords Party," 7; Young Lords Party and Abramson, 2.
52. *Ibid.*
53. *Ibid.*, 11.
54. *New York Times*, August 19, 1969.
55. Jack Newfield, *Village Voice*, December 4, 1969.
56. *Caribe*, 3, 14.
57. *Ibid.*, 14.
58. *New York Times*, December 15, 1969, Jan 8, 1970.
59. *New York Times*, January 8, 24, 1970; February 25, 1970.
60. *Caribe*, 3.
61. *New York Times*, June 7, 1970.
62. Young Lords Party, Abramson.
63. *Ibid.*
64. *Caribe*, 13.
65. *Ibid.*, 13.
66. Young Lords Party, Abramson; *New York Times*, September 5, 1970.
67. *New York Times*, October 19, 1970.
68. *New York Times*, October 19, 26, 29 1970; November 18, 1970, December 3, 1970.
69. *Caribe*, 3

70. Interview with Denise Oliver; Iris Morales, *Siempre Palante! The Young Lords*. New York, NY: Third World Newsreel, 1996.
71. Young Lords Party, Abramson.
72. *New York Daily News*, October 18, 1996.

Chapter 8

1. Interview with Marcos Dimas.
2. *New York Times*, June 30, 1970.
3. Interview with Jack Agueros.
4. Interview with Leo Bailey.
5. Document from the New York State Department of Civil Service, December 19, 1974.
6. *Ms.* Magazine, December, 1974.
7. Interview with Nicholas Mohr.
8. Interview with Humberto Cintron and Marcos Dimas.
9. Interview with Johnny Colon.
10. Ute Lenssen, *The Will to Plan East Harlem, 1937–1987: 50 Years of Missed Opportunities* (Thesis [M.S.]—Columbia University, 1990), 49–53.
11. www.answers.com/topic War on Poverty. Readers Companion to U.S. Women's History.
12. Jennings, and Rivera, 61.
13. Freeman, 407.
14. Jennings, and Rivera, 62–67.
15. *New York Times*, September 27, 1970.
16. *New York Times*, July 5, 1977.
17. *New York Times*, October 22, 1972.
18. Manhattan Community Board 11: Facts on East Harlem, by Urban Technical Assistance Project (UTAP) Columbia University Winter 2004.

Chapter 9

1. Interview with Eugene Lang; *New York Times*, February 17, 1985.
2. *New York Times*, October 19, 1985.
3. *New York Times*, December 8, 1985; Personal account of the IHAD's audience with Christopher Reeve.
4. *New York Times*, September 8, 1986.
5. *New York Times*, June 21, 1987; I Have a Dream Foundation National Fact Sheet.
6. History of the "I Have a Dream Foundation; "Fact Sheet, IHAD Concepts and Characteristics," "I Have A Dream" Celebrating 25 Years of Achievement.
7. "I Have a Dream" Foundation: Special Comments on the IHAD Program.
8. Interview with James De La Vega.

Chapter 10

1. Interview with Dr. Walter J. Turnbull. *New York Times* November 30, 1981; Dec. 19, 1996; March 17, 1997.
2. *New York Times*, September 22, 1994.
3. Architects' Renewal Committee in Harlem (New York, N.Y.). *East Harlem Triangle Plan*. New York: The Committee, 1968; Sexton, 85–91.
4. Architects' Renewal Committee in Harlem (New York, N.Y.).
5. *New York Times*, April 24, 1995.
6. *Ibid.*
7. *New York Times*, April 24, 28, 1995, August 23, 1997, April 28, 1999.
8. www.migrationinformation.org.
9. *New York Times*, December 24, 2007.
10. Manhattan Community Board 11: Facts on East Harlem, by Urban Technical Assistance Project (UTAP) Columbia University Winter 2004; 2000 Census; *New York Times*, September 6, 2003.
11. Arlene M. Dávila, Barrio Dreams: Puerto Ricans, Latinos, and the Neoliberal City (Berkeley, Calif: University of California Press, 2004), 157.

Epilogue

1. Manhattan Community Board 11: Facts on East Harlem, by Urban Technical Assistance Project (UTAP) Columbia University, Winter 2004.
2. *New York Times*, May 30, 2007.
3. Ute Lenssen.
4. www.nyc.gov/hpd/html/PR2006/PR-12-20-06.shtml. Mayor Bloomberg will sign compromise bill to reform 421a tax incentive into law.

Bibliography

Aponte-Pares, Luis. "Lessons from El Barrio—the East Harlem real great society/urban planning studio: A Puerto Rican chapter in the fight for urban self-determination." *New Political Science*. 20, no. 4: 399–420, 1998.
Burns, Ric. *New York: A Documentary Film*. PBS Home Video, Part 7, 2000.
Chenault, Lawrence Royce. *The Puerto Rican Migrant in New York City*. New York: Columbia University Press, 1938.
Covello, Leonard. *The Heart Is a Teacher*. New York: McGraw-Hill, 1958.
Dávila, Arlene M. *Barrio Dreams: Puerto Ricans, Latinos, and the Neoliberal City*. Berkeley: University of California Press, 2004.
Freeman, Robert Charles. "Exploring the Path of Community Change in East Harlem, 1870–1970: A Multifactor Approach." Ph.D. dissertation, Fordham University, 1994.
Glazer, Nathan, and Daniel Patrick Moynihan. *Beyond the Melting Pot: The Negroes, Puerto Ricans, Jews, Italians, and Irish of New York City*. Cambridge, Mass.: M.I.T. Press, 1963.
González, Juan. *Harvest of Empire: A History of Latinos in America*. New York: Viking, 2000.
Gurock, Jeffrey S. *When Harlem Was Jewish, 1870–1930*. New York: Columbia University Press, 1979.
Hoffnung-Garskof, Jesse. *The Migrations of Arturo Schomburg: On Being Antillano, Negro and Puerto Rican in New York, 1891–1938*. New Brunswick, N.J.: Transaction Periodicals Consortium, Rutgers University, 2001.
Homberger, Eric. *The Historical Atlas of New York City: A Visual Celebration of Nearly 400 Years of New York City's History*. New York: Henry Holt, 1994.
Jack, Hulan E. *Fifty Years a Democrat: The Autobiography of Hulan E. Jack*. New York: New Benjamin Franklin House, 1982.
Jacobs, Jane. *The Death and Life of Great American Cities*. New York: Random House, 1961.
Jennings, James, and Monte Rivera. *Puerto Rican Politics in Urban America*. Westport, Conn.: Greenwood Press, 1984.
Jesus, Carlos de. *That Old Gang of Mine*. New York: Filmakers Library, 1998.
Jiménez, Lillian, and Edward James Olmos. *Antonia Pantoja ¡Presente!* New York: Distributed by Women Make Movies, 2009.
Johnson, James Weldon. *Black Manhattan*. New York: A.A. Knopf, 1930.
Kenrick, Bruce. *Come Out the Wilderness: The Story of East Harlem Protestant Parish*. New York: Harper, 1962.
LaGumina, Salvatore John. *Vito Marcantonio, The People's Politician*. Dubuque, Iowa: Kendall/Hunt Pub. Co, 1969.
Lenssen, Ute. "The Will to Plan East Harlem, 1937–1987: 50 Years of Missed Opportunities." M.S. thesis, Columbia University, 1990.
Manhattan Development Committee and Harold Reeve Sleeper. *A Realistic Approach to Private Investment in Urban Redevelopment Applied to East Harlem As a Blighted Area*. New York: Architectural Forum, Time Inc., 1945.

Mann, Arthur. *La Guardia, a Fighter against His Times.* Philadelphia: Lippincott, 1959.
McCullough, David G. *Truman.* New York: Simon & Schuster, 1992.
Meyer, Gerald. *Vito Marcantonio: Radical Politician, 1902–1954.* Albany: State University of New York Press, 1989.
Morales, Iris. *Palante, Siempre Palante! The Young Lords.* New York: Third World Newsreel, 1996.
New York (N.Y.). *East Harlem Community Study. Mayor's Committee on City Planning in Cooperation with the Works Progress Administration,* 1937.
Orsi, Robert. *The Madonna of 115th Street: Faith and Community in Italian Harlem, 1880–1950.* New Haven: Yale University Press, 1985.
Osofsky, Gilbert. *Harlem: The Making of a Ghetto: Negro New York, 1890–1930.* New York: Harper & Row, 1971.
Pantoja, Antonia. *Memoir of a Visionary: Antonia Pantoja.* Houston: Arte Publico Press, 2002.
Plunz, Richard. *A History of Housing in New York City: Dwelling Type and Social Change in the American Metropolis.* New York: Columbia University Press, 1990.
Rampersad, Arnold. *The Life of Langston Hughes, Volume I : 1902–1941 : I, Too, Sing America.* New York: Oxford University Press, 1986.
———. *The Life of Langston Hughes, Volume II, 1941–1967, I Dream a World.* New York: Oxford University Press, 1988.
Riker, James. *History of Harlem. It Origins and its Annals.* Revised from notes and enlarged by Henry Pennington Toler. New York: New Harlem Pub. Co., 1904.
Rubenstein, Annette, ed. *I Vote My Conscience: Debates, Speeches and Writings of Vito Marcantonio.* New York: Vito Marcantonio Memorial, 1956.
Sánchez Korrol, Virginia. *From Colonia to Community: The History of Puerto Ricans in New York City, 1917–1948.* Westport, Conn.: Greenwood Press, 1983.
Schaffer, Alan. *Vito Marcantonio, Radical in Congress.* Syracuse, N.Y.: Syracuse University Press, 1966.
Schneider, Eric C. *Vampires, Dragons, and Egyptian Kings.* Princeton, N.J.: Princeton University Press, 1999.
Senior, Clarence Ollson. *Strangers — Then Neighbors: From Pilgrims to Puerto Ricans.* New York: Freedom Books, 1961.
Sexton, Patricia Cayo. *Spanish Harlem.* New York: Harper & Row, 1966.
Stelter, Lawrence, and Lothar Stelter. *By the El: Third Avenue and Its El at Mid-Century.* Flushing, N.Y.: H&M Productions, 1995.
Stewart, Donald. *A Short History of East Harlem.* New York: The Museum of the City of New York, 1972.
Torres, Rodolfo D., and George N. Katsiaficas. *Latino Social Movements: Historical and Theoretical Perspectives: A New Political Science Reader.* New York: Routledge, 1999.
Valentine, D. T. *Manual of the Corporation of the city of New York.* New York: Edmond Jones & Co., Printers, 1861.
Vega, Bernardo, and César Andreu Iglesias. *Memoirs of Bernardo Vega: A Contribution to the History of the Puerto Rican Community in New York.* New York: Monthly Review Press, 1984.
Wakefield, Dan. *Island in the city: The World of Spanish Harlem.* New York: Corinth Books, 1959.
Young Lords Party, and Michael Abramson. *Palante: Young Lords Party.* New York: McGraw-Hill, 1971.
Zipp, Samuel. *Manhattan Projects: The Rise and Fall of Urban Renewal in Cold War New York.* Oxford: Oxford University Press, 2010.

Index

Abdul, Rauol 83–88
Abraham Lincoln Houses 107
Abyssinian Baptist Church 210–211
African Methodist Episcopal Church 40
After Hours 190
Agueros, Jack 188
American Labor Party (ALP) 63, 66–68
Anaya-Cerda, Aurora 216–218
Anthony, Marc (Marco Antonio Muñiz) 195
Anti-Immigration Act (1921, 1924) 12, 33
Antonetti, Evelina 177
Antonini, Luigi 67
Apollo Theater 29
Arazo, Joseph 148
Arless, James 21–22, 53, 57
Art Workers Coalition 186
Aspira 150–154
Ateneo Obrero Hispano 38
Azteca Theatre 91–92

Badillo, Herman 146–148
Bailey, Leo 189–190
Baldwin, James 86–87
Barretto, Ray 195
Bauzá, Mario 101
Beckford, Victoria (Vickie) 81, 97
"Become Your Dream" 205–206
Belafonte, Harry 154
Benedict, Don 136–138, 140
Benjamin Franklin High School 26, 50, 99–100
Benjamin Franklin Houses (Franklin Plaza) 121
Berghaus, Audrey 24, 27, 121
Bethel African Methodist Church 40
Bethune, Mary McLoud 87
Black Panthers 171, 175
Blake, David 98
Bleakly, William 67
B'nai Brith 10
Bodega (store) 35
Boy's Choir of Harlem 207–208
Brockington, Hannah 208–209
Brockington, Katherine Miles 82
El Bronx Remembered 192
Brown, Earl 72
Bryan, Frederick Van Pelt 70

Bryant, James 42, 52–53, 56, 95, 97, 105, 108, 123–125, 128
Bunkley, Bob (Muntu) 171
Burgos, Julia De 187
Bush, Barbara 203
Bush, George W. 203

Cagney, James 27
Calabria 22
Calderon, Henry 198
Calvert, George 145
Campanilismo (Territorial) 24
Campos, Pedro Albizu 65
Candelario, Charlie 93
Cantor, Jacob 10
Carlito's Way 190
Carrero, José 151–153
La Carretta (Ox Cart) 193
Carson, Josephine 164
La Casa del Populo 26, 59
Central Jewish Institute 17
Central Park 94
Centro de Estudios de Puerto Rico (Center for Puerto Rican Studies) 33
Chambers Memorial Baptist Church 208
Channel Thirteen 193, 199
Chenault, Lawrence R. 32, 34
Cinquemani, Anthony 160–161
Cintron, Humberto 7, 53, 115–116, 193–194
Civil War 9, 31, 41
Clinton, Bill (William J.) 203
Colon, Johnny 5, 96, 109–110, 194–195
Colonia to Community 34
Colonias 34
Communist Party 66, 72
Coniff, Frank 72–73
Connie's Ballroom 81
Cosco 221
Cosmo Theatre 91, 118
Cotton Club 101
County Cook, Ireland 28
Covello, Leonard 26, 50, 59, 100
Crimmons, J.D. 17
The Crises 82
Cuneo, Ernest 63

Cuoamo (ship) 33–34
Curran, Thomas J. 68

Daily Mirror 65, 109
Daily News 109
Davis, Benjamin 72
Davis, Clarence 161–164
Davis, Miles 51
Davis, Sammy, Jr. 177
Death and Life of the Great American Cities 104
De Jesus, Carlos 69–70, 96, 106, 114, 129
De La Vega, James 204–206, 220
Deleon, Robert (Bob) 99, 122, 129
Denis, Nelson 211–213
Depression 3, 45
Dewey, Gov. Thomas E. 70
Dewitt Clinton Houses 115, 120
Diaz, Manny, Jr. 34, 45, 53–54, 63, 98, 127, 149
Di Martino, George 20, 23, 121
Dimas, Marcos 186–187, 198
DinCeccio, Father Alfred 74
Donovan, James 73, 135
Los Dos Antillas 31
DuBois, W.E.B. 82
Durante, Jimmy 111

Eagle Theatre 91, 198
East Harlem gangs 125–145
East Harlem Merchant's Association (EHMA) 118
East Harlem Real Great Society (EHRGS) 165
East Harlem Small Business Survey & Planning Committee (EHSBSC) 116
East Harlem Tenant's Council 168
East Harlem Tenant's League 109
East Harlem Triangle 208–209
East Harlem Tutorial Program (EHTP) 143–145
East River Houses 50–51, 68, 117
East River Plaza 214
Eddy, Rev. Norman C. 49, 69, 128, 130, 133, 138, 142–143, 175–176
Eisenhower, Dwight D. 54
El Bronx Remembered 192
Ellington, Duke 51, 101
Ellis, John 71
Ellison, Ralph 86
Espada, George 36, 108–109
Esperanza del Barrio 214
Espier, Robert 36, 119
Evans, Lois Pascale 23, 64, 121

Fabulous Latin House 165
Fair Employment Practices Commission (FEPC) 66
La Famiglia 24
Faulkner, Charles 130–131

Ferreira, Ramon 68, 95
Figueroa, Pablo 75, 100
First Spanish Methodist Church 175–177
Fitzgerald, Ella 101
Flores, Clemente 114–115
Flying Over 96th Street: Memoirs of a White Boy 159
Flynn, John 189
Fonda, Jane 177
Foran Act 1935 20
Forestiere (Foreigners) 24
Foster, Jacqueline 148
Fox Star Theatre (Boricua) 91–92
Frey, Martin J. 188

Gallo, Peter 127, 132
García, Adrián 187
García, Chino 165
Gaylord White Houses 115
gentrification 217, 220
George Washington Carver Houses 107–111, 116–117
George Washington Houses 108, 116–117, 121, 159
Gillespie, Dizzy 51, 101
Giordani, Angelo 166–170
Giuliani, Rudolph W. 211–212
Givens, David 88, 198, 210, 212–213
Goldstein, Herbert (Rabbi) 17
González, Angelo 165
Gonzalez, Juan 171–172, 176–177, 182–184
Good, Fred 166
"Goodbye Christ" (poem) 82, 85
Goodman, Marilyn 8, 81
Goodman, Roy 189
Gravanis, Calliope 88–90, 122
Great Society 165
The Greatest Generation 54
Grillo, Frank (Machito) 78, 101
Grist, Ray 50–51, 68, 129, 131
Guevara, Che (Ernesto) 51
Gurock, Jeffrey 13
Guzman, Francisco 214–216
Guzman, Pablo (Yoruba) 170–173

Hamilton, Jesse 42, 94–95
Hand in Hand 10
Handlin, Oscar 32
Hannigan, Patrick H. 70
Harlem Courthouse 26, 27, 28, 30
Harlem Federation 15
Harlem Hebrew Institute 49
Harlem Hebrew League 16
Harlem House 6, 26, 64, 135
Harlem Young Men's Hebrew Orthodox League 16
Harper, Emerson 83–84
Harper, Toy 83–84
Harper and Row 191–192
The Heart Is the Teacher 97

The Heckscher Foundation 53
Hell's Kitchen (Clinton) 28
Herbert H. Lehman Houses 115, 119
Hermandad Puertorriqueña (Porto Rican Brotherhood of America) 38
Hilquit, Morris 15
Hispanic Federation 150
Hope Community 145
Hughes, Carrie 82
Hughes, James 82
Hughes, Langston 1, 82–88; "Goodbye Christ" (poem) 82, 85

I Have a Dream Program (IHAD) 199–204
Italian American Student's League 26

Jack, Hulan 40, 122
Jacobs, Jane: *Death and Life of the Great American Cities* 104
James Weldon Johnson Houses 106–107, 120
Jenkins, William 172
Johnny's Colon Music School 194–195
Johnson, Lyndon B. 154, 163, 165

Kennedy, John F. 146–147, 154, 161
Kennedy, Martin J. 70
Kennedy, Robert F. 161
Kent State University 186
King, Martin Luther, Jr. 1, 154, 157, 161
Kirner, Emiliano 19
Korean War 55
Kornegay, Alice 208
Korrol, Virginia Sanchez E. 32; *Colonia to Community* 34
Kukle, Meyer 11, 16, 46, 49, 63, 66

LaGuardia, Fiorello H. 39, 50, 59–63, 65, 71, 117
Lambert, Wally 113–114
Lancaster, Burt 200
Lang, Eugene M. 199–204
Lanzetta, James 39, 62
Lebron, Lolita 187
Le Corbusier 104
Lefkowitz, Abraham 59
Lemus, George 172, 173
Lemus, Robert 172, 173
Lentini, Michael 25, 94, 96
Lexington Houses 107, 117
La Liga de Artesanos 31
La Liga Puertorriqueña e Hispana (LLPRH) 39
Linares, Guillermo 212
Lindsay, John V. (mayor) 154
Little Italy 1, 11, 23, 121
Local Initiatives Support Corporation (LISC) 208
Lopez, Willie 1, 5, 52, 66, 92–93, 113
Lorca, Federico Garcia 82
Louis, Joe 65

Loungo, Al 19, 111
Lower East Side 11, 13, 15, 166–167
Luciano, Felipe 99, 101, 172, 173, 174, 175, 176, 177, 179, 184, 197
Lucky Corner 63

Madonna di Constantinopoli (La Madonna) 18
Magellan, Ferdinand 71
Malcolm X 51, 154, 160
Mancino, Phillip 112
Manhattan Country School 156–159
Manhattan Development Committee 106
Marcantonio, Frank 58
Marcantonio, Sanario (Samuel) 58
Marcantonio, Vito 1, 40, 57–74, 117, 135, 137
Marin, Luis Muñoz 77
Marine Tiger 75
La Marqueta (Market) 35–36
Marristany, Hiram 188
Martí, Jose 31
Marzan, Efrain 34, 56 76, 78, 92, 96, 131
Massive Economic Neighborhood Development (MEND) 197, 208–209
Mayor's Committee on City Planning (MCCP) 46
McCants, Margaret 119
McCarthy, Joseph 72, 84–85
McCartney, Paul 207
McClellan Committee 169
McCullough, Robert (Bob) 209
McLaughlin, Mary 174
Medina, Albert 33, 35, 46
Melendez, Jesus (Papoleto) 97
Melendez, Mickey 167
Memoirs de Bernardo Vega 31
Mendez, Olga 190
Merli, John 118, 147
Messina (Italy) 27
Mexican American Workers Association (AMAT) 214
Mexican Community Center (CECMEX) 214
Mexican Unidos en Nueva York (UNIMEX) 214
Midler, Bette 177
Migration Division (Commonwealth Office) 77, 150
Miller, Dorie 65
Mills, Wright C. 77
Mitchell, John P. 104
Model Cities Program 167, 196
Mohr, Nicholasa 7, 68, 94; *El Bronx Remembered* 192; *Nilda* 190–92
Monserratt, Joe 33, 77 100
Montesi, Robert 126, 129–130, 133, 135
Morales, Hortencio 91–92
Morales, Rafael Colon 187
Morrisey, John P. 71
Moses, Robert 104–105
Mount Carmel Church 18–19

Index

Mount Morris Park (Marcus Garvey Park) 17, 31
Mount Sinai Hospital 209
Mucciolo, Charles 67
Municipal Theatre 91–92
Murphy, Vincent 27–31
El Museo del Barrio 1, 188–189
My Big Fat Greek Wedding 90

Naples 19–20, 22
Nardelli, Eugene (judge) 7, 51, 69, 101–102
National Labor Relations Board (NLRB) 62
National Recovery Act (NRA) 49
Negro Burial Ground 40
Neopolitans 20, 22
New Amsterdam 4
New Deal 62
New York: A Documentary Film 120
New York City Department of Planning 220
New York City Housing Authority (NYCHA) 50, 118
New York Times 110, 122
Newfield, Jack 174, 177
Nieuw Haarlem 4
Nilda 190–92
Nixon, Richard M. 186, 196
El Nuevo Barrio 168

Office of Economic Opportunity 166
Ogden, Codman 155
Oliver Perez, Denise 170, 171, 174–175, 179–181, 184
One Nation, One Standard 146
Orsi, Robert 23
Ortiz, Rafael 188
Osorio, Carlos 187
Otero, Manuel 187

padrones 1, 19, 20, 209
paesani 25
Pagan, Dylcia 159
Palmer, Robert C. 70
Palmieri, Charlie 78, 195
Pantoja, Antonia 148–154
Parker, Charlie 51
Pascale, Rose 21, 23, 25, 26, 27
Pathmark (supermarket) 210–213
Patsy's Pizzeria (restaurant) 21–22
Patton, Gen. George S. 54
Perez, Andrew 92, 95
Pérez, Armando 165
Perry, Wilhelmina 153
Pietri, Pedro 175
Poliseo, Ann 23–24
Polla 18
Poussaint, Dr. Alvin 5, 41, 43, 95, 97, 124–125, 129, 131–132
Powell, Adam Clayton, Jr. 1, 122
Pozo, Chano 101
public school 201

Public Works Administration (WPA) 49
Puco, Angela Bella 7, 18, 20
Puente, Tito (Ernesto) 78, 79, 101

Q & A 190
Quinones, Olga 36–37, 46, 52–53
Quintana, Harry 167

Radiant City 104
Realidades 192–194
Reeve, Christopher 202
Rene, Angel 78–79
Ricca, Frank J. 68
Rickoff, Juanita 32–34
Rivera, Mike 126, 131–132, 135, 172, 179, 183, 185
Rivera, Oscar Garcia 40
Robert F. Wagner, Sr., Houses 112, 116–117, 121
Robert Taft Houses 114, 117–118
Robles, Olguie 177, 180–184
Rodriguez, Al 210–212
Rodriquez, José 160–161
Rodriguez, Ray 37, 49, 55–56, 122–123, 140
Rodriguez, Rosendo 32
Rodriquez, Tito 78–79, 101
Roosevelt, Franklin D. 1, 4, 39, 45–46, 56, 66–67
Roosevelt, James 4
Roosevelt, Theodore 58
Rosaly, Luis 36, 106, 115, 122, 126, 128
Rosario, Josephina 76
Ross, Morty 9, 95
Rossetti, Frank 148
Rubenstein, Annette T. 63–64, 67, 69, 73
Rubio, Martín 187
Rudder, Helen Lichorish 43
Rufano, Peter (father) 5, 22–25, 45
Russo-Japanese War 11

St. Paul's Church 29
Salerno 18, 22
Sallicrup, Fernando 188
Sanchez, Yolanda 7, 150
Sanders, Miriam 60
Santangelo, Alfred 135, 147–148
Savatelli, Rose 20–23, 52, 93
Schneider, Eric: *Vampires, Dragons and Egyptian Kings* 125
Schomburg, Arturo Alfonso 32, 159
Schoonover, Melvin 208
Scottorigio, Joseph 70
Second Avenue El 5, 37
Segarra, Arnie 5, 107, 177, 197
Segarra, Manny 96, 111, 126
Selena (Quintanilla) (singer) 205
Senior, Clarence 77
Sicily 22
Simmons, Russell 51
Simone, Nina 81

Index

Simple (Semple), Jessie B. 83–84
Sinatra, Frank 65
Sklar, Eugene 11–12, 49
Smith, Gov. Al 104
Snipes, Wesley 51
Social Clubs 25
La Sociedad Beneficio Cubano y Puertorriqueña (Cuban and Puerto Rican Benevolent Society) 31
La Sociedad de Albizu Campos (SAC) 167, 170, 171
Solá, Michèle 158
Soto, Armando 187
Soto, Willie 177
Sotomayor, Sonia 103
Stern, Robert A.M. 120–121
stickball 93–94
Street Scene 83

Taft-Hartley Act (1947) 71
Taino Towers 168
Taller Boricua 1, 170, 186–188
Talmud Torah (Uptown) 10, 15
Tenement House Act (1901) 6
tenements 6, 78
Tepayac 215, 216
Tet Offensive 161
Third Avenue EL 5, 37
Thomas, Norman 15
Thomas, Piri 46, 65, 91 98, 119; *Down These Mean Streets* 1, 159–160, 190
Thomas Jefferson Houses 108, 111, 116, 117
Thomas Jefferson Park 26, 98–99
Thomas Jefferson Pool 26
Time (magazine) 64
Title 1 104, 118
Torres, Edwin (Judge): *After Hours* 190; *Carlito's Way* 190; *Q & A* 190
Torres, John 134–135
Torres, José (Chequi) 177
Townsend Harris High School 199–200
Trowbridge, Gus 154–158
Trowbridge, Marty 156
Trufino, Rafael 187
Truman, Harry S 1, 71, 73
Turnbull, Walter 207–208

Union Settlement 6, 26, 135
United Nations 181
Uptown Talmud Torah Association (UTTA) 15–16
Urban Planning Studio 168

Vampires, Dragons and Egyptian Kings 125
Van Pelt Bryan, Frederick 70
Vega, Bernardo 15, 31, 35; *Memoirs de Bernardo Vega* 31
Vega, Marta Moreno 188
Velez, Isidro (Ted) 92, 94, 109
Vietnam War 146, 161–165
Villegas, Raquel 53, 56–57, 91

Wagner, Robert F., Jr. (mayor) 143
Wagner, Sen. Robert F., Sr. 49
Waldorf Astoria 1
Wallace, Henry 72
Washburn Wire Factory 198
The Weary Blues 82
Webb, Chick 51, 101
Webber, Bill 136–137, 143, 145
Webber, Helen 143–145
Webber, Tom 159, 169–170
Weckquaesgeks 4
Westmoreland, Gen. William 162
White, Nate 83
Wilcox, Preston 15, 197
Wilson-Pakula Act (1947) 71
Woodrow Wilson Houses 112, 117–118, 159
Worker's Compensation Board 189
Workman's Circle Branch No. # 2 13, 49
Workman's Project Administration (WPA) 50
World War I 67
World War II 1, 31, 45, 50, 52–57, 106, 110, 120, 125, 127
Wright, Richard 86

Yoba, Malik 79
Young, Mahmoudah 80
Young Lords 170–185
Young Men's Hebrew Association (YMHA) 10

Zapata, Emilio 205

www.ingramcontent.com/pod-product-compliance
Ingram Content Group UK Ltd.
Pitfield, Milton Keynes, MK11 3LW, UK
UKHW041943140426
5217IPUK00014B/627